BEST WINES!
The Gold Medal Winners

1999

by Gail Bradney

A Print Project Book

Copyright © 1998
by Lowell Miller and Gail Bradney
All rights reserved. Third edition 1999
First edition copyrighted in 1996

ISSN 1088-8608
ISBN 0-9651750-2-2

Published by:
The Print Project
P.O. Box 703
Bearsville, NY 12409
bestwines@ulster.net

Distributed to the book trade by:
Independent Publishers Group
814 North Franklin Street
Chicago, IL 60610
(312) 337-0747

Printed and bound by:
McNaughton and Gunn, Inc., Saline, MI

Cover design by:
Howard Blume

Interior design by:
JoAnn Chamberlain, ¡GoJo Grafix!

Best Wines! can be purchased for educa-
tional, business, or sales promotional use.
For information please e-mail or write to
The Print Project at above address.

CONTENTS

ACKNOWLEDGMENTS

Each year *Best Wines!* has to be ready for press less than a month after the results are in from the last competition. This abbreviated production schedule insures that the wines featured in my book are current and available in stores. Doing the book this way wouldn't be possible without the cooperation, commitment, and competence of certain people who helped me on the 1999 edition.

At the top of that list is my number-one assistant, Joëlle Francis, whose dependability, sparkling intelligence, ebullient spirits, and brilliant capabilities helped make this the best edition yet.

I'd like to acknowledge as well the contributions of Michael Beames, whose research assistance was invaluable; JoAnn Chamberlain, who whips up beautiful layouts in a flash; and Howard Blume, who's created another knock-out cover.

Thanks also to the following persons: Jane Cunliffe, for her New Zealand expertise; Jan Stuebing, for unbeatable Australian know-how; Ken Onish, for help with South African producers; Nora Favelukes, for untangling some Chilean mysteries; and Billee Madsen and Pompeyo Carlos Layús, for answering Argentina-related queries.

I'm grateful to David Male and Andrew Sharp, co-directors of InterVin 1998, for granting me unlimited behind-the-scenes access to their exceptional wine competition in Toronto.

As always, I'm indebted to Susan Sewall and Harriet Bradney for their success in getting *Best Wines!* out into the world where readers can use it.

Once again, thank you, Lowell Miller, for standing by me. You're platinum.

And a kiss to little Finn, my inspiration.

INTRODUCTION

There are wine drinkers who subscribe to wine magazines, devour wine books, worship one or more wine guru, and enjoy ear-bending the local wine merchant with back-and-forth one-upsmanship about the relative merits of this vintage and that. They have dusty bottles in their basements worth a small fortune, and they turn up their nose at anything under $15.

And then there's the rest of us. Unless you're part of the wine snob culture, in which case you wouldn't admit to the following, you've no doubt experienced this: You enter a large, unfamiliar wine shop and your eyes glaze over. Too many choices.

I've spoken with all kinds of readers—those who consider themselves novices and those who've been buying and recognizing great wines for years. They all say the same thing: "I'll never be a wine expert. There's just too much to know."

Most wine enthusiasts feel overwhelmed by the subject of wine. In fact, the Wine Market Council recently conducted an interesting poll to determine why Generation Xers (the twenty- to mid-thirty-something crowd) prefer beer to wine. The result? These younger consumers feel there's too much to learn about wine, that it's too complicated. So they pop open a brewsky and they're happy campers.

I'd frame it slightly differently: Wine drinkers of all ages feel left out. Wine writers and wine publications mostly speak to those already in the know. And if you're not keen on reading about the stuff—you simply want to drink something good—the subject is indeed overwhelming. Every year (vintage) is different, and a single varietal of wine, say, Chardonnay, varies from one winemaking country to another—not to mention from one hillside to the next (the concept of *terroir*). Merlot is different from Cabernet Sauvignon, and on and on.

If you're like most wine lovers, you just want to walk into a wine shop and pick bottles that are delicious and affordable—but you don't want to become an expert to do it. You're annoyed that you could spend $12 on wine that's plonk. You're irked that there are no guarantees.

I was too, and that's how *Best Wines!* came to be, three years ago. I was certain there had to be a better way of finding good wines than to either immerse myself in the subject or to trust in the opinion of a single wine expert— whether a famous wine writer or Vinnie down at the corner shop. At the time, I was editing books by Robert Parker, America's most famous wine authority. And I only liked *his* recommendations about half of the time!

With this, the third annual edition of *Best Wines!*, I'm more convinced than ever that if you're looking for a foolproof method of choosing a great wine every time, buying gold medal wines is the way to do it. This year I scanned the world to find the toughest and most prestigious wine competitions, and *Best Wines! 1999* is the result—a compilation of the top-rated wines from the top-rated judgings. A gold medal from one or more of these leading competitions is as close to a guarantee of consistent high quality and satisfaction as any wine buyer will likely find.

These are the wines experts savored, and you will too. Best of all, you don't have to become an expert yourself to choose the "right" wine from among the hundreds of bottles in a typical liquor store or supermarket. In competitive wine judgings the real experts—Masters of Wine, sommeliers, winemakers, professors of oenology, wine scholars, and others for whom wine is their life—have done all the hard work for us. They've eliminated all but the very best wines, those that stood out from the pack in blind tastings—where the identity of the wines was kept anonymous. If you've been intimidated in the past when shopping for wine, I promise you won't be anymore.

I take a copy of *Best Wines!* with me whenever I visit the wine shop. I'm always confident about trying new types and new brands; I've yet to buy a disappointing bottle. The reason I'm so certain you'll have the same experience is because every wine in my book was the star among dozens and dozens of competing bottles. To be in my book a wine has to get the highest rating not from a single judge, but from a *panel* of judges, usually five or more; we're no longer talking about a single person's taste or preference. And since the wines are judged blind, you won't run into the snobbery, personal ego, media hype, or commercial bias found in other wine publications.

Many of the wines in my book received gold medals in more than one competition—some of them in three and more! That these wines will be unbelievably delicious is beyond doubt. I call these BBWs—Best of the Best Wines—and they're listed in Appendix 2. While you're at it, check out Appendix 1, Best Bargain Wines, which lists all wines in the book that are $15 or less. Imagine gold medal wines that don't cost their weight in gold! I love turning my friends on to these bargain gems.

This edition you'll find the wine winners from twelve international and eight national competitions, as well as the gold and platinum wines (rated 90 points and up) from Beverage Testing Institute's World Wine Championships, conducted more like an independent evaluating body than a competition. (To read about the Beverage Testing Institute, see page xiii.) A Key to Symbols and Abbreviations, on page xii, presents all the competitions I've included this edition and their abbreviations as they appear in the wine listings in Part II.

All of the wines in *Best Wines!* are "New World" wines. In winespeak *New World* is a term that means the winemaking regions of North and South America, South Africa, and Australia/New Zealand. Except for a few Canadian wines available only in Canada—indicated by (Can $) before the Canadian-dollar price—every foreign wine in the book has a U.S. importer/distributor. You'd be surprised how many wine books and publications don't bother to check whether the foreign wines they're reviewing are actually *available* to American wine consumers. It's all part of wine snob mentality: We'll get you revved up about a great Italian wine, but you'll never find it unless you visit a specific mountaintop village in Tuscany!

The chapters in Part I, What You Want to Know about Wine, reveal the secrets of how to taste wine, how to use the available space in your home for storing bottles, how to pair whatever you're cooking with its perfect wine mate, how to shop for gold medal wines, and so on. There are two chapters about wine competitions, one a behind-the-scenes look from my April 1998 weekend at InterVin, held in Toronto, the other a general piece about the pros and cons of wine competitions. Finally, I've updated the wine and health chapter with the latest findings about the benefits of moderate wine consumption.

In Part II you'll find the gold medal wines listed in broad categories, similar to the way a typical American wine shop is set up: reds, whites, blush, sparkling, and dessert all in their own sections, further categorized by varietal or type within those sections. Let's say you know that Shiraz and Zinfandel are both red wines, but you're not exactly sure how they're different. At the beginning of each new wine type is a detailed description of that varietal, including complementary dishes to serve with it. If you get bogged down with some of the wine terminology, refer to Appendix 3, A Glossary of Winespeak, for brief, accessible definitions and explanations of wine gobbledygoop.

For each gold medal winner in Part II you'll find the wine's full name, where it was made, how much it costs, and where it won the gold medal(s) and other special awards. To understand the competition abbreviations, see the Key to Symbols and Abbreviations, page xii.

If you live in an area that doesn't have high-quality wine shops, there's always the mail-order option. Appendix 4 is devoted to this subject, with a selective listing of wine vendors who've made mail-order wines their specialty. The laws around interstate shipping of wine are complicated, so be sure to find out first if it's legal in your state. The introduction to Appendix 4 explains more about this.

As I mentioned, I take my dog-eared copy of *Best Wines!* with me whenever I need to pick up a bottle or two. You'll discover that the reader-friendly wine index doubles as a handy shopping guide—with BBWs (✱), bargain wines (**$**), and foreign labels (℗) all flagged so you can quickly identify them.

Knowing how to buy a great bottle of wine every time has liberated me from the wine bullies. I thumb my nose at the wine snobs now, because I've found the secret to discovering wines the experts love most. I hope this book does the same for you.

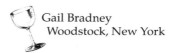
Gail Bradney
Woodstock, New York

KEY TO
SYMBOLS & ABBREVIATIONS

$	bargain wines—$15 and under
✳	Best of the Best Wines —3 or more gold medals
⚑	non-American wines
(Can $)	price in Canadian dollars; sold only in Canada

International Wine Competitions

BR	1998 Concours Mondial, Brussels
IV	1998 InterVin, Toronto
IW	1998 International Wine Challenge, London
NW	1998 New World International Wine Competition, Claremont, CA
PR	1998 Pacific Rim International Wine Competition, San Bernardino, CA
RI	1998 Riverside International Wine Competition, Riverside, CA
SM	1998 Selections Mondial, Montreal
SY	1998 Sydney International Wine Competition, Sydney
VI	1998 VinItaly, Verona
VL	1998 Vino Ljubljana, Slovenia
VN	1997 Vinandino, Mendoza
WS	1998 International Wine & Spirits Competition, London
WWC	1997–98 World Wine Championships, Beverage Testing Institute, Chicago (see below)

National or Regional (USA) Wine Competitions

CA	1998 California State Fair Commercial Wine Competition
DA	1998 Dallas Morning News Wine Competition
EN	1998 Enological Society of the Pacific Northwest Wine Competition
GH	1998 Grand Harvest Awards
LA	1998 Los Angeles County Wine Competition
OC	1998 Orange County Fair Wine Competition
SD	1998 San Diego National Wine Competition
WC	1998 West Coast Wine Competition

BEVERAGE TESTING INSTITUTE (WWC)

For the second year in a row, *Best Wines!* is honored to include the complete New World gold and platinum wines from Beverage Testing Institute's World Wine Championship judgings.

The tastings performed at the Beverage Testing Institute (BTI) are unlike the other competitions, which are annual events that take place over a short period of time. Any book that features the gold medal wines from the world's best judgings would be sorely lacking if it didn't include the higher-scoring wines from BTI.

The wineries I've spoken with all agreed: a 90-plus rating from BTI brings publicity, yes, but also loads of prestige, so revered are its panelists and impeccable its standards. Many of the top wineries that don't enter conventional wine competitions *do* participate with BTI.

The Beverage Testing Institute is an independent professional tasting body that reviews more than 6,000 wines from more than twenty different countries throughout their year-round tasting program. Panels consist of highly trained institute staff members and selected beverage industry professionals who've gained international recognition for their impartiality and professionalism.

The wines are tasted strictly on premise at the Chicago facility using procedures that minimize palate fatigue and psychological biases. Tastings are conducted weekday mornings, over a three-hour session, with a three-judge panel evaluating no more than thirty-five wines a day to avoid palate fatigue. All panelists taste "blind," aware only of the category being reviewed, not the brand. The wines are served in Riedel stemware and identified by a three-digit code on the base of the stem. Great care is taken to ensure that flawed samples aren't served.

The completed BTI evaluation includes highly structured tasting notes (for media sources of BTI's tasting notes, see below), as well as accurate scores based on a 100-point scale. Because of space constraints, *Best Wines!* includes the BTI score sans tasting notes.

Best Wines! readers can interpret BTI's point score according to the following:

96–100 Superlative ("Platinum")

90-95 Exceptional ("Gold")

The full reviews, including tasting notes and scores, are published electronically on the Internet at BTI's website, Tastings.com (http://www.tastings.com); on the Food & Drink Network

(America Online keyword: Tastings); and on Epicurious (http://www.epicurious.com), the website for *Gourmet* and *Bon Appétit* magazines.

In print they're published monthly as the Buying Guide of *Wine Enthusiast* magazine. Condensed portions of the reviews also appear in monthly features for *Restaurant Hospitality*.

For a hip site with a searchable database of all previous BTI reviews and a more detailed description of their scoring system, visit BTI's website, Tastings.com.

PART I

*What You Want
to Know About Wine*

Palate Secrets
HOW TO TASTE AND JUDGE WINE LIKE A PRO

've opened up a random page of a well-known wine monthly to get a sampling of how perky and precocious taste buds might experience the latest Oregonean Pinot Noirs. In one, a gamy edge rallies in on the fine finish. In another, a mouthful of plum notes feature silkiness lurking beneath slightly tannic scratchiness. Yipes!

Let's be honest. When wine flavors come in "hints," "suggestions," "touches," and "subtle notes," there's a good chance most of us will miss out. But must we? Can *we* learn to detect black currant flavors wrapped in an ethereal layer of sophisticated new oak? Can *our glass* conjure up cigarbox aromas?

It turns out that to properly taste wine, you have to understand two basic concepts. The first is that most of what we perceive as taste is actually more closely related to smell. And the second is that to fully appreciate a glass of wine, you have to consciously use your brain; i.e., think, consider, analyze, and then put it all together into language.

To prove the first point, all you have to do is think of that repulsive medicine your mother used to administer. If you pinched your nose while drinking it down, there was virtually no flavor. It's also why we have little appetite when our nose is congested with a cold. What's the point of eating when you can't taste?

The sorry news is that a hound dog is much better equipped than we are to pick up all the subtleties in a glass of wine, since dogs and other animals have more acute olfactory sensors than humans. Still, our olfactory receptors allow us to experience around ten thousand different aromas, which is nothing to snort at. These receptors are found in the nose but also in the retronasal passage, at the back of the mouth.

Our mouth, on the other hand, can pitifully distinguish but four kinds of taste: sweetness, on the tip of the tongue;

saltiness, a little further back on the sides; sourness, on the sides even further back; and bitterness, near the back center of the tongue.

So what does this anatomy lesson have to do with fine wine enjoyment? A lot. To fully experience the magic of what a great glass of wine can offer, you want to liberate as many aroma molecules as you can to maximize your senses of taste and smell. First, swirl the wine in the glass (didn't you always wonder why the heck you were doing this?) directly under your nose so you can sniff in the bouquet. If you happen to have a really *big* schnoz, distinctly advantageous under these circumstances, go ahead and stick it *into* the glass as far as it'll go.

Next, take a small sip and "whistle in" some air along with it to direct the vapors to that waiting retronasal passage. My fifty-something companion, a child of the sixties, likes to call this "bonging his wine." (Introducing the concept as such lets you know which of your dinner guests inhaled during their college days.) Don't worry about the noise. The slurpier it sounds, the better you'll taste the wine.

While the wine's in your mouth, "chew" it: Literally move your teeth and tongue around as though the wine were solid. The key here is to make sure it touches every part of your mouth and tongue before you let it slide down your throat. (If you were at a real wine tasting, you'd spit it out to avoid the goofy effects such multiple samplings would soon have on your judgment.)

Using all of the information you've just collected, now embark on the second part of the tasting equation—the thinking part. Unlike canines, who might engage in the following electrifying train of thought—*garbage . . . yum!*—we humans have the ability to analyze the whole experience and put it into language that transcends and elevates the thing itself.

It's not that hard. Think about the initial associations that came to mind when you first sniffed and swirled. These are the famous aromas described in professional tasting notes. Don't limit yourself to grapes. Complex wine may emit aromas as varied as flowers, weeds, fruits, vegetables, candy—even meat and tobacco. Your ability to describe what you perceive will improve with experience. Too, knowing the terms in which wine's various qualities are described will definitely help you think about and experience wine in a deeper way. At the very least, familiarize yourself with the wine terms in the back of this book (Appendix 3).

As for what happened "on the palate," as wine writers like to call the sensations inside the mouth, here's where the more cerebral stuff enters in. Saltiness isn't really a factor with wine. Sourness is experienced as acidity—a measure of how "zingy" the wine is. Sweetness is self-explanatory. And bitterness is something you shouldn't taste at all if you're drinking good wine.

But besides these, there are other qualities to consider. One respected authority calls the mouth more of a "measurer," which is an apt description. You can evaluate what the wine feels like inside the mouth: how "heavy" it feels (weight/body); how astringent or puckery it makes your mouth (from the tannins); how long the flavor and aroma components linger after you've swallowed (length). You might also consider such things as how much punch the alcohol delivers, and in the case of sparkling wines, how the mousse, or bubbles, feel on your tongue.

Most important is the *balance* of all these elements. When you consider all of the above, are any overwhelming? A really fabulous wine will have balance as well as complexity—which has the same meaning when describing wine as it does one's lover.

You might want to take notes just for the fun of it, especially when trying a new wine with a group of friends. After going through this process once or twice, you'll become more confident.

If you have the opportunity to sample several bottles at the same sitting (preferably all the same wine varietals), by all means do. Invited to sit and taste alongside the judges at InterVin 1998, I discovered to my surprise that my own nose and mouth are heuristic. That is, they get smarter with use, especially in a situation as intense as a professional wine judging, where five to six new wines are tasted every twenty minutes or so, all day long.

But even for the enthusiastic novice, once you've worked on *consciously* tasting wine, you'll never drink or think about wine quite the same way again.

Pantry Secrets
HOW TO CREATE YOUR OWN WINE CELLAR

f "a man's home is his castle" were literally true, none of us would have a wine-storing problem, as all castles come with underground catacombs that are vibration-free, dark, damp, and kept at a steady 55 degrees F. Ignore the muffled screams coming from the torture chamber one level down and you've got yourself one heck of a great place to show off, following a hearty repast with guests.

However, most of us have to make do with the Clorox-scented pantry, the old-shoe-leather closet, or the moldy basement in our home. If you're a rare-wine collector/investor, go get yourself a free-standing, obscenely expensive, custom-made wine cellar that regulates temperature and humidity—or have one built. If you're absolutely nuts, you can do what one California couple did: Turn your entire living space into a wine cellar. Sure, it's a bit cool and damp for entertaining, but with all those fabulous bottles around to sample, who'll even notice?

Seriously, though, if you're like most of us who wish to *drink* and *enjoy* the wine in the foreseeable future, you probably have a perfectly adequate "cellar" in your home already.

Wine is a living substance. Inside a wine bottle the water, acids, alcohol, and tannins interact in an exquisite dance. Hopefully, this performance will cause the maximum flavor, aroma, and body to evolve and emerge from the fruit in perfect balance. Your job is to not hinder this process.

Following are four main rules that will protect your wine from unnecessary ruin, whether you're storing it for next week or next year.

1. Keep wines at a constant temperature not exceeding 70 degrees F. More important than its temperature is the *constancy* of that temperature. Temperature changes should occur slowly; wild swings are undesirable. I cringe with embarrassment when I remember the once-iced champagne that sat outside in blistering 85-degree heat for two days after my wedding under the rental canopy. I actually returned cases to the wine shop for a refund! (I hope they're not reading this.) If you buy a bottle that really *needs* to evolve some more to reach its peak, know that a wine kept at 55 degrees will do so much more slowly than one kept at 70 degrees. (That's why some of the famous cellars in Europe have perfectly quaffable wine that seems ageless at forty or more years old; those catacombs are downright chilly!)

Tip: Common and seemingly appropriate wine-storing places in your home may not be the best in terms of temperature variation. A kitchen cabinet or shelf above your refrigerator is a poor choice since the refrigerator generates a lot of heat. Likewise, the furnace room in your basement, as well as the wall shared by the furnace room, isn't ideal. If you live in a northern climate, be aware that a closet or pantry that has an outside wall may experience significant dips in temperature. Remember: It's the *fluctuation in temperature degrees* that damage wine more often than actual storage temperature.

2. Keep wines in the dark. Light—especially direct sunlight—isn't good for wine. Ignore the appeal of those sunny kitchen counters you see in stylish living magazines, the ones with bowls of fruit, bouquets of flowers, and three or four wines artfully arranged in a wicker rack beneath the skylight. You can be sure that Martha Stewart will be *cooking* with that wine rather than drinking it if it's been there for any amount of time.

3. Keep wines in a humid place. Don't let those corks dry out. If they do, oxygen will get inside the bottle and turn your wine into vinegar. This is the same rationale behind storing bottles on their sides; contact with the wine keeps the corks moist and expanded. Humidity at about 50 percent is essential, and 70 to 75 percent is ideal.

4. Keep wines in a vibration-free place. Particularly true of Old World–style, more expensive wines, there will be sediments in the wine. If these get all stirred up, it upsets the delicate balancing act occurring inside the bottle.

Tip: Don't put your wine rack above a washing machine or in an insulated garage that doubles as a wood shop. Wines also hate to travel. If your wine has just been shipped to you or jostled on a car trip, let it settle down for a day or two before opening.

Wine Biz Secrets
WHY COMPETITIONS ARE VALUABLE

N early every time I do an author interview on radio, television, or for a print article, I have to spend valuable seconds and waste precious sound bites explaining the concept of wine competitions, why they're important for the consumer, and—even more basic—what they are. What gives? After all, the California State Fair Wine Competition has been around way longer than your grandfather—since 1854. In fact, all of the competitions included in *Best Wines!* are time-tested, get rave reviews from the many wine industry people with whom I've consulted, and are widely revered in the biz. So why is it that the people who enjoy wine don't know about wine competitions?

Thanks to ever-present ads and the unavoidable buzzing of the media in our ears, American consumers can tell you which toothpaste is recommended by four out of five dentists, which flick won the most Oscars this year, and which car is considered a bargain by *Consumer Reports*. But, dagnabbit, few wine lovers could name the wines that took home gold medals in the world's toughest and most prestigious wine competitions. Why not?

COMPETITIONS' IMAGE PROBLEM

Unfortunately, wine competitions suffer from an image problem. The award-winning wineries publish press releases about their medals, but that information stays largely within the wine industry. And even the wine press who publish the various competition results aren't sure what these results mean. Is a gold in one competition the same as a gold in another? Who judged the wines, and how were they judged? These are legitimate questions, ones I've had to address as I've polled the industry to determine which competitions are worthy of being included in *Best Wines!*

According to Andrew Sharp, co-director of InterVin, considered one of the stingiest international wine competitions when it comes to awarding gold medals, "it's a hard row to hoe to separate yourself from the bulk of competitions that are poor, those that are mediocre, and then the handful of good ones. We just won't compromise our standards."

And that's one of the problems: There isn't an industry standard to which all competitions must conform. Therefore, the many competitions out there are actually competing with *each other* to attract the best and most wineries to participate. It's confusing to the public and tends to dilute the message.

Moreover, it's popular for wine magazines and for wine writers to dis' wine competition results, claiming they're of little or no value. "The best wineries don't enter them," they say. Or, "only popular-style wines will be winners. The really interesting wines get knocked out of the race." Well, of course they'll say that. After all, if there's an *objective* and *reliable* source for discovering the best wines— a source free of advertising bias or personal ego—who's going to listen to the wine gurus and subscribe to the snobby magazines?

In short, the wine media are in competition with the competitions and often come out "against" them, but end up endorsing, praising, even gushing about the very same wines that won gold medals in the leading wine competitions. Go figure.

CRITICISMS OF WINE COMPETITIONS

Let's look at some of the most common criticisms leveled at wine competitions to see how they hold up.

"TOO FEW COMPETITORS, TOO MANY GOLDS"

All competitions are not created equal. Some are too small, which means that too many medals will be awarded to undeserving wines. Therefore, one of the criteria a competition must fit to be included in *Best Wines!* is a large wine base. Fifteen to eighteen hundred wines is an average and adequate pool. Some competitions include many more. The World Wine Championships out of Chicago and International WINE Challenge out of London, for example, are two of the largest in scope—with five to six thousand wine labels competing from around the world.

Some competitions award too many golds to mediocre wines because their standards are too low and their judges untrained. Even worse, other competitions have been known to award a high percentage of medals in order to "reward" the wineries who've paid to enter (don't forget that most competitions are for-profit events), thus offering an unspoken guarantee to wineries that they'll walk away with a medal or two, as long as they pay the fee to enter.

Because the overall quality of wines is improving, there are bound to be more gold medals being awarded than ever before. Yet competitions that give out too many gold medals don't help the consumer decide which wines are truly outstanding. From my point of view, the stingiest competitions are the best ones. On average, the competitions deemed worthy for inclusion in *Best Wines!* award about five to seven golds for every hundred wines.

"QUIRKY WINES DON'T WIN GOLD MEDALS"

How about the argument that competition medals, because they're awarded by panels of judges, never go to the most unique or unusual wines? Here's a legitimate complaint, one that some competitions haven't addressed. It's undisputable that all wines in *Best Wines!* will be excellent, since every one is a gold medal winner—rated top in its category by no less than five judges, and in some cases by fifteen to twenty judges when it won multiple gold medals in two or three different competitions.

But what happens if a really stupendous yet decidedly oddball Cabernet steps onto the field with some ultradistinguished and refined fellow Cabs? Will this weirdo wine be pushed out of the game? Possibly, if the judges use the "hedonistic" method of rating wines. Based on an "I like it/I don't like it" system, the hedonistic approach eliminates some of the more interesting examples of a varietal. Likewise, it's judges' human nature to compare samples rather than to consider each wine on its own merits. So, again, a rebellious genius may not fare so well next to the silk-underwear type.

But if in the end the Cab that takes home the gold medal in this contest is a terrific, well-made, classy example of the varietal, what consumer has reason to complain? That is, in essence, what wine competitions are good for: determining really top-notch wines in each category.

InterVin is a competition that takes a different approach than most. Rather than the hedonistic approach, InterVin judges are required to judge each wine individually according to a sophisticated numerical scale known a I.N.E.S. (InterVin Numerical Evaluation System), which directs the tasters to analyze and score the wine in each of eighteen different categories that determine Visual, Olfactory, Tactile, Flavor, and Overall Quality ratings. Further, InterVin judges are instructed not to make comparisons between wines; rather, they taste and score each wine according to its own merits, and don't add up their own scores. At InterVin, a fabulous but quirky wine has a much greater chance of being awarded a gold medal than it might elsewhere, provided it scores well in each of the I.N.E.S. categories.

"TOP WINERIES DON'T ENTER WINE COMPETITIONS"

Here's a familiar dig. While it's true that Lafite-Rothschild doesn't need to enter wine competitions to prove to the world that it can produce gold-medal-caliber Bordeaux, it's also true that most wine drinkers already know about the wines of Lafite (and know that it'll be a cold day in hell before they'll shell out $500 a bottle to buy it).

On the other hand, winning a gold medal in a wine competition is one of the least expensive ways for an up-and-coming boutique winery from California or a new

Argentina label, both relatively unknown but making fabulous wines nevertheless, to get a lot of bang for their media buck. By winning a gold medal, these wines will get written up in the wine media, will get picked up by distributors, and will get featured in my book (!). So wine competition results are a great place to find out about the sleeper wines, the boutique wines, the best-kept-secret wines, and the bargain wines—inexpensive wines that beat out bottles twice and three times their price.

Again, InterVin has led the way in instituting policies to encourage the world's top wineries to participate—at no risk. (Other competitions would be wise to follow suit if they wish to attract more prestige wineries.) To compete at InterVin, wineries can request that the results be kept confidential—unless they win a gold. This prevents a very well known and recognized producer from the embarrassment of winning a bronze while a little California upstart half its price gets a gold medal.

Orange County Fair Wine Competition tackles this problem from a different angle. If the competition organizers see that a particular category of wines entered isn't representative of what the average Orange County wine buyer might find at the corner market, they'll purchase and enter bottles themselves to "fill out" the category. In this way, their judges get a chance to taste and evaluate the widest range of wines, from the least known to the best.

"SOME GOLD MEDALS SEEM BETTER THAN OTHERS"

True. That's because they are. Competitions are like everything else—some are corrupt, others are run by incompetents. The competitions included in *Best Wines!* have to meet impeccable criteria. Every wine competition in my book is unique, but all share the distinction of being widely considered excellent venues for setting exceedingly high market standards for New World wines.

To be in *Best Wines!*, the competitions have to conduct the tastings blind. That is, their judges aren't permitted to see the bottles, names, or labels until after the medals are awarded.

Some conduct tastings over an abbreviated time period—three or four days. The World Wine Championships conducts tastings over the course of a year and judges them by region. Many wine competitions have the judges taste wine by price category, the reasoning being that a $10 wine isn't meant to compete with a $50 bottle. Others, like InterVin, are opposed to judging wine by price or region, believing that a $15 and a $35 bottle should be able to compete side by side; so should, the reasoning goes, a French and an Oregon wine. This system reaps some interesting results. If a $15 bottle wins a gold at InterVin, it's an amazing achievement, and you'd better run out and buy up every bottle you can, since it means that this bargain wine excelled over some pricy competitors.

There are other differences, too. International Wine & Spirits Competition does a chemical analysis of each wine, the results of which are factored into the judges' scores at the end. Sydney International serves complementary food alongside the wines being evaluated, both because it's different and exotic, but also because most wines are consumed with food, so, they figure, why shouldn't they be judged that way? Grand Harvest, a newcomer to *Best Wines!* this edition, groups the wines according to appellation of origin rather than in classes such as "Chardonnay." The idea here is to determine the best example of both winemaking and the regional characteristics the wines share (also known as *terroir*).

IN PRAISE OF WINE COMPETITIONS

Okay, so there are good competitions as well as bad. Still, you might ask, why are gold medal wines any better than the wines my wine monger recommends, or those that get high scores and great write-ups in wine magazines?

A WINE "EXPERT" HAS BUT ONE POINT OF VIEW

Wine retailers are often more knowledgeable than the majority of wine drinkers. After all, they spend a great deal of time tasting and evaluating wines to decide which ones to stock. In my little town, the wine shop proprietors are honest and offer fabulous recommendations most of the time. Still, it's just one person's opinion. And unless he or she knows the type of wine you like, there's a fifty-fifty chance that you'll be disappointed.

How about wine writers? Again, wine writers have very specific tastes and aren't always neutral. They often get free samples, perks such as paid trips and meals, and can be influenced by flashy PR materials sent by wine producers to seduce the wine press. But even assuming that most wine writers have nothing but the best and most forthright intentions, you still face the problems of one person's palate preferences diverging wildly from your own.

To see what I mean, just open up any issue of the famous *Wine Spectator* to the readers' letters section. You'll nearly always see a letter complaining that so-and-so rated a wine 90 points in one issue while that same wine was given an "unacceptable" rating of 76 two months later. How could the ratings be so different, they ask? The editor's reply is always something like "every taster on our staff has his own palate biases and preferences." That's precisely the problem with relying on a single person's opinion.

On the other hand, consider a wine that has won a gold medal. It means that out of a field of perhaps a hundred similar wines, this bottle was deemed "best" by five to six judges who had no idea what wine they were tasting.

Now consider a wine that's won two or more gold medals, of which there are many in my book. A minimum of ten judges, half of them tasting that wine in a different time and place, within a different field of competitors, all named this wine leader in its class. It's quite hard to argue with these circumstances. This baby's an undisputed champion, and the chances that you'll love it are greater than if it were recommended by a single person.

DOLLARS CORRUPT

Vinnie down at the corner wine shop has just gotten in a large shipment of some cheap Chilean wine. It's a dog.

However, he knows his customers like bargains, so he "recommends" it. They can't argue with the price, so the stuff disappears off his shelf faster than he can order more. It's a sad but true fact that some wine retailers' recommendations may be dictated by the immediate need for more shelf or cellar space. If you're serious about wine, try to find a wine seller who shares your values and understands your palate preferences and pocketbook.

As for wine magazines—arghh, don't get me started! I'll pose it to you this way: A large wine producer buys a full-page ad in a well-known bimonthly wine magazine for $15,000. (That's the fee for an ad that runs just two weeks, remember.) That issue's focus is California Chardonnays. Well, it turns out that this winery produces a lot of popular-style Chardonnay. And it also turns out that this wine producer is a semi-regular advertiser—spends upwards of $300,000 a year on ads. When the magazine's staff writers get together to sample and score the California Chardonnays, what are the chances that one of their best advertisers will get panned? All I can say is, "Doy."

If you don't believe me, talk to any wine retailer familiar with the top wine media and they'll tell you the same thing. Talk to the competition judges, as I have, and they'll tell you the same thing. Read the Internet chat pages and letters to the editor of a big wine magazine and you'll see the same question over and over: "Is there any relationship between the high scores you give and the amount and frequency of a wine producer's ads in your magazine?" The editors always deny it, yet those pesky readers persist in asking the question month after month. I wonder why.

This type of conflict of interest isn't all that unusual. In fact, the same thing happens in other businesses all the time—take the broker who recommends his firm's own funds to clients who came to him for some neutral advice. The commission's there, the product's good. So why not, he figures? While I have the highest respect for most of the wine writers out there, the magazines they work for may not share their same scruples and integrity. Therefore, don't view wine magazines' recommendations through rosé-colored glasses.

Wine competitions would face a similar dilemma if judging weren't conducted blind. The reason the best competition organizers go to such lengths to assure the wineries' anonymity while the products are being judged is because objectivity, combined with expertise, is really the only thing they have to offer wineries. If wine producers suspect that a competition is fixed, a gold medal from that competition loses its cachet, and the competition might as well advertise that it's looking for mediocre wines, since those are the only ones that will be entered.

Consequently, a wine consumer can be confident that a gold medal wine from a high-quality competition—namely, one featured in *Best Wines!*—got that award on its own merits. Gold medals are earned, not bought.

THE EXPERTS' CHOICE

Wine competitions provide a way for consumers to discover the wines the experts love most. Those who judge at the toughest and most prestigious wine competitions have to be experts in their fields—people who've spent their lives learning about wine, many of them wine scholars, wine writers, winemakers, Masters of Wine, sommeliers, restaurateurs, teachers, and so on. Panels of these experts serve as judges and determine which wines merit gold medals, following the strictest and most impeccable procedures to guarantee excellent tasting conditions and reliable results. In my view, a consumer won't find a more dependable and unbiased method for choosing a great bottle every time.

Competition Secrets
BEHIND THE SCENES AT INTERVIN 1998

B y now you're at least familiar with the concept of the wine competition—if you weren't before—and you also hopefully understand why gold medal winners from these events are reliably among the best wines.

But how do competitions really work? Who are the judges, for example? Are they red-bulbous-nosed men in suits with pretentious vocabularies? Who decided *they* were qualified? How could anyone accurately assess the value of sixty to seventy different wines in one day? How can a *panel* of judges decide which wine merits a gold medal? And what criteria are used to reach that decision?

Good questions! The truth is, few people get to find out what goes on behind the scenes at a really top-notch international wine competition because the judgings are usually closed to the public and cloaked in secrecy. Behind the scenes at InterVin 1998, one of the most highly respected international wine competitions, I got to snoop among the staff, interview the directors, and sit for six hours right alongside the judges, with whom I sniffed, swirled, slurped, spat, and gossiped.

INTERVIN'S JUDGES

A competition is only as good as its judges. To be selected as a judge for InterVin you can be a truck driver or a professor of oenology—as long as you pass the three-hour judge's test. Few do. In fact, the April weekend I was there, Andrew Sharp, InterVin's Canadian co-director, had just administered the test to 169 people. Of those, 49 passed. Of the 49 who advanced to the next phase—to be performance-monitored on an actual tasting panel—12 had to be subsequently removed from the panels they sat on. In the end, only 37 of the original 169 tested passed both the palate exam and the first sitting at InterVin. That's only a 22 percent success rate in this case.

Being a competitive type, I had to know *exactly* what this judge's test consisted of. (Could *I,* a mere compiler of wine statistics, pass it? Do I perhaps possess an *extremely talented* palate, one that the wine world needs to hear about?)

THE JUDGE'S TEST

InterVin has a *waiting list* of people eager to most likely fail this test. Why? Because getting certified as an InterVin judge qualifies you for other renowned wine-judgings that recognize the certificate. Being a judge at a major wine competition is prestigious, mildly profitable (judges are paid, wined and dined, and put up in fancy hotels), and—most of all—fun.

The judge's test exposes how many brain cells you lost as a teen or after your first marriage ended. "It's not something you can prepare for," explains Andrew Sharp. The author of *Winetaster's Secrets,* Sharp has made a career out of understanding how the palate works, how it can be trained, and how to communicate this knowledge to consumers. "We need to know, before we put our judges down into a regular list of judges, two fundamental things: first, do they have a palate that works and how well does it work? And then does it work over a long period of time? You and I and lots of people can sit down and taste a wine and we can give it a pretty accurate evaluation. Can you do that sixty times a day, four days in a row?"

A candidate is given four wines, starting with whites, that are extremely similar—same vintage, same viticultural area. Each glass is identical except for a small code number. He gets fifteen minutes to write down any notes he likes. The wines are then pulled away, recoded, and resequenced. Now he has to go back and re-identify the four original wines. They're pulled away again after another fifteen minutes, repoured in new recoded glasses, set down again before the tester in a new order, and have to be correctly identified once more.

Judge candidates go through this process with a series of reds and a series of whites. There's a right and a wrong answer—no room for opinions. This portion of the judge's test measures his consistency, concentration, and how well he can detect slight nuances and subtle differences in character.

On to the next phase of the exam: a four-part threshold test. "We take the four common wine components—sweetness, acid, what causes body or structure, and tannins. We take the same wine and vary it with four different levels of that component, serve them in random order, and they have to start from the lowest to the highest and put them in order," explains Sharp.

Next phase: The test-takers are served up five glasses of wine with five of the nine most common wine faults, caused by such things as unwanted yeast activity, spoilage, agricultural contaminants, or unclean barrels. InterVin gets actual faulty samples from a laboratory that does research and testing for wineries. The tasters have to figure out what's wrong with each sample by exactly identifying the flaw.

Most test takers by now have failed. The ones who've passed get another chance to fail; this time they'll be tracked by computer.

Sharp is a perfectionist. While he understands that wine tasting is an aesthetic act performed by human beings with personalities, biases, and frailties, he also believes that those human qualities can be classified, charted, and channeled to create a sort of scientific balance.

With a programmer Sharp created a computerized monitoring system that charts each judge's scores according to regional bias, wine-type bias, percentage lowest or highest score on a panel, consistency (how he unknowingly scores the same wine twice), etc.

"They will sit on one competition and we track them again with the computer. We test them for how many times they've been thrown out, how far away their averages are from the mean. We'll replace wines that they've tasted before to see how they score. Their scores count exactly the same as the other panelists'. For the first couple of panels we will look at them and if they are seriously out then we'll remove them right away."

ONCE A JUDGE, ALWAYS A JUDGE?

At InterVin, the testing and monitoring never end. All judges—even long-time veterans—sign their names to the score sheets. Each judge's composite score for every wine tasted is entered into a computer and then analyzed to determine the judge's level of palate fatigue, consistency, and even how his palate this year compares with that of last year.

"Last year," says Sharp, "they might have been a marvelous taster, but this year through maybe illness, through age, whatever, their palate has changed. It's a constantly changing thing. Once you pass the test it doesn't mean you're there forever. You're constantly monitored every year. And if your judging standard falls down too far, you're out."

I wondered if the degradation of one's taste buds necessarily follows from age. "It depends on what experience you've gained along the road," was his answer. "Because if you're older, you'll get weaker. But if you get older in gaining experience, then that experience fills in what you're losing in sensitivity."

CUSTOM-DESIGNED PANELS AND FLIGHTS

Sharp knows every judge's palate strengths and weaknesses, and thus devotes great attention to the composition of the panels and the wines selected for each panel— something a computer program can't do. For every wine, there will be five score sheets, one from each of the judges who tasted it. The high and low scores are knocked out. The remaining three are averaged to determine that wine's score. Thus a judge sitting on a five-judge panel has a 40 percent chance of being knocked out for any given wine. "Anything above 40 percent of your being rejected means you're in trouble here. You're getting rejected more than what you should," says Sharp. "So now what happens is we can take that figure of rejection and we find out how he does against Cabernets. Well, if he's getting tossed out 80 percent of the time with Cabernets, and only 20 percent of the time with Chardonnays, we know he's tasting better on Chardonnays. So then we go back and make sure that the panel he's on gets a higher number of Chardonnays than Cabernets."

Judges from different parts of the globe have unavoidable style preferences as well. "We make sure that we don't get an imbalance on a panel that would overly skew it to one side or another," says Sharp.

INTERVIN'S SCORING SYSTEM

InterVin judges follow the 100-point InterVin Numerical Evaluation System (I.N.E.S.). As it's described in the literature, I.N.E.S. is "designed for competition purposes . . . [with the] objective to assess the various components of wine and how well those components harmonize. Combined, the 18 elements of the I.N.E.S. express an evaluation of a wine sample in *numerical* terms."

The fundamental judging concept is expressed in three basic ideas. First, that each wine be judged on its own merits—not by how it compares to any other wine, or how well it represents a "typical" wine of its grape variety or region of origin. (Don't think for a second that these judges can't spot, say, a New York Chardonnay, even though the wines' identities are kept secret.) Second, that each wine be judged for what it is *at the time of judging*—not for what it may become in the future. (Consumers should exclaim "Hallelujah!" to that.) And third, that judges express their qualitative assessments in only five degrees—great, fine, ordinary, poor, unacceptable—and that they not add up their own scores. This avoids the natural temptation to compare scores, thus adding numerical bias.

According to Sharp, "While *total* objectivity cannot realistically be achieved, our goal is to move in this direction as far as possible, and away from the 'hedonistic' approach."

Sharp argues, rightly I think, that the "I like it/I don't like it" (a.k.a. hedonistic) approach skews the results of blind tastings. It tends to eliminate original and bold styles, and even whole classes of wine, such as native American wines, which deserve to be judged on their own merits, not in comparison with the great vinifera, or fine wines, to which most oenophiles are accustomed.

So think of a multiple choice test with 18 questions, each requiring one of five answers—from great to unacceptable. Judges are asked to linger on the four-part "Visual" portion of the evaluation first, which includes rating the wine's Surface; Clarity/Limpidity; Depth/Luminance; and Tint/ Hue. The "Olfactory" section is next, where Intensity/Purity; Aroma; Bouquet; and Harmony/Balance are each scored. The two-part "Tactile" section includes Body as well as Astringency. Under "Taste" the judges evaluate the wine's Intensity/Purity; Sweetness; Acidity; Bitterness; and Harmony/Balance. The "Flavor" portion comprises Aftertaste and Persistence. And the final score is given to "Overall Quality."

Not all categories are weighted equally. For instance, a "Great" score under Clarity/Limpidity counts for 4 points, while a "Great" score under Body counts as 8 points.

If you think this is easy, try to distinguish between aroma and bouquet, for instance. To be honest, I would have been thrown out by the monitors had they been checking my scores for competence. It takes real palate talent and tremendous concentration to tell the difference between, say, intensity and body, or to separate out a quality such as purity from that of balance and to identify where a wine falls on the spectrum between great and unacceptable.

INTERVIN'S GOLD MEDAL WINES

There are only 9 points (on a 100-point scale) separating a bronze from a gold medal at InterVin, which is unusual. To merit an InterVin gold, a wine has to achieve a score of 90 points. Then it gets retasted by a second panel of judges. If it can achieve 90 points *twice*, it's awarded a gold medal.

Wow! If no wines earn 90 or more, no golds are awarded. This policy is *exceedingly* unusual among wine competitions.

Some have criticized InterVin for being too tough, saying that the competition holds wines to an impossibly high standard. Andrew Sharp responds: "Our mission is to raise the quality of all wine. By putting them in open competition with each other, by raising the bar every couple of years, it pushes them, stimulating the wineries to do better and better."

Further, since wines aren't judged by price or by region, every bottle has to stand on its own, which helps to eliminate the possibility of regional bias or lowered standards.

One thing is for certain: I wouldn't hesitate to buy any gold medal wine from InterVin. For that matter, I'd buy an InterVin bronze or silver wine too.

I WAS THERE

So what was it like to pretend to be a judge for a day? In case anyone out there is thinking of starting a wine competition fantasy camp, don't bother. It's fairly grueling to taste upwards of 70 wines in six hours. While I found the experience fascinating, it was also humbling.

InterVin '98 was held on the 25th floor of the Metropolitan Hotel in downtown Toronto. It's 8:30 Saturday morning, and I slip into the large kitchen down the hall from the tasting rooms, where the staff people are readying for a long day of tasting. Today, each of five panels, consisting of five to six judges apiece, will taste 60 to 70 different wines. Since each panel evaluates their own set of wines, that's over 300 bottles that will be opened and scrutinized today.

Take those 300 bottles, multiply by five to six glasses, and you have 1,500 to 1,800 glasses that need to be clean, dry, spot-free, labeled with the same number as the corresponding bottle, poured, placed in the correct order on a cart, wheeled into the judging room, and then re-placed in front of the proper table of judges in the proper sequence. After the flight is judged, they have to be wheeled away, washed, dried, relabeled, and so on.

It's *not* a no-brainer; the sheer volume of bottles and glasses makes you realize that a misplaced list, a transposed number on a code, a bottle out of order—any of these could screw up the fairness and objectivity, a wine competition's hallmark.

This morning co-director David Male, the New York half of the team, is overseeing the preparations, answering questions, troubleshooting, and making sure that everything goes as planned.

Should a judge sneak a peek in the kitchen, intentional or not, it could result in his or her recognizing a label, inevitably tainting later judgment or concentration during the tastings.

Because the human mind is so complex, great care is taken to assure identical conditions for the tasters every flight, every day. That is, every glass is exactly the same—except of course for the small number that identifies it to the competition staff. A flaw in the glass, a water spot, a wine that's slightly warmer or colder than the one before it—all of these factors can contribute to real or imagined differences in the wine and thus the score it's given.

"We take it as a trust that is given to us by the wineries, who send their wine in, pay us to do this, and then if we can't give them a perfect environment in the sense of an *even* environment with everyone else, then we're not being fair," explains Sharp. "Because the wineries want an even playing field, and we have to do everything we can to make sure the temperature's the same, to make sure the humidity is the same, the glasses are the same, that they're washed and cleaned the same, and presented in the same way."

I walk into the next room to await the first flight of wines to be evaluated today. I'm seated with Panel E, consisting of five judges: four men and one woman besides myself. (That's not uncommon in the wine industry, dominated by males, most of them white.) Everyone at my table, I later find out, is associated with the wine industry in one way or another.

The five judges' tables are covered in white tablecloths so you can view the wine's color against a white background. At each place is a small lamp, bottle of spring water, spittoon, and score sheets. (My score sheets, thank goodness, are for my eyes only; they won't count.)

For each flight, which consists of five to six wines, a half hour is allotted—or about six minutes per glass. We have three such flights scheduled, then a midmorning food and coffee break. Three more flights then lunch. Three more then a mid-afternoon food and tea break. One more set of three flights concludes our day.

At first I'm tentative about my ability to evaluate these wines. For one, it isn't easy to avoid comparisons, which is frowned upon at InterVin. I'm tempted to look at, smell, and taste all of them, one after another, to see which one is "best."

It's not the only difficult part. Try spending six minutes contemplating two ounces of wine—wine you won't be able to swallow!

Around the fifteenth wine or so I begin to "see" luminescence, detect a wide array of aromas, discern subtle qualities such as weight and depth, understand the difference between tannic and hard—and I'm not even under the influence, having spit out every mouthful! (By the way, spitting with finesse is an art, one I'm still mastering.)

Like a baby in a rich and stimulating environment, I am rapidly learning. I discover that my nose is tremendously sensitive, and that the range of smells I'm now perceiving is limited only by my ability to express myself. For instance, when I think I recognize the delicate scent of violets in one of the red wines, I'm thrilled to remember that violets are in fact one identifiable and desirable trait of a certain red varietal (Cabernet Sauvignon). Taking my time with an ounce of wine leads me to enjoy the experience of other sensations, such as that of finish—how long the mingled effects of the acid, alcohol, fruit, and tannins linger at the back of my throat and on my tongue. It's like anything else: Practice makes perfect. Anyone's palate, I'm convinced, can be educated.

Did you ever open a wine you thought might have a flaw, but weren't sure enough to return it? I even got so that I could *grimace* with confidence when my table received three flawed wines during the day—two with corkiness, one with "geranium." A corky wine is unmistakable once you've smelled its wet dog and soggy newspaper aroma, caused by a bacterial growth on the cork. A geranium wine has a distinctive odor resembling the pungent flower, caused by a bacterial degradation of sorbic acid.

JUDGES, JUDGINGS, AND RELIABILITY

I was really impressed by the judges at InterVin, who were articulate, thoughtful, and unbelievably knowledgeable. Wine people don't get into this profession by accident. *They really do love wine*, the major theme in their lives.

Having spent a day in the company of such fine wine-careerists, having experienced firsthand the professionalism of a leading wine competition—the organizer's competence and the gravity and reverence with which they approach their task—I'm comfortable relying on the judgments of these tasters, and you should be too.

That's what this book is all about.

Health Secrets
BENEFITS OF MODERATE WINE CONSUMPTION

I f you haven't heard the good news about the benefits of moderate wine consumption to your health, you probably live in a cave. There are many positive ramifications associated with having one to three glasses per day, particularly when consumed with your dinner. Isn't it great to know that, for once, what you love is actually good for you?

I researched and compiled the following information from a number of sources, including leading medical journals, major wine references, mainstream newsmagazines, wine trade monthlies, and Internet sites of top university oenology departments and leading wine organizations. The studies from which the data were collected go back as far as 1947 and are as recent as 1998—from respected medical researchers around the world.

WINE AND THE HEART

Read the U.S. Government Dietary Guidelines for Americans and you'll get the mainstream view on wine and health. Surprisingly, it states that moderate drinking is associated with a lower risk for coronary heart disease. If Uncle Sam approves, you've got to believe that rigorous testing and analysis are behind that statement.

People from all over the world—including Japanese men living in Hawaii; Chicago General Electric workers; the good folks of Framingham, Massachusetts; Aussies in Busselton, Western Australia; elderly villagers in rural Greece; Californians in Alameda County; thousands of doctors and nurses; and of course the famous 13,000 French people of "French Paradox" fame—have been poked, prodded, monitored, and questioned in studies related to alcohol consumption and the heart. The results are consistent and positive: Moderate drinking is good for your heart in a number of ways.

Lowers risk for angina. Data from Harvard's ongoing Health Study reveals that among 22,000 male physicians participating in the study, those who drank two drinks per day had a 56 percent lower risk for angina pectoris (chest pain). Angina, caused by a lack of blood to the heart, is considered a warning sign for heart attack risk.

Prevents arterial clotting. Wine, especially red wine, contains phenolic compounds, which are effective antioxidants. These are the compounds that impart bitterness and astringency to wine, and allow for long aging (which makes sense, since the antioxidants counteract the oxygen that ruins wine over time). In our bodies, these phenolic compounds, particularly resveratrol and flavonoids, inhibit clotting of the arteries and other internal blood clots, such as those that cause strokes. Wine's ability to inhibit the clotting activity of platelets, a condition known as thrombosis, substantially reduces the risk of heart attack.

Improves cholesterol levels. Having wine with your meal can counter the adverse effects of fat in your bloodstream by positively affecting your cholesterol levels. Along with the alcohol, phenolics found in wine alter blood lipid (fat) levels by lowering your LDL levels, the "bad" cholesterol that's implicated in arterial clogging, and by raising your HDL, the so-called good cholesterol. What's more, one study discovered that those who drank wine with their dinner, as opposed to those who drank mineral water, not only experienced improved cholesterol numbers, but the effects were still detectable early the next morning. Researchers believe that cholesterol oxidizes in the blood, causing it to settle on arterial walls. The antioxidant properties of wine—or specifically, tannins—keep that from happening.

Lowers blood pressure. Experts agree that high blood pressure contributes to coronary heart disease and overall mortality. New evidence points to another aspect of wine's cardioprotective benefits: its ability to positively affect systolic and diasystolic blood pressure. The lowest blood pressure levels in subjects of a recent Harvard study were found in those who consumed one to three drinks per day (wine or alcoholic spirits), even factoring in such things as smoking, a family history of hypertension, adjustments for pulse rate, and medication use.

WINE AND STROKES

Just as moderate wine drinking benefits the heart by helping to prevent the formation of arterial plaque, which can clog arteries and blood vessels, it also aids in preventing cerebrovascular disease caused by internal blood clotting. Several renowned researchers have determined, in a number of different studies, that wine drinkers enjoy a dramatically reduced risk of the most common type of stroke. In fact, a recent paper published by the American Heart Association showed that risk of stroke for abstainers from alcohol is double that for moderate drinkers.

WINE AND PERIPHERAL ARTERY DISEASE

I may sound like a doctor, but I'm not. The fact is, I'd never heard of Peripheral Artery Disease (PAD) until I did wine-and-health research. But now that I know it refers to the clogging of arteries in places other than the heart—the legs, for example—and that it's a notable cause of death among the elderly, I'm happy to know that a glass or two of wine a day can greatly decrease my risk for PAD. If you're a man, particularly, and you have poor circulation in your legs, moderate wine drinking could reduce your risk for PAD by as much as 32 percent.

WINE AND AGING/MORTALITY

What mortality studies come down to is this: Given that 100 percent of the population die 100 percent of the time, what's the percentage who die from X disease and why?

Mortality researchers have launched a number of studies to determine wine's role in longevity (now that I've passed my fortieth birthday, I prefer the term *longevity* to *aging*). The most recent and largest study to date investigating the link between alcohol consumption and health has determined that one drink a day can lower mortality among elderly and middle-aged persons by 20 percent.

The 12-Year Copenhagen Study, perhaps the most famous of wine-and-health studies, found a 49 percent reduction in mortality among the study's participants who drank three to five glasses of wine per day (not exactly moderate, in my opinion). It was those flavonoids again, with their antioxidant properties, that were found to have a significant preventive effect on diseases of the heart as well as some forms of cancer.

Another recent study monitored 8,000 people for ten years and found that people who drink one or two glasses of wine per day live longer and are less likely to die from all causes than either abstainers or heavy drinkers. In fact, no study to date has shown that total abstainers have lower mortality from all causes than light drinkers.

Yet another study focused on factors important in predicting healthy aging, defined as living independently at a high level of physical and mental function, without requiring outside aid. Except for being a nonsmoker, the most important factor predicting healthy aging was being a moderate drinker.

Finally, the lifestyles and diets of elderly inhabitants of three rural Greek villages were studied to see if they could find the secret to these old folks' "fountain of youth." It turned out that these elderly people ate a healthy diet consisting of legumes, fruits, vegetables, grains, monounsaturated fats (mostly olive oil), small amounts of meat and dairy, and a daily moderate amount of wine with meals. The researchers concluded that wine, an integral part of their diet, was an essential element in helping these elderly villagers live to such ripe old ages.

WINE AND BRAIN FUNCTION

A ten-year-old study from France has just concluded that elderly persons who were also moderate drinkers showed a 75 percent decrease in Alzheimer's disease. Additionally, these elderly folks had an 80 percent decrease in the rate of dementia compared with nondrinkers.

In a study of elderly male twins, standard cognitive reasoning tests were administered to two brothers, one a moderate drinker, the other a total abstainer. The brother who consumed alcohol scored higher on a regular basis. Still other studies have shown that moderate drinkers are less likely to suffer from depression when under stress.

WINE AND CANCER

Oversimplified, antioxidants are substances that are thought to prevent cancer. There are compounds in the body known as free radicals, which are highly reactive forms of molecules that can weaken cell walls, thus allowing those cells to oxidize. When cells are oxidized, they die or are subject to mutation, which can result in cancer. Phenolics, found in red wine, block free radicals, thus preventing harmful oxidation. Researchers emphasize the importance of polyphenols as anticancer agents, and wine is rich in both the quality and quantity of polyphenols.

A recent article published by the *Journal of the National Cancer Institute* reported that in a study assessing tobacco, alcohol, and socio-economic status on four types of cancers of the stomach and esophagus, wine drinkers were found to have 40 percent less risk for all four cancers.

In one University of Davis study, specially bred mice were fed dealcoholized wine solids and were found to be free of tumors 40 percent longer than their siblings with no wine in their diets.

The Harvard University Nurses' Health Study found that while excessive alcohol consumption increases the risk of developing many cancers, light to moderate wine drinking significantly decreased cancer risk in the subjects. A new study conducted on the Chinese population confirms that death rates for moderate drinkers (middle-aged men) were 19 percent lower for cancer and noncancer causes than for nondrinking men.

WINE AND BACTERIAL DISEASES

An exciting recent study done at West Virginia University found that wine can protect you from the kinds of bacterial diseases one can get from tainted shellfish, bad water, and spoiled meat or poultry—i.e., food poisoning. The three culprits studied were E. coli, salmonella, and shigella. The researchers found that wine kills these bacteria.

Wine was tested alongside pure alcohol, tequila, and bismuth salicytate (the active ingredient in Pepto Bismol) to see what effect each had on 10 million colony-forming units of shigella, salmonella, and E. coli. Wine was the most effective in destroying these critters, with good old Pepto Bismol coming in a distant second, and alcohol and tequila bringing up the rear. In other words, it's something specific in wine, not just the alcohol, that has this beneficial effect.

WINE'S OTHER BENEFITS

There's a long list of other maladies that may be prevented or beneficially affected by moderate wine drinking, and the list will get longer, since money is being funneled into these studies by governments, drug companies, and large university medical departments. Here's a short list:

Treats iron-deficient anemia. Wine has long been prescribed to treat anemia. It helps vegetarians and others by stimulating the body's ability to absorb minerals and other nutrients.

Lowers risk for bone/joint diseases. More studies continue to suggest that moderate wine consumption by postmenopausal women may help prevent osteoporosis, since these women have higher levels of estrogen-related hormones. (Estrogen deficiency is a key factor in the development of osteoporosis.) One study found that five to fourteen drinks a week decreased the risk of rheumatoid arthritis for women. Further, moderate amounts of wine in the diet may also increase bone density, especially among the elderly. Another group of researchers even found that older women who drank moderately performed better in tests designed to measure agility, coordination, and balance than did either abstainers or heavy drinkers.

Reduces the likelihood of diabetes. Two recent reports have confirmed earlier reports that moderate drinkers (in this case, wine or spirits) experience a 40 percent decrease in the likelihood that they will develop adult onset diabetes.

Reduces the risk of gallbladder disease. It's been shown that red- and white-wine drinkers benefit from a one-third reduced risk of developing gallstones and the subsequent complications of gallbladder disease.

Reduces the formation of kidney stones. A recent study compared wine with twenty-one other beverages to determine which were most strongly associated with decreased risk for the formation of painful kidney stones. Wine came out ahead, reducing the risk of stone formation by 39 percent. Another study found that alcohol in general was associated with a lower incidence of kidney stones.

EMERGING HEALTH BENEFITS

In addition to the above, there are a number of ongoing studies that have found moderate wine consumption to have potentially beneficial effects on the following:

- Common cold
- Insulin sensitivity
- Parkinson's disease
- Bone fractures
- Digestive ailments
- Pancreatic cancer
- Hepatitis A
- Stress and depression

While new and exciting research will no doubt uncover even more health benefits related to moderate wine drinking, one thing seems clear: There's no need to count your daily glass of wine as a vice.

To your health, bottoms up, cheers, and all that.

Chef Secrets
DEMYSTIFYING WINE-AND-FOOD PAIRING

One of the two questions I'm asked most frequently in interviews is, "What wine should I serve with (*fill in the blank*)?" During preholiday interviews it's "Thanksgiving turkey" or "Christmas ham." (My listeners never seem to want me to wax poetic about how a small-town gal hiked up the hardscrabble paths of life to get to where I am today. Ho-hum—such is the exciting life of an author.)

I then impart little gems of wisdom and send my fans out in radioland scampering to their nearest wine shop, list in hand, full of newfound confidence that finally they have the secret to matching the best wine with the meal they'll be slaving over for family and friends. (The other most commonly asked question is "What's the best such-and-such for under ten dollars?" For the answer, see Appendix 1, "Best Bargain Wines.")

The real secret to mastering food-and-wine pairing lies in: (1) understanding the concepts of "weight" as it relates to wine and "richness" as it relates to food; (2) knowing some basic "rules" about food ingredients that enhance or detract from wine; and (3) having the confidence in your own preferences and taste to discard tired and outdated myths about food-and-wine compatibility.

MATCHING WEIGHT AND FLAVOR INTENSITY

What is meant by a wine's "weight"? Go back to the Palate Secrets chapter (I'll be quizzing you later) and you'll remember that a lot happens inside your mouth when you're trying to assess a wine. Was the red wine astringent? Did the fruits taste rich and dark or were they refreshing and light? Was your white wine zesty and fresh or smooth and round? Did it have smoky or buttery flavors, or was it citrusy and sassy? Did the wine's flavor and effect linger in your mouth or disappear quickly? Did the wine have a chewy or thick texture, or was it more delicate and subtle? Did it deliver a punch or a light kiss?

These are all goofy questions to which you'll finally intuit the answers if you go through the tasting process described in the first chapter, and familiarize yourself with some of the terms used to describe wine (see the glossary in Appendix 3). The answers to these questions will give you an idea of the wine's weight and general character.

While different winemaking processes result in different wine styles, there are certain varietals that generally occupy the "heavy" or "light" range of the spectrum. For instance, Cabernet Sauvignon, red Bordeaux-style blends, and Shiraz are usually rich, weighty, robust red wines; Chardonnay aged in oak and white Meritage are examples of white wines that have some heft. Beaujolais-style reds are lightweight, as are Chenin Blancs, which are white, as well as most rosés. If you're unsure about where a red or white wine falls in this spectrum, refer to the listings in Part II, where the first page of each section describes the varietal's typical characteristics.

What does this have to do with food? Common sense tells us that a bulldozer personality won't pair well with an ultrasensitive type. When it comes to food and wine, consider the richness of the dish you're preparing in relation to its potential wine mate. Broiled steak, grilled oily seafood, roasted wild game, and heavily creamed sauces are examples of rich dishes. Steamed vegetables, tofu stir-fry, baked lemon sole, and picnic sandwiches are examples of lighter fare. Garlicky, tomato-based pasta dishes, pizza, and fried chicken fall somewhere in the middle. Get it?

If you pay attention that your wine and your food are of equal weight, the food doesn't overpower the wine, and vice versa. Following this one rule makes it possible to find the right wine match for any food, no matter your expertise. Hearty, robust dishes match up well with equally full-bodied wines, which is why young, tannic reds go well with grilled game and red meat, or why fruity, round, soft, uncomplicated wines should be consumed with equally simple foods, such as nonspicy vegetarian dishes or picnic fare.

But don't make blanket generalizations about foods. For example, stir-fry chicken doesn't have the heft of roast chicken served in a dark wild mushroom sauce. Always consider the way the food is prepared when determining how to find its perfect wine matchup.

Similarly, know that every food and wine has an intensity or density of flavor. A food that's sweet, for example, needs a wine that's at least as sweet. A lemony seafood dish would call for a zesty, lively wine with a lot of acidity, but medium-bodied with not so much oakiness, such as certain Sauvignon Blancs. Salty foods go nicely with sparkling wines and, traditionally, aperitifs such as sherry. Very spicy foods may be light, yet intensely flavored. Therefore, choose a wine that is also light-bodied but intense, such as a semi-sweet Riesling or Gewurztraminer.

HELPFUL OR MEDDLESOME INGREDIENTS

I wonder how long I can beat this food/wine marriage metaphor before it dies? Well here goes. There are some basic ingredients you'll want to get to know better, since they interact with wine in ways that enhance the enjoyability of the interplay. And there are those you'll want to cross off your list of potential wine mates.

One of the best articles I've read on the subject was in *Wine Spectator,* where the American writer dined with a French chef who kept fooling with the food to see how the writer would experience his wine. While I would have liked to see more drama in the piece (e.g., the French chef poisoning the upstart American wine writer: "Adieu, monsieur! Hah hah!"), it helped me and the writer understand just how potent is food's effect on wine.

For example, an extremely tart and acidic white wine tasted softer and mellower after the chef squeezed lemon juice on the fish dish that accompanied it.

When the chef added a little sweetness or bitterness to the food, such as a sweet fruit sauce or some grated lemon zest, the wine seemed more acidic or astringent.

Some more general rules: Salty and sour foods tend to make wine taste milder. A squeeze of lemon and bit of salt can

restore balance to the marriage if the problem is wine bitterness. A French chef might melt a little butter over a steak
to add fat, which will mellow a harsh red wine. When it
comes to wine with dessert, if the wine is only slightly
sweet, try serving a dessert with fruit purée rather than
sugar sauce.

In other words, seasonings and sauces may be more cru-
cial to food-and-wine matching than is the main ingredient (i.e., fish, poultry, or meat).

FOODS THAT MAKE WINE TASTE WEIRD

Vinegar is incompatible with wine, period. Try to use wine
or lemon salad dressings if you're serving salads with wine.

It's long been known that artichokes and asparagus are
wine-unfriendly. In the case of the former, artichokes contain a substance called cynarin that makes water taste sweet
and wine, metallic. Some people report that asparagus does
the same.

Chocolate is the subject of great debate. Slick ads for an
"Evening of Wine and Chocolate" occasionally land in my
post office box, and are worded as if the event organizers
are meeting in a speakeasy and plotting the overthrow of
the government. I mean, is it seditious to consider such a
pairing? Apparently so. For one, it's hard to find a wine
that's sweeter than chocolate. Also, chocolate coats the
mouth, which is deadly for wine tasting.

Cheeses are also a problem for some wine lovers, specifically because they're often salty, strong-flavored, high in
fat, and because they coat the mouth. Many experts agree
that sweet wines are generally the best wines to drink with
cheeses, and white wines fare better than do reds. But of
course the variety of cheeses makes it impossible to make
sweeping recommendations. So either steer clear or be
willing to experiment.

You'll no doubt notice in the introductory descriptions of
each wine type in Part II that cheese and chocolate are nevertheless mentioned as good companions to certain wines.

The fact is that all kinds of people recommend these pairings, so who am I to argue?

DEBUNKING THE MYTHS

True or false: Red wine goes best with red meat, white wine with white meat. If you answered true, then you either need to go back to the beginning and reread this chapter, or I need to track down my murderous French chef and arrange to have him serve me a last meal. The truth is that the old myths are no longer followed—by me or by anyone else. A food's richness and flavor intensity will determine what type of wine to serve. Rich foods go with robust, full-bodied wines. Delicate foods go with soft and mellow wines. Spicy foods should be served with spicy wines. Sweetness, saltiness, fat content as well as the type of sauces and cooking methods used are important when determining which wine to serve alongside a dish.

But the single most important factor when choosing the right wine, unless you're entertaining wine snobs who will secretly be marking scorecards under the table, is whether or not it's a good wine and whether or not you like it. Be creative, know the "rules," then buy something you enjoy. That's what wining and dining are about, after all.

My Secrets
HOW TO BUY A GREAT WINE EVERY TIME

O nce I realized that buying gold medal wines was a surefire way to avoid a disappointing bottle every time (without having to become an expert), I decided to write this book for others like myself who are tired of being pushed around by the wine bully culture.

But as I became the user of my own book I uncovered some of the pitfalls of gold medal wine shopping. Here are some tried-and-true shopping tips to help avoid frustration.

RIGHT BRAND AND TYPE, WRONG VINTAGE

Not an uncommon problem. Let's say the wine you want is a 1997. But your wine shop is still carrying 1996. It's because that's the vintage his or her distributor stocks. Until the distributor sells out of 1996s, you may be out of luck, at least at that wine shop. I've found that wine retailers in smaller towns and particularly East Coast towns carry earlier vintages. West Coast and large-city wine retailers sell out the fastest and have the most current vintages.

Before trying one of the other options below, ask the owners if they can order that particular vintage. Depending on how sophisticated their connections are, they may be able to call any one of several distributors to track down that vintage for you. And wine shops are happy to do it. It never occurred to me before I began this project that I could get absolutely any wine I wanted most of the time. All I had to do was ask.

You can also try another area wine shop. Many times wine stores in a single town will have different distributors, which means they may stock a different vintage than their competitors.

Another option is to contact the winery directly. Most wineries have 800 numbers, so calling information is also free (800-555-1212). Many wineries also have websites. Either way, getting in touch with the winery directly can be lots of fun. The majority of wineries have free newletters that keep you informed about great deals, fun events, and other wine news. And most of them aren't snobbish in the least. In fact, they'll usually treat you like gold. If you live in a *reciprocal state* (see Appendix 4 for more information on this), they may be able to ship you bottles at a price that might top what you'd find at the wine shop.

Yet another way is to hook up with a mail-order or Internet wine retailer (see Appendix 4 for a selective listing) and they might stock the gold medal wine you seek. Again, if you live in a state that doesn't enforce restrictive alcohol-shipping laws, they'll be able to send you the bottles quickly, usually next-day or two-day.

Last, but not necessarily as a last resort, you can buy the vintage your winemonger stocks even though it's not listed in this edition. Since 1995, when I started the *Best Wines!* project, I've researched hundreds of gold medal wines. Not surprisingly, it's really the wineries, not the wines, that are winning the golds. Every year there are surprises, but generally speaking the very best wineries produce gold medal winning wines year after year. If a wine won two gold medals, you can be confident that an earlier or later vintage of that same wine will be delicious. The later vintage is apt to pick up a gold medal itself.

A winemaker who knows how to produce a stunning Zinfandel one year will most assuredly be able to do it again the next year too. If that weren't true, wineries would go out of business.

"TINYTOWN WINES" DOESN'T CARRY IT

My folks live in a fairly small town in Central Illinois. Jug wines often occupy more shelf space than fine wines in rural areas and smaller towns. The solution to this problem is basically the same as above. First talk to the wine merchant. Next, try outside sources.

THE PRICE LISTED IN BOOK ISN'T RIGHT

Shame on you. Would an Episcopalian-raised former Mid-westerner lie to her readers? Well, sure. All writers are liars. But I wouldn't lie about the wine prices. The prices listed in this book reflect *suggested retail prices* and were provided by the wineries themselves, or in some cases by the competitions, who themselves obtained the price from the winery. But buyers beware. Even in little Woodstock, New York, the same wine can vary as much as three dollars from wine shop to wine shop.

One solution is to do some competitive shopping if you can. Try different shops; try some alternatives to wine shops mentioned above if interstate shipping isn't a problem in your state. The best solution is to just buy up a gold medal winner when you see it. Gold medal wines sell out quickly.

NOW, ON TO THE PLEASURES

The real fun of writing this book for me has been the freedom I now feel to experiment with new wines. If a merchant doesn't carry the brand you want, look in the book for alternatives. In other words, don't get hung up on the same label, region, or type of wine to which you're accustomed.

Since every wine in this book won the highest award against dozens, sometimes hundreds, of competitors, you can be confident that you won't be disappointed. Want an inexpensive Cabernet? Try one from Chile or Washington instead of California. Want a zingy Chardonnay? Look to Canada or Australia. Love red wine? Try a Bordeaux-style blend or an Italian-American varietal. Try serving a sparkling wine before dinner to your guests. Have a chilled ice wine rather than parfaits for dessert.

I recently went to a celebration for a friend's MBA party. My companion and I were asked to bring red wine for twenty people. Book in hand, we strolled down the aisles of a large wine retailer and picked out six gold medal winners, ranging from a bargain $6 Chilean Merlot to a moderate $10 California Petite Sirah to an extravagant $24 Oregonean Pinot Noir. We also chose a Zinfandel, a Cabernet, and an Australian Shiraz, each around $15. Wonderfully, although we hadn't tried any of these wines, we knew they'd be a smash—and they were.

If I want to buy an inexpensive wine, I either scan the list of Best Bargain Wines in Appendix 1, or I look to the index for the "$15 and under" symbol (**$**). When I want a wine that will dazzle even the most biased wine drinker, I buy a bottle that's won three or more gold medals—also known as a BBW, Best of the Best Wines. You'll find BBWs listed separately in Appendix 2. Or you can easily find them in the index, where the BBW symbol (✹) identifies them as wines that have won the most golds.

Another pleasure associated with using this book is the gratifiying feeling of being a savvy shopper. For instance, there are a lots of wineries in the book that picked up numerous golds. Because they're listed alphabetically by type, you can compare a "regular" Pinot Noir, say, with a Reserve Pinot Noir. Often, the less expensive one may have more golds and more special awards. By all means, buy the cheaper one!

I got out of my wine-buying rut by exploring gold medal wines instead. You can too!

PART II

The Gold Medal Winners

Red Wines

Beaujolais-style Reds
Cabernet Franc
Cabernet Sauvignon
Italian Varietals
Malbec
Merlot
Miscellaneous Varietal Reds
Native Reds & French-American Hybrids
Petite Sirah
Pinot Noir
Red Blends
Syrah/Shiraz
Zinfandel

BEAUJOLAIS-STYLE REDS

The "Beaujolais-style" reds collectively known as American Gamays are no relation to the French grape, Gamay Noir à Jus Blanc, of the Beaujolais region. And in fact, the French wine community is as grouchy about Americans calling their wine Gamay, Napa Gamay, or Gamay Beaujolais as they are with our generic term *champagne* for sparkling wines. A recent lawsuit filed by the French resulted in a ruling: Within five years American wine producers must retire the above terms.

Some wineries are already experimenting with calling Napa Gamay by its real name: Valdiguié, which to me sounds a bit like a Medieval dragon slayer. On the other hand, only time will tell what Gamay and Gamay Beaujolais, which aren't even related to Napa Gamay (a.k.a. Valdiguié) and are actually made from a lesser relative of Pinot Noir, will be called.

Regardless of the confusion that surrounds their name and origin, American Gamays are in fact reminiscent of a nice French Beaujolais (go ahead—arrest me) in that they're light, fruity, simple, and generally inexpensive. Gamays are meant to be consumed young. They're wines to drink— not sip—out of cool, frosted glasses.

Food companions: Serve Beaujolais-style reds slightly chilled with uncomplicated food such as picnic platters of cold meats, salads, and light cheeses. Gamays also complement grilled meats, poultry, veal, hamburger, chili, and turkey soup.

Amity Vineyards 1997 Gamay Noir
Region: Oregon $9
Golds/Awards: Gold (EN)

Beringer 1996 Gamay Beaujolais
Region: California $8
Golds/Awards: Gold (WC)

Gallo Sonoma 1995 Barelli Creek Vineyard Valdiguié
Region: California, Alexander Valley $12
Golds/Awards: Gold (WC, NW)

Glen Ellen 1996 Proprietor's Reserve Gamay Beaujolais
Region: California $5
Golds/Awards: Gold (RI)

Did You Know...?

The French government sued the U.S.
government to prevent our wine growers
from using "their" term: *Gamay Beaujolais*. They won,
but the ruling doesn't go into effect until 2007.

**Gundlach-Bundschu Winery 1997 Rhinefarm Vineyards
Gamay Beaujolais**
Region: California, Sonoma Valley $9
Golds/Awards: Gold (PR)

J. Lohr 1997 Estate Wildflower Valdiguié
Region: California $7.50
Golds/Awards: Gold (LA); Best of Class (LA)

Navarro 1996 Napa Gamay
Region: California, Mendocino $12
Golds/Awards: Gold (NW)

V. Sattui 1997 Gamay Rouge
Region: California $12.75
Golds/Awards: Gold (CA); Best of Class (CA)

Weinstock Cellars 1997 Gamay
Region: California, Paso Robles $5.99
Golds/Awards: Gold (CA); Best of Class (CA)

CABERNET FRANC

One of the primary blending varieties, Cabernet Franc is most often paired with Cabernet Sauvignon to add cedary, raspberry, and floral suggestions to its more assertive cousin in Bordeaux-style red blends (also known in America as red Meritage). In the New World, over the last twenty years, California and Australia in particular have upped their plantings of this variety, and are using it widely to add dimension to their Cabernet Sauvignons. In the Old World it has been used this way for many decades.

However, interest in making Cabernet Franc as a varietal wine has also increased in the New World, particularly in California, Long Island, Argentina, Washington State, and New Zealand.

Compared with Cabernet Sauvignon, Cabernet Franc is light to medium bodied, fruitier, lighter in color, and less tannic.

Food companions: Cabernet Franc pairs well with aromatic herbs such as basil and sage, Mediterranean-style pasta dishes, baked chèvre in olive leaves, spring lamb, and game such as venison.

Arciero Winery 1995 Estate Bottled Cabernet Franc
Region: California, Paso Robles $10.50
Golds/Awards: Gold (DA)

Buttonwood Farm Winery 1995 Cabernet Franc
Region: California, Santa Ynez Valley $18
Golds/Awards: Gold (NW); Best of Class (NW)

Did You Know...?

In a hurry for your collector bottle of wine
to age so you can drink it? There are magnet
gadgets on the market to put around the bottle
to supposedly simulate aging by altering the
chemical composition of the wine inside. Try it on
a bottle of snake oil first!

Columbia Winery 1994 Red Willow Vineyard Cabernet Franc
Region: Washington, Yakima Valley $23.99
Golds/Awards: Gold (WWC-91 pts)

Columbia Winery 1995 Red Willow Vineyard Cabernet Franc
Region: Washington, Yakima Valley $19.99
Golds/Awards: Gold (NW); Best of Class (NW)

Douglas Hill Winery 1995 Cabernet Franc
Region: California, Napa Valley $14.99
Golds/Awards: Gold (NW); Best of Class (NW)

Gainey 1995 Cabernet Franc
Region: California, Santa Ynez Valley $20
Golds/Awards: Gold (WWC-90 pts)

Geyser Peak 1995 Trione Vineyard Winemaker's Selection Cabernet Franc
Region: California, Alexander Valley $19.99
Golds/Awards: Gold (WWC-90 pts, CA); Best of Class (CA)

Hart Winery 1996 Estate Bottled Unfiltered, Unfined Cabernet Franc
Region: California, Temecula $20
Golds/Awards: Gold (OC)

Cabernet Franc

RED

Indian Springs Vineyards 1996 Cabernet Franc
Region: California, Nevada County $15
Golds/Awards: Gold (OC)

Jarvis 1994 Cabernet Franc
Region: California, Napa Valley $45
Golds/Awards: Gold (WWC-90 pts)

Jekel 1994 Cabernet Franc
Region: California, Arroyo Seco $25
Golds/Awards: Gold (NW)

Kendall-Jackson 1995 Grand Reserve Cabernet Franc
Region: California $18
Golds/Awards: Gold (SD)

Kendall-Jackson 1995 Buckeye Vineyard Cabernet Franc
Region: California, Alexander Valley $24
Golds/Awards: Gold (SD)

Pepperwood Grove 1996 Cabernet Franc
Region: California $6.99
Golds/Awards: Gold (OC)

Savannah 1995 Chanel Vineyards Cabernet Franc
Region: California, Santa Cruz Mountains $26
Golds/Awards: Gold (WC); Best of Class (WC)

Stonelake 1996 Reserva Cabernet Franc
Region: Chile, Lontue $18
Golds/Awards: Gold (BR)

Wildhurst Vineyards 1996 Cabernet Franc
Region: California, Clear Lake $13
Golds/Awards: Gold (LA)

Did You Know...?

Tips from an experienced Manhattan couple
who've amassed an impressive wine collection
at auction that's doubled in value since they
began collecting just two years ago: Buy at auction
in the afternoon, after everyone's tired and the initial
excitement is over. You'll get the best bang for your buck.

CABERNET SAUVIGNON

For most of the world, Cabernet Sauvignon is king of the reds. Widely grown in the New World for more than a century, its popularity never wanes. Blockbuster Cabs produced in California in particular are giving some of France's famous wineries the jitters as they outperform their old cousins in blind tastings. Cabernet Sauvignon is the principal component of Bordeaux-style red blends, often called "Meritage" in this country.

While Cabs vary from country to country and vineyard to vineyard, one can characterize them generally. They tend to be deeply colored, richly fruity, with complex structure, which means lots of acid and plenty of tannin. Some terms used to describe Cabs are: black cherry, blackberry, plums, herbs, green olives, truffles, loamy earth, tobacco, leather, violet, mint, eucalyptus, tea, cedar, bell pepper, tar, and chocolate. These aren't subtle flavors and aromas!

A great Cab is capable of long aging in your cellar. Yet many New World examples can be complex and age worthy yet ready for early drinking. The Reservas from Chile represent great value and have lots of personality; Argentina has some wonderful and approachable Cabernets too.

Because of its assertive personality, Cabernet Sauvignon is frequently blended with other varieties, most commonly Merlot and Cabernet Franc. (As long as it's 75 percent Cab, the wine can be called Cabernet Sauvignon in the U.S.)

Food companions: Cabernet Sauvignon pairs best with simple, hearty foods such as roast or grilled red meat, pork, veal, lamb, and duck. Charcoal-boiled steak smeared with blue cheese or imbedded with peppercorns; wild game such as grouse or carabou; swordfish; ceasar salad; and pesto are other good complements. With medium- to lighter-style Cabs, try fruit-based sauces (on meat), wild mushroom dishes, garlicky Mediterranean cuisine, hard cheeses, even dark chocolate and chocolate chip cookies.

Cabernet Sauvignon

Adelaida 1993 Cabernet Sauvignon
Region: California, San Luis Obispo County $19
Golds/Awards: Gold (WWC-91 pts)

**Anderson's Conn Valley Vineyards 1994 Estate Reserve
Cabernet Sauvignon**
Region: California, Napa Valley $40
Golds/Awards: Gold (WWC-90 pts)

Did You Know...?

What is ullage? The ullage level is the amount of air
between the top of the wine and the cork. The more
ullage in an old bottle, the greater chance that oxidation
has occurred. If you see significant ullage in a new
bottle, definitely don't buy it.

Andrew Will 1994 Cabernet Sauvignon
Region: Washington $30
Golds/Awards: Gold (WWC-90 pts)

Andrew Will 1994 Reserve Cabernet Sauvignon
Region: Washington $40
Golds/Awards: Gold (WWC-91 pts)

Apex 1994 Cabernet Sauvignon
Region: Washington, Columbia Valley $35
Golds/Awards: Gold (WWC-92 pts)

B.R. Cohn 1994 Olive Hill Vineyard Cabernet Sauvignon
Region: California, Sonoma Valley $32
Golds/Awards: Gold (WWC-92 pts)

**Bartholomew Park Winery 1996 Parks Vineyard Cabernet
Sauvignon**
Region: California, Napa Valley $29
Golds/Awards: Gold (PR); Best of Class (PR)

Beaucanon 1995 Cabernet Sauvignon
Region: California, Napa Valley $14
Golds/Awards: Gold (LA)

Beaulieu Vineyard 1994 Georges de Latour Private Reserve Cabernet Sauvignon
Region: California, Napa Valley $50
Golds/Awards: Gold (SD, LA, WWC-92 pts); Best of Class (LA)

Beaulieu Vineyard 1995 Cabernet Sauvignon
Region: California, Coastal Region $9.99
Golds/Awards: Gold (OC)

Belvedere 1995 Cabernet Sauvignon
Region: California, Dry Creek Valley $17
Golds/Awards: Gold (LA, OC, PR)

Benziger 1994 Estate Grown Reserve Cabernet Sauvignon
Region: California, Sonoma Mountain $35
Golds/Awards: Gold (SD, WC)

Benziger 1995 Ash Creek Vineyard Reserve Cabernet Sauvignon
Region: California, Alexander Valley $30
Golds/Awards: Gold (WC)

Benziger 1995 Cabernet Sauvignon
Region: California, Sonoma County $15.99
Golds/Awards: Gold (PR, WWC-90 pts)

Benziger 1996 Cabernet Sauvignon
Region: California, Sonoma County $17
Golds/Awards: Gold (SD)

Beringer 1993 Private Reserve Cabernet Sauvignon
Region: California, Napa Valley $65
Golds/Awards: Gold (WWC-94 pts)

Beringer 1995 Cabernet Sauvignon
Region: California, Knight's Valley $18
Golds/Awards: Gold (LA)

Did You Know...?

"There are people who have been known to prefer bad wine to good, just as there are men who are fascinated by bad women."
—André L. Simon

Bogle 1996 Cabernet Sauvignon
Region: California $9
Golds/Awards: Gold (LA, CA)

Bonterra 1995 Organically Grown Grapes Cab. Sauvignon
Region: California, North Coast $15
Golds/Awards: Gold (PR, NW)

Buehler Vineyards 1995 Cabernet Sauvignon
Region: California, Napa Valley $20
Golds/Awards: Gold (LA, CA)

Byington 1994 Twin Mountains Cabernet Sauvignon
Region: California, Santa Cruz Mountains $14.50
Golds/Awards: Gold (WWC-91 pts)

Caballero de la Cepa 1993 Mendoza Reserve Cabernet Sauvignon
Region: Argentina $9.95
Golds/Awards: Gold (VN)

Calina 1996 Valle Central Cabernet Sauvignon
Region: Chile $9
Golds/Awards: Gold (RI)

Callaway 1995 Cabernet Sauvignon
Region: California $11
Golds/Awards: Gold (WC); Best of Class (WC)

Canyon Road 1995 Reserve Cabernet Sauvignon
Region: California, Sonoma County $16
Golds/Awards: Gold (DA, LA)

Did You Know...?

According to the largest study yet investigating the effect of alcohol consumption on health, one drink a day can lower the mortality rate among the middle-aged and elderly population by 20 percent. Most of the health benefits were ascribed to a 30–40% decline in death rates associated with cardiovascular disease.

Carmen Vineyards 1996 Cabernet Sauvignon
Region: Chile $6.99
Golds/Awards: Gold (NW); Best of Class (NW)

Did You Know...?

Rick Berman, executive producer of *Star Trek* films, is also a wine buff. Trekkies know that there are often small wine references peppered throughout the newer *Trek* movies, as well as the *Next Generation* and *Voyager* series. The upcoming *Star Trek* movie takes place on an agrarian planet renowned for its vineyards.

Caymus 1994 Cabernet Sauvignon
Region: California, Napa Valley $35
Golds/Awards: Gold (WWC-92 pts)

Cedar Mountain 1993 Cabernet Sauvignon
Region: California, Livermore Valley $25
Golds/Awards: Gold (WWC-91 pts)

Cedar Mountain 1994 Cabernet Sauvignon
Region: California, Livermore Valley $20
Golds/Awards: Gold (WWC-90 pts)

Chalk Hill 1994 Cabernet Sauvignon
Region: California $26
Golds/Awards: Gold (IW)

Chalk Hill 1995 Cabernet Sauvignon
Region: California $26
Golds/Awards: Gold (IW)

Chapel Hill 1996 Cabernet Sauvignon
Region: Australia $16
Golds/Awards: Gold (IW)

Chateau La Joya 1997 Cabernet Sauvignon
Region: Chile, Colchagua Valley $8.99
Golds/Awards: Gold (BR)

Chateau Los Boldos 1996 Cabernet Sauvignon Vielles Vignes
Region: Chile $8.99
Golds/Awards: Gold (VN)

Chateau Montelena 1993 Estate Cabernet Sauvignon
Region: California, Napa Valley $38
Golds/Awards: Gold (WWC-90 pts)

Chateau St. Jean 1992 Reserve Cabernet Sauvignon
Region: California, Sonoma County $45
Golds/Awards: Gold (PR, WWC-93 pts)

Chateau St. Jean 1994 Cinq Cepages
Region: California, Sonoma County $24
Golds/Awards: Gold (NW, WC, GH)

Did You Know...?

California's winemaking industry is over 200 years old,
even though wines from this region have only come to
prominence in the last twenty years or so.

Chateau Souverain 1994 Winemaker's Reserve Cabernet Sauvignon
Region: California, Alexander Valley $35
Golds/Awards: Gold (NW, SD, OC, WC, WWC-90 pts)

Chimney Rock 1994 Reserve Cabernet Sauvignon
Region: California, Stags Leap District $50
Golds/Awards: Gold (WWC-90 pts)

Cinnabar 1994 Saratoga Vineyard Cabernet Sauvignon
Region: California, Santa Cruz Mountains $25
Golds/Awards: Gold (WWC-94 pts)

Clos du Bois 1994 Briarcrest Vineyard Cabernet Sauvignon
Region: California, Alexander Valley $23
Golds/Awards: Gold (NW)

Clos du Bois 1995 Alexander Valley Selection Cabernet Sauvignon
Region: California, Alexander Valley $21
Golds/Awards: Gold (RI, WC)

Clos du Val 1993 Reserve Cabernet Sauvignon
Region: California, Napa Valley $48
Golds/Awards: Gold (NW, BR, WWC-91)

Clos LaChance 1994 Cabernet Sauvignon
Region: California, Santa Cruz Mountains $22
Golds/Awards: Gold (WWC-90 pts)

Clos Malverne 1994 Cabernet Sauvignon
Region: South Africa, Stellenbosch $14.99
Golds/Awards: Gold (WWC-90 pts)

Clos Malverne 1995 Cabernet Sauvignon
Region: South Africa, Stellenbosch $14.99
Golds/Awards: Gold (WWC-90)

Clos Pegase 1994 Hommage Reserve Cabernet Sauvignon
Region: California, Napa Valley $40
Golds/Awards: Gold (WWC-93 pts)

Did You Know...?

"Islam prohibits alcoholic drinks. Drinking makes people lose their heads and impedes clear thinking. Even music dulls the mind."
–Ayatollah Khomeini

Cooper-Garrod 1994 Cabernet Sauvignon
Region: California, Santa Cruz Mountains $20
Golds/Awards: Gold (WWC-90 pts)

Cooper-Garrod 1995 Estate Bottled Cabernet Sauvignon
Region: California, Santa Cruz Mountains $25
Golds/Awards: Gold (RI); Chairman's Award (RI)

Cornerstone 1993 Beatty Ranch Cabernet Sauvignon
Region: California, Howell Mountain $32
Golds/Awards: Gold (WWC-91 pts)

Cosentino 1994 Reserve Cabernet Sauvignon
Region: California, Napa Valley $40
Golds/Awards: Gold (WWC-90 pts)

Cottonwood Canyon 1994 Cabernet Sauvignon
Region: California, Central Coast $24.50
Golds/Awards: Gold (WWC-90 pts)

Cuvaison Winery 1994 Twenty-fifth Anniversary Cabernet Sauvignon
Region: California, Napa Valley $28
Golds/Awards: Gold (LA, WWC-93 pts)

Dalla Valle 1993 Cabernet Sauvignon
Region: California, Napa Valley $40
Golds/Awards: Gold (WWC-90 pts)

Did You Know...?

Many would be surprised to learn that the makers of those $500-plus bottles receive only a small percentage of the inflated price. For instance, vintner Christian Moueix, of Pétrus fame, never receives more than $50 a bottle (whole-sale) for his famous and much-sought-after wines.

David Bruce 1994 Reserve Cabernet Sauvignon
Region: California, Santa Cruz Mountains $20
Golds/Awards: Gold (WWC-90 pts)

Davis Bynum 1994 Hedin Vineyard Cabernet Sauvignon
Region: California, Russian River Valley $24
Golds/Awards: Gold (NW)

De Bortoli 1995 Cabernet Sauvignon
Region: Australia, Yarra Valley $21
Golds/Awards: Gold (SY)

Deer Valley 1995 Cabernet Sauvignon
Region: California $4.99
Golds/Awards: Gold (NW)

DeLoach 1993 O.F.S. Cabernet Sauvignon
Region: California, Russian River Valley $25
Golds/Awards: Gold (WWC-92 pts)

DeLoach 1994 O.F.S. Estate Bottled Cabernet Sauvignon
Region: California, Russian River Valley $27.50
Golds/Awards: Gold (WC, WWC-90 pts)

Cabernet Sauvignon RED

Diamond Creek 1994 Volcanic Hill Cabernet Sauvignon
Region: California, Napa Valley $50
Golds/Awards: Gold (WWC-90 pts)

Dr. Konstantin Frank 1995 Cabernet Sauvignon
Region: New York, Finger Lakes $22
Golds/Awards: Gold (NW)

Dry Creek Vineyard 1995 Reserve Cabernet Sauvignon
Region: California, Dry Creek Valley $27
Golds/Awards: Gold (WWC-92 pts)

Dunn 1993 Cabernet Sauvignon
Region: California, Napa Valley $35
Golds/Awards: Gold (WWC-92 pts)

Dunnewood 1995 Cabernet Sauvignon
Region: California, North Coast $8.50
Golds/Awards: Gold (PR)

Edgewood 1994 Cabernet Sauvignon
Region: California, Napa Valley $20
Golds/Awards: Gold (PR, DA)

Edgewood 1995 Cabernet Sauvignon
Region: California, Napa Valley $18
Golds/Awards: Gold (RI, LA)

Did You Know...?

During Prohibition savvy businessmen sold and shipped grape concentrate to eager buyers on the East Coast. Lest the buyers not know what to do with their innocent grape juice once it arrived, the "recipe" was right on the top of the container in the form of a warning: "Caution: Do NOT add sugar or yeast or else fermentation will take place!"

Etchart 1995 Cafayate Cabernet Sauvignon
Region: Argentina $6.99
Golds/Awards: Gold (VL)

Etchart 1995 Rio de Plata Cabernet Sauvignon
Region: Argentina $6.99
Golds/Awards: Gold (VN)

Etchart 1996 Rio de Plata Cabernet Sauvignon
Region: Argentina $6.99
Golds/Awards: Gold (VL)

> Did You Know...?
>
> Grape pickers in Argentina work 12-hour days, and make $10 a day.

Evans & Tate 1995 Cabernet Sauvignon
Region: Australia, Margaret River $19
Golds/Awards: Gold (SY)

Far Niente 1994 Cabernet Sauvignon
Region: California, Napa Valley $55
Golds/Awards: Gold (WWC-90 pts)

Fenestra 1994 Cabernet Sauvignon
Region: California, Livermore Valley $13.50
Golds/Awards: Gold (CA); Best of Class (CA)

Ferrari Carano 1993 Cabernet Sauvignon
Region: California, Sonoma County $22.50
Golds/Awards: Gold (WWC-90 pts)

Fetzer 1985 Reserve Cabernet Sauvignon
Region: California, Sonoma County $75
Golds/Awards: Double Gold (CA)

Fetzer 1994 Usibelli Vineyard Reserve Cabernet Sauvignon
Region: California, Napa Valley $24
Golds/Awards: Gold (OC, WC, WWC-90 pts, CA); Best of
California, Best of Class (CA)

Fetzer 1995 Valley Oaks Cabernet Sauvignon
Region: California $8.99
Golds/Awards: Gold (NW, LA, WC)

Fife 1995 Reserve Cabernet Sauvignon
Region: California, Spring Mountain $35
Golds/Awards: Gold (CA)

Fisher 1994 Lamb Vineyard Cabernet Sauvignon
Region: California, Napa Valley $50
Golds/Awards: Gold (WWC-95 pts)

Flichman 1995 Cabernet Sauvignon
Region: Argentina $6.95
Golds/Awards: Gold (VN)

Flora Springs 1995 Cypress Ranch Cabernet Sauvignon
Region: California, Napa Valley $35
Golds/Awards: Gold (LA); Best of Class (LA)

Foxridge 1996 Cabernet Sauvignon
Region: Chile $10
Golds/Awards: Gold (WS)

Franciscan Oakville Estate 1994 Cabernet Sauvignon
Region: California, Napa Valley $17
Golds/Awards: Gold (WWC-90 pts)

Freemark Abbey 1992 Bosché Estate Cabernet Sauvignon
Region: California, Napa Valley $27.99
Golds/Awards: Gold (WWC-92 pts)

Freemark Abbey 1992 Sycamore Vineyard Cabernet Sauvignon
Region: California, Napa Valley $26.50
Golds/Awards: Gold (WWC-90 pts)

Did You Know...?

Need a hobby? The International Correspondence of
Corkscrew Addicts, an elite organization of 50 collectors,
requires members to publish six illustrated documents a
year. Week-long outings to the Alps, Venice, and Barcelona
are not unusual for these jet-setting 'screw-geeks.

Gallo Sonoma 1992 Estate Cabernet Sauvignon
Region: California, Northern Sonoma $40
Golds/Awards: Gold (BR, VI)

Gallo Sonoma 1993 Estate Cabernet Sauvignon
Region: California, Northern Sonoma $45
Golds/Awards: Gold (OC, WC, WWC-90 pts)

Gallo Sonoma 1993 Frei Ranch Vineyard Cabernet Sauvignon
Region: California, Dry Creek Valley $18
Golds/Awards: Gold (WWC-91 pts)

Gallo Sonoma 1994 Barelli Creek Vineyard Cabernet Sauvignon
Region: California, Alexander Valley $20
Golds/Awards: Four Star Gold (OC)

Gallo Sonoma 1994 Frei Ranch Vineyard Cabernet Sauvignon
Region: California $18
Golds/Awards: Gold (NW, BR, IV, LA); Four Star Gold (OC)

Did You Know...?

Agoston Haraszthy, a Hungarian refugee, came to
California in 1856, bought land, started a
vineyard, and imported thousands of premium European grapevine cuttings. When his
fortunes failed, he distributed cuttings
throughout the state, selling them to defray his
debts. Thus, some say, began California's fine
wine industry.

Gary Farrell 1995 Hillside Selection Cabernet Sauvignon
Region: California, Sonoma County $24
Golds/Awards: Gold (NW, SD)

Geyser Peak 1995 Cabernet Sauvignon
Region: California, Sonoma County $15
Golds/Awards: Gold (PR, LA)

Geyser Peak 1995 Reserve Cabernet Sauvignon
Region: California, Alexander Valley $28
Golds/Awards: Gold (LA)

Girard 1994 Cabernet Sauvignon
Region: California, Napa Valley $25
Golds/Awards: Gold (WWC-90 pts)

Girard 1994 Reserve Cabernet Sauvignon
Region: California, Napa Valley $40
Golds/Awards: Gold (WWC-91 pts)

Did You Know...?

How was wine invented? Yeast is found naturally
on the skin of a grape. Crush or step on a bunch
of grapes and the yeast will find its way into
the sugary grape juice. When sugar meets
yeast, the process of fermentation
begins—all by itself.

Goundrey 1996 Reserve Cabernet Sauvignon
Region: Australia, Mount Barker $22
Golds/Awards: Gold (WS)

**Greenwood Ridge Vineyards 1995 Estate Bottled
Cabernet Sauvignon**
Region: California, Anderson Valley $32
Golds/Awards: Gold (SD); Best of Class (SD)

Grgich Hills 1994 Cabernet Sauvignon
Region: California, Napa Valley $35
Golds/Awards: Gold (SD, WWC-91 pts); Best of Class (SD)

Grove Street Winery 1996 Cabernet Sauvignon
Region: Argentina/California $17
Golds/Awards: Gold (NW)

**Guenoc 1994 Bella Vista Vineyard Reserve Cabernet
Sauvignon**
Region: California, Napa Valley $30
Golds/Awards: Gold (PR, NW, RI, WC); Chairman's Award (RI)

Guenoc 1995 Cabernet Sauvignon
Region: California, North Coast $15.50
Golds/Awards: Gold (SD, IV, LA)

Hagafen 1995 Cabernet Sauvignon
Region: California, Napa Valley $20
Golds/Awards: Gold (LA, OC)

Hardys 1992 Thomas Hardy Cabernet Sauvignon
Region: Australia, Coonawarra $54.99
Golds/Awards: Gold (WWC-91 pts)

Hardys 1995 Coonawara Cabernet Sauvignon
Region: Australia $17.99
Golds/Awards: Gold (IW)

Heitz 1992 Martha's Vineyard Cabernet Sauvignon
Region: California, Napa Valley $68
Golds/Awards: Gold (WWC-93 pts)

Helena View 1992 Cabernet Sauvignon
Region: California, Napa Valley $20
Golds/Awards: Gold (WWC-90 pts)

Hendry 1993 Block 8 Cabernet Sauvignon
Region: California, Napa Valley $22
Golds/Awards: Gold (WWC-93 pts)

Herzog 1994 Special Reserve Cabernet Sauvignon
Region: California, Alexander Valley $26.69
Golds/Awards: Gold (WWC-91 pts)

Did You Know...?

To make wine kosher, it has to be heated or pasteurized in order to render it ritually impervious to desecration. Winemaker Peter Stern of Royal Wine Company has found a way to flash heat his wine, keeping the rabbis happy while retaining the integrity of the grapes' gift. The result is Herzog wines, kosher wines that don't taste like Chateau Welch's.

Hess Collection 1993 Cabernet Sauvignon
Region: California, Napa Valley $20
Golds/Awards: Gold (WWC-94 pts)

Did You Know...?

Many attribute the red wine boom in the U.S. to the November 17, 1991, *60 Minutes* program that introduced the concept of "The French Paradox" to the American public. (Red wine's apparent role in preventing heart disease.)

Hillebrand Estates 1995 V.Q.A. Cabernet Sauvignon
Region: Canada, Niagara Peninsula $9.95
Golds/Awards: Gold (VI); Grand Gold Medal (VI)

Hyatt Vineyards 1995 Reserve Cabernet Sauvignon
Region: Washington, Yakima Valley $24.95
Golds/Awards: Gold (NW)

J. Lohr 1995 Cypress Cabernet Sauvignon
Region: California $8.75
Golds/Awards: Gold (LA)

J. Lohr 1995 Seven Oaks Cabernet Sauvignon
Region: California, Paso Robles $14
Golds/Awards: Gold (NW)

Jarvis 1993 Cabernet Sauvignon
Region: California, Napa Valley $55
Golds/Awards: Gold (WWC-93 pts)

Jekel 1995 Cabernet Sauvignon
Region: California, Monterey $16
Golds/Awards: Gold (NW)

Joseph Phelps 1994 Backus Vineyard Cabernet Sauvignon
Region: California, Napa Valley $70
Golds/Awards: Gold (WWC-92 pts)

Joseph Phelps 1994 Cabernet Sauvignon
Region: California, Napa Valley $24
Golds/Awards: Gold (WWC-90 pts)

Kathryn Kennedy 1994 Cabernet Sauvignon
Region: California, Santa Cruz Mountains $75
Golds/Awards: Gold (WWC-95 pts)

Kendall-Jackson 1994 Grand Reserve Cabernet Sauvignon
Region: California $42
Golds/Awards: Gold (BR)

Kendall-Jackson 1995 Buckeye Vineyard Cabernet Sauvignon
Region: California, Alexander Valley $24
Golds/Awards: Gold (RI); Chairman's Award (RI)

Kenwood 1994 Jack London Vineyard Cabernet Sauvignon
Region: California, Sonoma Valley $25
Golds/Awards: Gold (WWC-91 pts)

Kiona 1993 Reserve Cabernet Sauvignon
Region: Washington, Yakima Valley $19.99
Golds/Awards: Gold (WWC-90 pts)

Kiona 1996 Cabernet Sauvignon
Region: Washington $17.99
Golds/Awards: Gold (NW)

Korbel 1994 Cabernet Sauvignon
Region: California, Alexander Valley $18.99
Golds/Awards: Gold (WWC-90 pts)

Kunde 1994 Cabernet Sauvignon
Region: California, Sonoma Valley $17
Golds/Awards: Gold (WWC-90 pts)

KWV Cathedral Cellar 1995 Cabernet Sauvignon
Region: South Africa, Coastal Region $12
Golds/Awards: Gold (SM, BR)

Did You Know...?

Jabulani Ntshangase is South Africa's first black wine producer. With three other men, he bought nearly a thousand vineyard acres to create "Spice Route," as the organization is called. Spring 1998 marks their first harvest.

La Garza 1996 Cabernet Sauvignon
Region: Oregon, Umpqua Valley $15
Golds/Awards: Gold (EN)

Laborie Estate 1996 Cabernet Sauvignon
Region: South Africa $14
Golds/Awards: Gold (VI)

Did You Know...?

The Wine Market Council is hoping that their upcoming $20 million advertising campaign will reach the under-40 audience, who are still at a stage in life where they're determining personal style and taste.

Lakespring 1994 Cabernet Sauvignon
Region: California, Napa County $10
Golds/Awards: Gold (OC)

Laurel Glen 1994 Cabernet Sauvignon
Region: California, Sonoma Mountain $38
Golds/Awards: Gold (WWC-90 pts)

L'Ecole No. 41 1994 Cabernet Sauvignon
Region: Washington, Columbia Valley $24
Golds/Awards: Gold (WWC-90 pts)

Le Ducq 1995 Sylviane Cabernet Sauvignon
Region: California, Napa Valley $30
Golds/Awards: Gold (LA); Best of Class (LA)

Leonetti 1994 Cabernet Sauvignon
Region: Washington, Columbia Valley $45
Golds/Awards: Gold (WWC-93 pts)

Lindemans 1994 "St. George" Cabernet Sauvignon
Region: Australia, Coonawarra $27.85
Golds/Awards: Gold (SY)

Lockwood 1995 Estate Bottled & Grown Cabernet Sauvignon
Region: California, Monterey $16
Golds/Awards: Gold (NW)

Louis M. Martini 1994 Monte Rosso Vineyard Selection Cabernet Sauvignon
Region: California, Sonoma Mountain $30
Golds/Awards: Gold (WWC-92 pts)

Magnotta 1994 Gran Riserva Red Cabernet Sauvignon
Region: Canada, Niagara Peninsula   (Can $) 23.95
Golds/Awards: Gold (BR, WS)

Did You Know...?

Why is my wine glowing? Three Italians, in a joint venture with the Cuban government, are producing wines at a high-tech facility in Cuba near the former nuclear missile site constructed by the Soviet Union.

Manso De Velasco 1995 Cabernet Sauvignon
Region: Chile, Septima $18.99
Golds/Awards: Gold (IW, WS)

Marcelina 1993 Cabernet Sauvignon
Region: California, Napa Valley $20
Golds/Awards: Gold (WC)

Meerlust 1991 Cabernet Sauvignon
Region: South Africa, Stellenbosch $22
Golds/Awards: Gold (WWC-91 pts)

Meridian 1994 Coastal Reserve Cabernet Sauvignon
Region: California $20
Golds/Awards: Gold (RI, OC, SD); Chairman's Award (RI)

Meridian 1995 Cabernet Sauvignon
Region: California $12
Golds/Awards: Gold (LA); Best of Class (LA)

Merryvale Vineyards 1995 Merryvale Reserve Cabernet Sauvignon
Region: California, Napa Valley $32
Golds/Awards: Gold (LA)

Michel-Schlumberger 1993 Reserve Cabernet Sauvignon
Region: California, Dry Creek Valley $35
Golds/Awards: Gold (DA, RI)

Cabernet Sauvignon RED

Michel-Schlumberger 1994 Benchland Cabernet Sauvignon
Region: California, Dry Creek Valley $19.50
Golds/Awards: Gold (OC)

Miguel Torres 1996 Santa Digna Cabernet Sauvignon
Region: Chile $8.99
Golds/Awards: Gold (VN)

Mill Creek 1996 Cabernet Sauvignon
Region: California, Sonoma County $18
Golds/Awards: Gold (RI)

Monthaven 1995 Cabernet Sauvignon
Region: California, Napa Valley $9.99
Golds/Awards: Gold (LA)

Mount Eden 1993 Old Vine Reserve Cabernet Sauvignon
Region: California, Santa Cruz Mountains $35
Golds/Awards: Gold (WWC-94 pts)

Murphy-Goode 1994 Brenda Block Cabernet Sauvignon
Region: California, Alexander Valley $30
Golds/Awards: Gold (WWC-91 pts)

Napa Ridge 1994 Reserve Cabernet Sauvignon
Region: California, Napa Valley $15
Golds/Awards: Gold (NW)

Napa Ridge 1996 Oak Barrel Cabernet Sauvignon
Region: California, Central Coast $10
Golds/Awards: Gold (SD, LA); Best of Class (SD, LA)

Navarro 1993 Cabernet Sauvignon
Region: California, Mendocino $20
Golds/Awards: Gold (PR); Best of Class (PR)

Neil Ellis 1993 Cabernet Sauvignon
Region: South Africa, Stellenbosch $16.99
Golds/Awards: Gold (WWC-90 pts)

Did You Know...?

Tannin, found mostly in red wine, is an antioxidant.

Did You Know...?

There were only 1,000 cases of Pétrus produced annually during the 1960s. Most of that wine was probably guzzled immediately, since Pétrus didn't become famous until the 1970s. How could there still be so much 1960s Pétrus being auctioned? Experts believe more than a few of these bottles are fakes.

Norman Vineyards 1995 Estate Bottled Cabernet Sauvignon
Region: California, Paso Robles $17
Golds/Awards: Gold (NW)

Norman's 1996 Chais Clarendon Cabernet Sauvignon
Region: Australia, McLaren Vale $17.99
Golds/Awards: Gold (WS)

Norman's 1996 White Label Cabernet Sauvignon
Region: Australia $9.99
Golds/Awards: Gold (IW)

Orlando 1993 St. Hugo Cabernet Sauvignon
Region: Australia, Coonawarra $28.99
Golds/Awards: Gold (WWC-90 pts)

Orlando 1994 St. Hugo Cabernet Sauvignon
Region: Australia, Coonawarra $28.99
Golds/Awards: Gold (IW)

Parker 1994 Terra Rossa First Growth (Cabernet Sauvignon)
Region: Australia, Coonawarra $45
Golds/Awards: Gold (WWC-91 pts)

Pedroncelli 1995 Three Vineyards Cabernet Sauvignon
Region: California, Northern Sonoma $11.50
Golds/Awards: Gold (GH)

Pedroncelli 1996 Vintage Selection Cabernet Sauvignon
Region: California, Dry Creek Valley $10
Golds/Awards: Gold (RI)

Peju Province 1994 H.B. Vineyard Cabernet Sauvignon
Region: California, Napa Valley $55
Golds/Awards: Gold (WWC-94 pts)

Penley Estate 1994 Cabernet Sauvignon
Region: Australia, Coonawarra $45
Golds/Awards: Gold (SY)

Peter Lehmann 1995 Cabernet Sauvignon
Region: Australia, Barossa Valley $17
Golds/Awards: Gold (WWC-90 pts)

Peter Lehmann 1996 Cabernet Sauvignon
Region: Australia $17
Golds/Awards: Gold (IW)

Phoenix Vineyards 1995 Cabernet Sauvignon
Region: California, Napa Valley $19
Golds/Awards: Gold (RI, CA); Best of Class (CA)

Pine Ridge 1994 Cabernet Sauvignon
Region: California, Howell Mountain $35
Golds/Awards: Gold (WWC-91 pts)

Plam 1994 Vintner's Reserve Cabernet Sauvignon
Region: California, Napa Valley $30
Golds/Awards: Gold (WWC-90 pts)

Plam 1995 Vintner's Reserve Cabernet Sauvignon
Region: California, Napa Valley $30
Golds/Awards: Gold (LA)

Did You Know...?

Alcohol, no matter what its form, contains
about 7 calories per gram, so about 164
calories for an 8-ounce glass of wine.

Portteus 1994 Reserve Cabernet Sauvignon
Region: Washington, Yakima Valley $26
Golds/Awards: Gold (WWC-90 pts)

Preston 1995 Reserve Cabernet Sauvignon
Region: Washington, Columbia Valley $20
Golds/Awards: Gold (EN)

Quail Ridge 1993 Volker Eisele Vineyard Reserve Cabernet Sauvignon
Region: California, Napa Valley $39.99
Golds/Awards: Gold (WWC-92 pts)

Raymond Vineyard 1995 Raymond Estates Cabernet Sauvignon
Region: California, Napa Valley $13
Golds/Awards: Gold (WC)

Raymond Vineyard 1995 Raymond Reserve Cabernet Sauvignon
Region: California $20
Golds/Awards: Gold (LA)

Renaissance 1995 Cabernet Sauvignon
Region: California, North Yuba $13.99
Golds/Awards: Gold (CA); Best of Class (CA)

Ridge 1993 Monte Bello Cabernet Sauvignon
Region: California, Santa Cruz Mountains $55
Golds/Awards: Platinum (WWC-96 pts)

Did You Know...?

One reason California produces so many different kinds of wines is because California has so many different climates.

Ridge 1994 Monte Bello Cabernet Sauvignon
Region: California, Santa Cruz Mountains $50
Golds/Awards: Platinum (WWC-97 pts)

Ridge 1995 Cabernet Sauvignon
Region: California, Santa Cruz Mountains $22
Golds/Awards: Gold (WWC-93 pts)

Robertson's Well 1996 Cabernet Sauvignon
Region: Australia, Coonawarra $16
Golds/Awards: Gold (SY)

Rodney Strong 1993 Reserve Cabernet Sauvignon
Region: California, Northern Sonoma $40
Golds/Awards: Gold (NW)

Did You Know...?

The Duke and Duchess of Windsor kept a pair
of handwritten ledger books, recently sold at
auction, that featured a running inventory of
every bottle of wine and spirits that entered and
exited the Windsor households from 1954 until 1986.

Rodney Strong 1994 Reserve Cabernet Sauvignon
Region: California, Northern Sonoma $35
Golds/Awards: Gold (RI)

Rodney Strong 1995 Cabernet Sauvignon
Region: California, Sonoma County $13
Golds/Awards: Gold (WC)

**Rosenblum 1995 Hendry Vineyard Reserve Cabernet
Sauvignon**
Region: California, Napa Valley $40
Golds/Awards: Gold (WWC-90 pts)

Rutherford Ranch 1994 Cabernet Sauvignon
Region: California, Napa Valley $10
Golds/Awards: Gold (OC)

Rymill Winery 1995 Cabernet Sauvignon
Region: Australia, Coonawarra $16.50
Golds/Awards: Gold (SY)

**S. Anderson 1994 Richard Chambers Vineyard Cabernet
Sauvignon**
Region: California, Stags Leap District $54
Golds/Awards: Gold (WWC-95 pts)

Saddleback Cellars 1995 Cabernet Sauvignon
Region: California, Napa Valley $27
Golds/Awards: Gold (OC)

St. Clement 1994 Cabernet Sauvignon
Region: California, Napa Valley $25
Golds/Awards: Gold (WWC-90 pts)

St. Clement 1994 Cabernet Sauvignon
Region: California, Howell Mountain $45
Golds/Awards: Gold (WWC-92 pts)

St. Francis 1994 Reserve Cabernet Sauvignon
Region: California, Sonoma Valley $30
Golds/Awards: Platinum (WWC-96 pts)

St. Francis 1995 Cabernet Sauvignon
Region: California, Sonoma Valley $12
Golds/Awards: Gold (BR)

St. Supéry 1994 Cabernet Sauvignon
Region: California, Napa Valley $90
Golds/Awards: Gold (WWC-90 pts)

Ste. Chapelle Winery 1995 Cabernet Sauvignon
Region: Idaho $11.50
Golds/Awards: Gold (PR, NW)

Santa Ana 1996 Cabernet Sauvignon
Region: Argentina $5.99
Golds/Awards: Gold (SY)

Santa Rita 1994 Casa Real Old Vines Cabernet Sauvignon
Region: Chile, Maipo Valley $23
Golds/Awards: Gold (WWC-90 pts)

Santa Rita 1995 Casa Real Old Vines Cabernet Sauvignon
Region: Chile, Maipo Valley $29.99
Golds/Awards: Gold (WWC-91)

Sea Ridge Coastal Winery 1995 Barrel Fermented Cabernet Sauvignon
Region: California $10
Golds/Awards: Gold (WC); Best of Class (WC)

Seavey 1993 Cabernet Sauvignon
Region: California, Napa Valley $28
Golds/Awards: Gold (WWC-90 pts)

Did You Know...?

Only 211 people in the world have a Masters of Wine, the most coveted and difficult wine title to achieve.

Sebastiani 1994 Estate Bottled Cherryblock Cabernet Sauvignon
Region: California, Sonoma County $50
Golds/Awards: Gold (NW, DA); Best of Class (NW)

Seppelt 1993 "Dorrien" Cabernet Sauvignon
Region: Australia, Barossa $30
Golds/Awards: Gold (SY)

Sequoia Grove 1995 Cabernet Sauvignon
Region: California, Napa Valley $22
Golds/Awards: Gold (BR)

> *Did You Know...?*
>
> "Black goo," a substance that kills grapevines by withholding water and nutrients, is making growers nervous, since it mirrors the symptoms of Pierce's Disease and can live in a healthy vine for several years without any outward signs.

Shafer 1993 Hillside Select Cabernet Sauvignon
Region: California, Stags Leap District, Napa Valley $60
Golds/Awards: Gold (WWC-93 pts)

Shafer 1994 Cabernet Sauvignon
Region: California, Stags Leap District, Napa Valley $28
Golds/Awards: Gold (WWC-90 pts)

Sierra Vista 1994 Five Star Reserve Cabernet Sauvignon
Region: California, El Dorado $24
Golds/Awards: Gold (WWC-90 pts)

Signorello 1994 Cabernet Sauvignon
Region: California, Napa Valley $30
Golds/Awards: Gold (WWC-90 pts)

Signorello 1994 Founder's Reserve Cabernet Sauvignon
Region: California, Napa Valley $55
Golds/Awards: Gold (WWC-93 pts)

Silver Oak 1993 Cabernet Sauvignon
Region: California, Alexander Valley $38
Golds/Awards: Gold (WWC-92 pts)

Silver Oak 1993 Napa Cabernet Sauvignon
Region: California, Napa Valley $50
Golds/Awards: Gold (WWC-90 pts)

Silver Oak 1994 Cabernet Sauvignon
Region: California, Alexander Valley $45
Golds/Awards: Gold (OC)

Silverado 1994 Cabernet Sauvignon
Region: California, Napa Valley $22.50
Golds/Awards: Gold (WWC-91 pts)

Did You Know...?

There is still a Women's Christian Temperance Association.

Silverado 1994 Limited Reserve Cabernet Sauvignon
Region: California, Napa Valley $50
Golds/Awards: Gold (WWC-93 pts)

Silverado Hill Cellars 1995 Premium Black Label Cabernet Sauvignon
Region: California, Napa Valley $15
Golds/Awards: Gold (PR)

Smith & Hook 1994 Masterpiece Edition Cabernet Sauvignon
Region: California, Santa Lucia Highlands $35
Golds/Awards: Gold (WWC-90 pts)

Sonoma Creek Winery 1995 Ranch Salina Vineyard Cabernet Sauvignon
Region: California $28.95
Golds/Awards: Gold (PR); Best of Class (PR)

Soquel 1994 Partner's Reserve Cabernet Sauvignon
Region: California, Santa Cruz Mountains $40
Golds/Awards: Gold (WWC-91 pts)

Spottswoode 1994 Cabernet Sauvignon
Region: California, Napa Valley $45
Golds/Awards: Gold (WWC-93 pts)

Stag's Leap Wine Cellars 1994 Cask 23 Cabernet Sauvignon
Region: California, Napa Valley $100
Golds/Awards: Platinum (WWC-96 pts)

Stag's Leap Wine Cellars 1994 Fay Vineyard Cabernet Sauvignon
Region: California, Napa Valley $50
Golds/Awards: Gold (WWC-94 pts)

Stag's Leap Wine Cellars 1994 SLV Cabernet Sauvignon
Region: California, Napa Valley $50
Golds/Awards: Gold (WWC-93 pts)

Stag's Leap Wine Cellars 1995 Cabernet Sauvignon
Region: California, Napa Valley $28
Golds/Awards: Gold (DA, WC); Best of Class (WC)

Staton Hills Winery 1995 Cabernet Sauvignon
Region: Washington, Columbia Valley $15.95
Golds/Awards: Gold (LA)

Sterling Vineyards 1995 Cabernet Sauvignon
Region: California, Napa Valley $14
Golds/Awards: Gold (CA)

Stevenot Winery 1995 Cabernet Sauvignon
Region: California, Sierra Foothills $15
Golds/Awards: Gold (NW)

Stonelake 1996 Reserva Cabernet Sauvignon
Region: Chile, Lontue $13
Golds/Awards: Gold (BR)

Did You Know...?

"A lady temperance candidate concluded her passionate oration, 'I would rather commit adultery than take a glass of beer.' Whereupon a clear voice from the audience asked, 'Who wouldn't?'"
—Adlai Stevenson

Cabernet Sauvignon RED

Stonestreet 1994 Cabernet Sauvignon
Region: California, Alexander Valley $35
Golds/Awards: Gold (WWC-90 pts)

Stonestreet 1995 Cabernet Sauvignon
Region: California, Alexander Valley $37
Golds/Awards: Gold (PR, DA)

Sumac Ridge 1995 Cabernet Sauvignon
Region: Canada, Okanagan Valley (Can $) 18.95
Golds/Awards: Gold (NW, SM)

Swartland 1994 Cabernet Sauvignon
Region: South Africa, Swartland $9.99
Golds/Awards: Gold (WWC-90 pts)

Tittarelli 1994 Cabernet Sauvignon
Region: Argentina $8.99
Golds/Awards: Gold (VN)

Titus 1994 Cabernet Sauvignon
Region: California, Napa Valley $22
Golds/Awards: Gold (WWC-90 pts)

Trellis Vineyards 1996 Cabernet Sauvignon
Region: California, Alexander Valley $13.99
Golds/Awards: Gold (WC)

  *Did You Know...?*

Women are buying more wine than men,
but they're buying it at a low price point in
supermarkets. Fine wine (read: expensive) is
still a male preserve.

Trentadue 1995 Estate Bottled Cabernet Sauvignon
Region: California, Dry Creek Valley $22
Golds/Awards: Gold (RI)

V. Sattui Winery 1994 Rosenbrand Reserve Cabernet Sauvignon
Region: California, Napa Valley $27
Golds/Awards: Gold (NW, WS)

V. Sattui Winery 1995 Cabernet Sauvignon
Region: California, Napa Valley $17.50
Golds/Awards: Gold (NW, LA)

V. Sattui Winery 1995 Morisoli Vineyard Cabernet Sauvignon
Region: California, Napa Valley $25
Golds/Awards: Gold (NW, DA)

Did You Know...?

The word *spirit* in reference to alcoholic drinks has ancient Germanic roots—scholars believed that consuming alcohol allowed one to commune with the netherworld.

V. Sattui Winery 1995 Preston Vineyard Cabernet Sauvignon
Region: California, Napa Valley $27
Golds/Awards: Gold (WC)

V. Sattui Winery 1996 Suzanne's Vineyard Cabernet Sauvignon
Region: California, Napa Valley $22.50
Golds/Awards: Gold (RI, LA, WC); Best of Class (LA)

Venezia 1996 Meola Vineyards Cabernet Sauvignon
Region: California, Alexander Valley $19.99
Golds/Awards: Gold (PR, NW, SD, RI)

Vichon 1990 Cabernet Sauvignon
Region: California, Napa Valley $25
Golds/Awards: Gold (IW)

Villa Mt. Eden 1994 Signature Series Cabernet Sauvignon
Region: California, Mendocino $50
Golds/Awards: Gold (WWC-90 pts)

Villa Mt. Eden 1995 Grand Reserve Cabernet Sauvignon
Region: California, Napa Valley $20
Golds/Awards: Gold (LA)

Viña Tarapaca 1992 Gran Reserva Cabernet Sauvignon
Region: Chile, Maipo Valley $15
Golds/Awards: Gold (WWC-90 pts)

Viña Tarapaca 1996 Cabernet Sauvignon
Region: Chile, Valle Central $7
Golds/Awards: Gold (NW)

> Did You Know...?
>
> W.C. Fields, commenting on his trip to Afghanistan:
> "We lost our corkscrew and were compelled to live
> on food and water for several days."

Von Strasser 1994 Diamond Mountain Cabernet Sauvignon
Region: California, Napa Valley $32
Golds/Awards: Gold (WWC-90 pts)

Weinstock Cellars 1996 Cabernet Sauvignon
Region: California, Paso Robles $10.99
Golds/Awards: Gold (CA); Best of Class (CA)

Wellington Vineyards 1994 Random Ridge Cabernet Sauvignon
Region: California, Napa Valley $18
Golds/Awards: Gold (NW, OC)

Whitehall Lane 1994 Morisoli Vineyard Reserve Cabernet Sauvignon
Region: California, Napa Valley $36
Golds/Awards: Gold (WWC-92 pts)

Whitehall Lane 1995 Reserve Cabernet Sauvignon
Region: California, Napa Valley $38
Golds/Awards: Gold (SD, WC)

Windsor 1994 Private Reserve Cabernet Sauvignon
Region: California, Alexander Valley $22
Golds/Awards: Gold (NW, WWC-90 pts); Best of Class, Best of Varietal (NW)

Windsor 1994 Shelton Signature Cabernet Sauvignon
Region: California, Sonoma Valley $21
Golds/Awards: Gold (NW)

Windsor 1995 Preference Vineyard Cabernet Sauvignon
Region: California, North Coast $13
Golds/Awards: Gold (RI, CA); Best of Class (CA)

Windsor 1995 Private Reserve Cabernet Sauvignon
Region: California, North Coast $20
Golds/Awards: Gold (LA)

Woodside 1993 Cabernet Sauvignon
Region: California, Santa Cruz Mountains $18
Golds/Awards: Gold (WWC-90 pts)

Woodward Canyon 1994 Captain Z.K. Straight Cabernet Sauvignon
Region: Washington, Columbia Valley $35
Golds/Awards: Gold (WWC-92 pts)

Wyndham Estates 1996 Bin 444 Cabernet Sauvignon
Region: Australia, Southeastern Region $12.99
Golds/Awards: Gold (PR, BR)

Wynns 1993 John Riddoch Cabernet Sauvignon
Region: Australia, Coonawarra $40
Golds/Awards: Gold (WWC-93 pts)

Wynns 1994 Coonawarra Estate Cabernet Sauvignon
Region: Australia, Coonawarra $13.99
Golds/Awards: Gold (RI); Chairman's Award (RI)

Wynns 1994 John Riddoch Cabernet Sauvignon
Region: Australia, Coonawarra $40
Golds/Awards: Gold (IW)

Yalumba 1993 The Menzies Cabernet Sauvignon
Region: Australia, Coonawarra $21
Golds/Awards: Gold (WWC-92 pts)

ZD Wines 1993 Reserve Cabernet Sauvignon
Region: California, Napa Valley $45
Golds/Awards: Gold (WWC-90 pts)

Did You Know...?

"Wine is like sex in that few men will admit not knowing all about it."

—Hugh Johnson

ITALIAN VARIETALS

I f you're looking for a "new" red wine, don't overlook the great Italian varietals coming out of California and to a lesser degree Argentina. Transplanted Italian winemakers introduced these varieties to American soil and have started a trend that's meeting with commercial success and worldwide recognition.

Aglianico Not common in southern Italy, and even less common in California, this variety can produce deep ruby red wines with full flavor and powerful, intense aromas.

Barbera This was the fourth leading red wine variety grown in California until twenty-some years ago. Until recently it was relegated to the role of jug wine, or merely a blending agent to enhance its more powerful cousins, Nebbiolo and Sangiovese. But Barbera is now undergoing a change in reputation similar to that of Sauvignon Blanc, as fine California and Argentinean Barberas hit the market. In cooler regions Barbera becomes rich and complex; in hot climates it produces a light fruity wine.

Charbono See Dolcetto.

Dolcetto Common in Italy, this grape produces easygoing, fruity, fragrant reds with flavors and aromas reminiscent of almonds and licorice. This variety is known as Charbono in California.

Nebbiolo This is one of Italy's two finest grapes, Sangiovese being the other. It is responsible for some of that country's best wines, among them world-famous Barbaresco and Barolo. In both South and North America, Nebbiolo is making its presence known. A great Nebbiolo can be long-lived, tannic, acidic, alcoholic, richly textured, and big, big, big. Nebbiolo almost always requires aging in order to reach its full potential.

Sangiovese Because it ripens slowly and late, the Sangiovese variety can yield rich, alcoholic, long-lived red

wines with cherry and plummy flavors. It can also be made into light, fresh and fruity, early-drinking reds.

Food companions: Italian-style wines stand up to hearty dishes such as grilled meat and vegetable skewers, prime rib, sausage, veal, rabbit, and of course garlicky, tomato-sauced Italian cuisine. Mature cheeses that aren't too strong, such as fontina, make good companions to these delicious wines as well.

Adelaida 1995 Sangiovese
Region: California, San Luis Obispo $24
Golds/Awards: Gold (WWC-90 pts)

Adler Fels 1996 Sangiovese
Region: California, Mendocino $20
Golds/Awards: Gold (NW)

Altamura 1994 Sangiovese
Region: California, Napa Valley $28
Golds/Awards: Gold (WWC-90 pts)

Atlas Peak 1995 Reserve Sangiovese
Region: California $24
Golds/Awards: Gold (WS); Best Sangiovese (WS)

Beaulieu Vineyard 1995 Sangiovese Signet Collection
Region: California, Napa $16
Golds/Awards: Gold (RI)

Bella Vista 1995 Sangiovese
Region: California, Solano County $20
Golds/Awards: Gold (WWC-90 pts)

Benziger 1994 Imagery Series Largo Vista Vineyard Sangiovese
Region: California, Dry Creek Valley $20
Golds/Awards: Gold (WWC-92 pts)

Benziger 1995 Imagery Series Barbera
Region: California, Sonoma Valley $22.99
Golds/Awards: Gold (PR); Best of Class (PR)

Boeger 1995 Charbono
Region: California $15
Golds/Awards: Gold (LA)

Did You Know...?

The University of California at Davis (one of
California's and the world's top oenology
schools) graduated only 5 students from
their oenology department in 1966.

Boeger 1996 Barbera
Region: California, El Dorado $13.50
Golds/Awards: Gold (OC, CA)

Bonterra 1994 Sangiovese
Region: California, Mendocino County $22
Golds/Awards: Gold (WWC-90 pts)

Bonterra 1995 Sangiovese
Region: California, Mendocino County $23
Golds/Awards: Gold (CA); Best of Class (CA)

Did You Know...?

"It's such a great feeling to be able to go out in the
vineyard and see all kinds of wildlife and actually taste
the fruit without worrying about whether it was just
sprayed and if I should even be out there at all."
— winemaker Bob Blue, of organic Bonterra Vineyards

Callaway 1994 Nebbiolo
Region: California, Temecula $12
Golds/Awards: Gold (NW)

Cambria 1996 Tepusquet Vineyard Sangiovese
Region: California, Santa Maria Valley $18
Golds/Awards: Gold (WC); Best of Class (WC)

Chameleon Cellars 1996 Sangiovese
Region: California, North Coast $16
Golds/Awards: Gold (RI); Chairman's Award (RI)

Charles Krug 1995 Family Reserve Sangiovese
Region: California, Napa Valley $16
Golds/Awards: Gold (WC)

Coturri 1995 Poggio alla Pietra Vineyards Sangiovese
Region: California, Sonoma Valley $35
Golds/Awards: Gold (WWC-91 pts)

Ehlers Grove 1996 Dolcetto
Region: California, Napa Valley $14
Golds/Awards: Gold (CA); Best of Class (CA)

Flora Springs 1996 Sangiovese
Region: California, Napa Valley $18
Golds/Awards: Gold (LA)

Martin Brothers 1994 Vecchio Nebbiolo
Region: California, Central Coast $20
Golds/Awards: Gold (WWC-94 pts)

Martin Brothers 1996 Nebbiolo
Region: California, Central Coast $11
Golds/Awards: Gold (DA)

Montevina Winery 1995 Terra D'Oro Barbera
Region: California, Amador County $18
Golds/Awards: Gold (NW); Best of Class (NW)

Obester 1995 Twentieth Anniversary Sangiovese
Region: California, Mendocino County $13.95
Golds/Awards: Gold (CA); Best of California, Best of Class (CA)

Parducci 1994 Old Vines Charbono
Region: California, Mendocino $10.75
Golds/Awards: Gold (CA); Best of Class (CA)

Renwood 1995 Linsteadt Vineyard Barbera
Region: California, Amador County $24
Golds/Awards: Gold (WWC-90 pts)

Did You Know...?

Q: Who is the U.S. regulatory agency that
regulates all aspects of wine production
and sets minimum standards that have
to be observed?
A: The Bureau of Alcohol, Tobacco,
and Firearms.

Renwood 1996 Barbera
Region: California, Amador County $18.95
Golds/Awards: Gold (CA); Best of Class (CA)

Robert Pepi 1995 Colline Di Sassi Sangiovese
Region: California, Napa Valley $25
Golds/Awards: Gold (RI, LA, WC); Best of Class (LA)

Robert Pepi 1995 Two-Heart Canopy Sangiovese
Region: California, Santa Rosa $18
Golds/Awards: Gold (NW); Best of Class, Best of Varietal (NW)

Rutherford Hill 1995 21ˢᵗ Anniversary Sangiovese
Region: California, Napa Valley $30
Golds/Awards: Gold (WWC-91 pts)

Staglin 1996 Stagliano Sangiovese
Region: California, Rutherford $35
Golds/Awards: Gold (WWC-90 pts)

Storrs 1996 San Lucas Vineyard Sangiovese
Region: California, Central Coast $20
Golds/Awards: Gold (OC)

Swanson 1995 Estate Bottled Sangiovese
Region: California, Napa Valley $24
Golds/Awards: Gold (NW)

Temecula Crest 1996 Nebbiolo
Region: California, Temecula $18
Golds/Awards: Gold (RI, NW); Best of Class, Best of
Varietal (NW)

Thomas Fogarty 1996 Estate Reserve Sangiovese
Region: California, Santa Cruz Mountains $27.50
Golds/Awards: Gold (WWC-91 pts)

Venezia 1996 Alegria Vineyards Sangiovese
Region: California, Russian River Valley $19.99
Golds/Awards: Gold (CA); Best of California, Best of Class (CA)

Vino Noceto 1995 Sangiovese
Region: California $12
Golds/Awards: Gold (IW)

Windwalker Vineyards 1996 Cooper Vineyard Barbera
Region: California, Amador County $12.50
Golds/Awards: Gold (PR, RI)

Did You Know...?

In 1920 there were 700 wineries in California. By the end of Prohibition there were 160.

MALBEC

Between last edition and this, Malbec has grown enough in popularity to merit its own chapter. South America has led the way in the New World when it comes to this rustic red. It is one of the component grapes used to make many Bordeaux blends, but until recently had been losing popularity. Now in California, in particular, and to a lesser degree South Africa and Australia, wine producers are starting again to make full-bodied red wines predominantly out of Malbec.

You're apt to see more and more of this varietal, particularly as Argentina wines gain ground here. Malbec at its best is richly concentrated with gamy, intense flavors and great aging potential because of its high tannin levels.

Food companions: Pair Malbec with steak, tomato-based spaghetti dishes, venison, and rich gravies and sauces. It makes a brilliant dessert wine—great with chocolate cheesecake. Argentine Malbec lovers have it with empañadas—pastries filled with minced beef, chopped olives, raisins, and boiled eggs.

Columbia Winery 1996 Red Willow Vineyard Malbec
Region: Washington, Yakima Valley $24.99
Golds/Awards: Gold (SD)

Edgewood 1995 Malbec
Region: California, Napa Valley $18
Golds/Awards: Gold (OC)

Geyser Peak 1995 Winemaker's Selection Malbec
Region: California, Alexander Valley $20
Golds/Awards: Gold (PR, NW, IV, WC, CA); Best of Class
(PR, NW, WC); Best of Varietal (NW); Best Red Wine (PR)

Humberto Canale 1997 Malbec
Region: Argentina $7.99
Golds/Awards: Gold (VN)

Jekel 1994 Sanctuary Estate Malbec
Region: California, Arroyo Seco $30
Golds/Awards: Gold (NW, DA)

Santa Julia 1996 Mendoza Malbec
Region: Argentina $5.99
Golds/Awards: Gold (VN)

Tupungato 1996 Mariposa Malbec
Region: Argentina $9.95
Golds/Awards: Gold (VN, NW)

Viu Manent 1996 Malbec
Region: Chile $8
Golds/Awards: Gold (VN)

Did You Know...?

Argentina is one of the best places on earth
for ripening red wine grapes—and foreign
capitalists are taking notice. It has endless hours
of sun, low humidity, and virtually no disease.

MERLOT

I s there anyone who doesn't like Merlot? This charming varietal is soft, fruity, and has a supple personality characterized by an array of wonderful flavors and aromas, among them black cherries, plums, fruitcake, caramel, herbs, and sometimes a hint of orange peel. A typical Merlot may also often have high alcohol and a lush, chewy texture.

California, Washington State, and increasingly Long Island, New York, are among the New World regions where the Merlot grape is grown, as well as New Zealand, Australia, and South America—particularly Chile, where amazing bargains can be found.

In the next few years consumers are apt to see this varietal more and more. It's enjoying such a surge in popularity that some call Merlot "the new Chardonnay"; it's as easy to drink but offers the health benefits of red wine.

Because it has what Cabernet Sauvignon lacks, Merlot is often used to soften the latter in Bordeaux-style blends (also known as red Meritage). But more and more it's found the other way around: as the base varietal, with small amounts of Cabernet Sauvignon added to the Merlot to give it more structure and focus. Less tannic than Cab, Merlot can be enjoyed sooner rather than cellared for years.

Food companions: Serve Merlot with chicken, duck, ham, and turkey, as well as Mediterranean dishes and even spicy Chinese foods. Or sip it before dinner alongside soft cheeses. It also goes well with onion soup, meatloaf, roast beef, pork chops, Manhattan-style clam chowder, pasta with red sauce, teriyaki, and tandoori chicken.

Alderbrook 1996 Kunde Vineyard Merlot
Region: California, Sonoma Valley $22
Golds/Awards: Gold (RI); Chairman's Award (RI)

Andrew Will 1995 Merlot
Region: Washington $28
Golds/Awards: Gold (WWC-90 pts)

Andrew Will 1995 Reserve Merlot
Region: Washington $32
Golds/Awards: Platinum (WWC-96 pts)

Antares 1995 Merlot
Region: California $24.99
Golds/Awards: Gold (WWC-90 pts)

Apex 1995 Merlot
Region: Washington, Columbia Valley $40
Golds/Awards: Gold (WWC-92 pts)

Barnard Griffin 1995 Reserve Merlot
Region: Washington, Columbia Valley $26.95
Golds/Awards: Gold (WWC-90 pts)

Bartholomew Park Winery 1996 Alta Vista Vineyards Merlot
Region: California, Sonoma Valley $18
Golds/Awards: Gold (SD, LA, CA); Best of Class (SD)

Bartholomew Park Winery 1996 Desnudos Vineyards Merlot
Region: California, Sonoma County $30
Golds/Awards: Gold (LA)

Bartholomew Park Winery 1996 Parks Vineyard Merlot
Region: California, Napa Valley $25
Golds/Awards: Gold (DA)

Did You Know...?

British wine writer Sarah Kemp (*Decanter*) bemoans the fact that British wine drinkers are increasingly interested in bargain rather than high-quality wines. As proof, she cites the best-selling 1997 wine book in Britain—a book called *Superplonk*.

Benziger 1995 Reserve Merlot
Region: California, Sonoma County $32
Golds/Awards: Gold (WWC-92 pts, PR, DA)

Benziger 1996 Merlot
Region: California, Sonoma County $16.99
Golds/Awards: Gold (LA, RI); Best of Class (LA);
Chairman's Award (RI)

Beringer 1994 Bancroft Ranch Merlot
Region: California, Howell Mountain $45
Golds/Awards: Gold (WWC-92 pts)

Brutocao 1995 Estate Bottled Unfiltered & Unfined Merlot
Region: California, Mendocino $18
Golds/Awards: Gold (DA, LA); Best of Class (LA)

Carta Vieja 1996 Reservado Merlot
Region: Chile $9
Golds/Awards: Gold (VL)

Casa LaPostolle 1996 Cuvée Alexandre Merlot
Region: Chile, Rapel Valley $16
Golds/Awards: Gold (WWC-90 pts, IW)

Casa LaPostolle 1996 Merlot
Region: Chile, Rapel Valley $10
Golds/Awards: Gold (WWC-90)

Did You Know...?

Bob Thompson of *Decanter* magazine describes
Chilean Merlot as "one of those jolly girls who
has all her clothes off before the door is closed."

Charles Shaw 1995 Barrel Select Merlot
Region: California $8.99
Golds/Awards: Gold (WWC-90 pts)

Chateau La Joya 1995 Gran Reserva Merlot
Region: Chile $12.99
Golds/Awards: Gold (VN)

Merlot RED

Did You Know...?

"Contains sulfites": How do sulfites get into wine? It's dusted and sprayed on vines to prevent disease. It's used on barrels to rid them of harmful bacteria. It's often added to juice to prevent browning and to inhibit the growth of certain unwanted yeast strains.

Chateau La Joya 1996 Gran Reserva Merlot
Region: Chile, Colchagua Valley $12.99
Golds/Awards: Gold (SM)

Chateau La Joya 1996 Premium Merlot
Region: Chile $8.99
Golds/Awards: Gold (VN)

Chateau St. Jean 1993 Reserve Merlot
Region: California, Sonoma County $40
Golds/Awards: Gold (PR)

Chateau St. Jean 1995 Merlot
Region: California, Sonoma County $18
Golds/Awards: Gold (RI, OC); Chairman's Award (RI)

Chateau Ste. Michelle 1995 Canoe Ridge Estate Vineyard Merlot
Region: Washington, Columbia Valley $31
Golds/Awards: Gold (WWC-90 pts)

Chateau Ste. Michelle 1995 Merlot
Region: Washington, Columbia Valley $17.99
Golds/Awards: Gold (PR)

Chateau Ste. Michelle 1995 Reserve Merlot
Region: Washington, Columbia Valley $42
Golds/Awards: Gold (WWC-92 pts)

Chateau Souverain 1995 Merlot
Region: California, Alexander Valley $16.50
Golds/Awards: Gold (WC, WWC-90 pts); Best of Class (WC)

Cilurzo 1997 Reserve Merlot
Region: California, Temecula $12.95
Golds/Awards: Four Star Gold (OC)

Merlot   RED

Clarendon Hills 1996 Merlot
Region: Australia $45
Golds/Awards: Gold (IW)

Clos Du Bois 1995 Selection Merlot
Region: California, Alexander Valley $20
Golds/Awards: Gold (WWC-91 pts)

Clos Du Val 1995 Merlot
Region: California, Napa Valley $28
Golds/Awards: Gold (WWC-91 pts)

Did You Know...?

The average American consumes six times more beer
and twenty times more soft drinks than wine.

Columbia Crest 1995 Merlot
Region: Washington, Columbia Valley $15.99
Golds/Awards: Gold (NW)

Columbia Winery 1995 Red Willow Vineyard Merlot
Region: Washington, Columbia Valley $23
Golds/Awards: Gold (WWC-90 pts)

Concannon 1995 Limited Merlot
Region: California, Alameda County $16.95
Golds/Awards: Gold (LA); Best of Class (LA)

Cosentino 1996 Reserve Merlot
Region: California, Napa Valley $34
Golds/Awards: Gold (LA); Best of Class (LA)

Cuisine Cellars 1996 Merlot
Region: California, Sonoma $8.99
Golds/Awards: Gold (LA)

Davis Bynum 1995 Laureles Vineyard Merlot
Region: California, Russian River Valley $22
Golds/Awards: Gold (CA)

DeLoach 1996 Estate Bottled Merlot
Region: California, Russian River Valley $18
Golds/Awards: Gold (RI, WC); Chairman's Award (RI)

Dry Creek Vineyard 1995 Reserve Merlot
Region: California, Dry Creek Valley $30
Golds/Awards: Gold (NW, LA); Best of Class (NW)

Duckhorn 1993 Merlot
Region: California, Howell Mountain $30
Golds/Awards: Gold (WWC-90 pts)

Duckhorn 1995 Merlot
Region: California, Napa Valley $28
Golds/Awards: Gold (WWC-90 pts)

Eikendal 1996 Merlot
Region: South Africa $17.99
Golds/Awards: Gold (VL)

Estancia 1995 Merlot
Region: California, Alexander Valley $14
Golds/Awards: Gold (WWC-90 pts)

Fairview 1994 Merlot
Region: South Africa, Paarl $14.99
Golds/Awards: Gold (WWC-90 pts)

Did You Know...?

Charles Back, owner of South Africa's Fairview, hated
the condition that exists on many wine farms, where
black, or more commonly colored (brown-skinned
people not of African descent, such as Indians),
are housed by the farmers and thus kept
landless. In 1997 he bought a farm in
Paarl and with the help of the ANC
government, sold it to his workers.

Fetzer 1995 Barrel Select Merlot
Region: California, Sonoma County $14
Golds/Awards: Gold (PR)

Fetzer 1996 Eagle Peak Merlot
Region: California $8.99
Golds/Awards: Gold (WC)

Merlot   RED

Did You Know...?
There were only two acres of Merlot planted in California in 1960.

Firestone 1995 Winemaker's Reserve Merlot
Region: California, Santa Ynez Valley $25
Golds/Awards: Gold (NW, DA)

Flora Springs 1995 Windfall Vineyard Merlot
Region: California, Napa Valley $32
Golds/Awards: Gold (WWC-93 pts)

Flora Springs 1996 Merlot
Region: California, Napa Valley $20
Golds/Awards: Gold (LA)

Freemark Abbey 1995 Merlot
Region: California, Napa Valley $21
Golds/Awards: Gold (OC)

Frick 1995 Merlot
Region: California, Dry Creek Valley $20
Golds/Awards: Gold (OC)

Gallo Sonoma 1995 Merlot
Region: California, Sonoma County $11
Golds/Awards: Gold (LA)

Geyser Peak 1995 Merlot
Region: California, Sonoma County $14.99
Golds/Awards: Gold (GH)

Geyser Peak 1995 Reserve Merlot
Region: California, Alexander Valley $29.99
Golds/Awards: Gold (WWC-92 pts)

Geyser Peak 1996 Merlot
Region: California, Sonoma County $16
Golds/Awards: Gold (PR, BR); Best of Class (PR)

Glen Ellen 1995 Expressions Merlot
Region: California, Sonoma $12.99
Golds/Awards: Gold (LA)

Godwin 1995 River Ranch Vineyard Merlot
Region: California, Alexander Valley $20
Golds/Awards: Gold (OC)

Greenwood Ridge Vineyards 1995 Estate Bottled Merlot
Region: California, Anderson Valley $22
Golds/Awards: Gold (LA, OC, WC); Best of Class (WC)

Hogue 1995 Barrel Select Merlot
Region: Washington $15
Golds/Awards: Gold (LA)

J. Lohr 1996 Cypress Merlot
Region: California $12
Golds/Awards: Gold (LA)

Jekel 1996 Sanctuary Estate Reserve Merlot
Region: California $15
Golds/Awards: Gold (CA); Best of Class (CA)

Joseph Phelps 1995 Merlot
Region: California, Napa Valley $26
Golds/Awards: Gold (WWC-90 pts)

Katnook Estate 1995 Merlot
Region: Australia $24.99
Golds/Awards: Gold (IW)

Kendall-Jackson 1994 Vintner's Reserve Merlot
Region: California $19
Golds/Awards: Gold (BR)

Kenwood 1996 Merlot
Region: California, Sonoma County $20
Golds/Awards: Gold (OC)

KWV 1995 Cathedral Cellar Merlot
Region: South Africa, Coastal Region $12
Golds/Awards: Gold (WS); Best Merlot (WS)

Did You Know...?

Merlot for breakfast? "There is no doubt that the olfactory senses and palate are far more keen and alert in the morning than in the late afternoon." —Robert Parker

Lambert Bridge 1995 Merlot
Region: California, Sonoma County $20
Golds/Awards: Gold (SD, WWC-90 pts); Best of Class (SD)

Le Ducq 1994 Sylviane Merlot
Region: California, Napa Valley $30
Golds/Awards: Gold (WWC-90 pts)

L'Ecole No. 41 1995 Merlot
Region: Washington, Columbia Valley $24
Golds/Awards: Gold (WWC-92 pts)

Lockwood 1995 Estate Bottled and Grown Merlot
Region: California, Monterey $18
Golds/Awards: Gold (NW, WWC-90 pts); Best of Class (NW)

Lockwood 1995 Partners' Reserve Merlot
Region: California, Monterey County $24
Golds/Awards: Gold (WWC-92 pts)

Louis M. Martini 1994 Reserve Merlot
Region: California $18
Golds/Awards: Gold (IW)

Meerlust 1994 Merlot
Region: South Africa, Stellenbosch $11
Golds/Awards: Gold (WWC-90)

Merryvale 1995 Reserve Merlot
Region: California, Napa Valley $32
Golds/Awards: Gold (WWC-90 pts)

Mission Hill 1996 Private Reserve Merlot
Region: Canada, Okanagan Valley   (Can $) 14.95
Golds/Awards: Gold (LA)

Did You Know...?

"Is Nothing Sacred" Department:
A French cognac producer has decided that
African-Americans who celebrate Kwanzaa
are a great target market for their new
passion-fruit beverage blended with cognac.
Last year they launched their campaign with
"Kwanzaa Gift Bags."

Monticello 1994 Corley Reserve Merlot
Region: California, Napa Valley $28
Golds/Awards: Gold (WWC-90 pts)

Nelson Estate 1995 Merlot
Region: California, Sonoma Valley $19
Golds/Awards: Gold (OC)

Niebaum-Coppola 1995 Francis Coppola Family Merlot
Region: California, Napa Valley $32
Golds/Awards: Gold (WWC-92 pts)

Orfila Vineyards & Winery 1996 Merlot
Region: California, San Diego $15.98
Golds/Awards: Gold (WC)

Palmer 1995 Reserve Merlot
Region: New York, North Fork Long Island $29.99
Golds/Awards: Gold (DA)

Peconic Bay 1995 Epic Acre Merlot
Region: New York, North Fork Long Island $24.99
Golds/Awards: Gold (WWC-90 pts)

Did You Know...?

Wine investors are looking to Long Island, New York, as one of the next best places to sink their money. Merlot is star here, and one great collaboration is already in the works between one of France's top winemakers and an up-and-coming vineyard that will focus solely on Merlot. Stay tuned.

Pine Ridge 1995 Merlot
Region: California, Carneros $33.50
Golds/Awards: Gold (WWC-94 pts)

Plam 1995 Vintner's Reserve Merlot
Region: California, Napa Valley $25
Golds/Awards: Gold (WWC-93 pts)

Portteus 1995 Merlot
Region: Washington, Yakima Valley $16
Golds/Awards: Gold (WWC-90 pts)

Did You Know...?

The Chinese government's official policy is to encourage wine consumption over beer or distilled spirits. Why? To conserve grain for food products and to discourage growing levels of national consumption of high alcohol-content beverages.

Portteus 1995 Reserve Merlot
Region: Washington, Yakima Valley $29
Golds/Awards: Gold (WWC-91 pts)

Preston 1994 Reserve Merlot
Region: Washington, Columbia Valley $21
Golds/Awards: Gold (WWC-90 pts)

Prince Michel Vineyards 1997 De Virginia Merlot
Region: Virginia $18.95
Golds/Awards: Gold (LA)

Quail Ridge 1996 Merlot
Region: California $16.99
Golds/Awards: Gold (OC)

Quatro 1994 Merlot
Region: California, Sonoma County $12.99
Golds/Awards: Gold (PR, DA)

Raymond Vineyard 1995 Reserve Merlot
Region: California, Napa Valley $20
Golds/Awards: Gold (OC, WC)

Richardson Vineyards 1996 Sangiacomo Vineyard Merlot
Region: California, Los Carneros $19
Golds/Awards: Gold (CA); Best of California, Best of Class (CA)

Ridge 1995 Merlot
Region: California, Santa Cruz Mountains $40
Golds/Awards: Gold (WWC-90 pts)

River Run Vintners 1996 Merlot
Region: California $15
Golds/Awards: Gold (NW); Best of Class, Best of Varietal, Best New World Merlot (NW)

Robert Keenan Winery 1995 Merlot
Region: California, Napa Valley $30
Golds/Awards: Gold (CA); Best of Class (CA)

Rosenblum 1995 Lone Oak Vineyard Merlot
Region: California, Russian River Valley $20
Golds/Awards: Gold (LA, WWC-90 pts)

Rutherford Hill 1995 Reserve Merlot
Region: California, Napa Valley $44
Golds/Awards: Gold (WWC-90 pts, LA)

Rutherford Vintners 1996 Barrel Select Merlot
Region: California $8.99
Golds/Awards: Gold (WC); Best of Class (WC)

St. Clement 1995 Merlot
Region: California $24
Golds/Awards: Gold (RI, WWC-90 pts)

St. Francis 1994 Reserve Merlot
Region: California, Sonoma Valley $29
Golds/Awards: Gold (WWC-93 pts)

St. Francis 1995 Merlot
Region: California, Sonoma Valley $18
Golds/Awards: Gold (BR)

Did You Know...?

Polyphenols, found in wine, are powerful germ killers. Early Greek writings indicate that wine was used to treat battlefield wounds.

Seven Hills 1995 Klipsun Vineyards Merlot
Region: Oregon, Columbia River $24
Golds/Awards: Gold (WWC-93 pts)

Seven Hills 1995 Seven Hills Vineyard Merlot
Region: Oregon, Walla Walla Valley $24
Golds/Awards: Gold (WWC-90 pts)

Silverado 1995 Merlot
Region: California, Napa Valley $22.50
Golds/Awards: Gold (WWC-94 pts)

Silver Ridge 1996 Barrel Select Merlot
Region: California $10
Golds/Awards: Gold (DA)

Solis Winery 1995 Reserve Merlot
Region: California, Santa Clara Valley $22
Golds/Awards: Gold (CA); Best of Region, Best of Class (CA)

Sumac Ridge 1995 Merlot
Region: Canada, Okanagan Valley   (Can $) 17.95
Golds/Awards: Gold (EN)

Swanson 1995 Merlot
Region: California, Napa Valley $24
Golds/Awards: Gold (WWC-91 pts)

Swanson 1996 Merlot
Region: California, Napa Valley $26
Golds/Awards: Gold (LA, WWC-94 pts); Best of Class (LA)

Talus 1995 Merlot
Region: California $8
Golds/Awards: Gold (LA)

Tefft Cellars NV Merlot
Region: Washington, Columbia Valley $15
Golds/Awards: Gold (IV)

Turning Leaf 1995 Reserve Merlot
Region: California, Sonoma County $9.99
Golds/Awards: Gold (LA)

Viña Calina 1995 Seleccion de las Lomas Merlot
Region: Chile $20
Golds/Awards: Gold (NW)

Did You Know...?

The recent explosion in wine sales created both a
planting and Pierce's Disease boom; vineyards in
California are being sited closer to creeks and rivers that
host the bug that carries Pierce's.

Waterbrook 1995 Reserve Merlot
Region: Washington, Columbia Valley $32
Golds/Awards: Gold (WWC-92 pts)

Whitehall Lane 1995 Leonardini Vineyard Reserve Merlot
Region: California, Napa Valley $36
Golds/Awards: Gold (WWC-93 pts)

Windsor 1995 Shelton Signature Series Merlot
Region: California, Sonoma County $23.50
Golds/Awards: Gold (PR, WWC-90 pts); Best of Class (PR)

Woodward Canyon 1995 Merlot
Region: Washington, Columbia Valley $30
Golds/Awards: Gold (WWC-95 pts)

Yakima River 1994 Winemaker's Reserve Merlot
Region: Washington, Yakima Valley $28
Golds/Awards: Gold (WWC-90 pts)

Did You Know...?

Can wine be macho? In China, wine is
traditionally considered the beverage of
choice for women, an obstacle that U.S. PR
firms representing American wineries are
trying to overcome.

MISCELLANEOUS VARIETAL REDS

There are many varietals of wine in the world, but the ones most of us see—and buy—in the store constitute a more modest selection. In fact, I was recently chatting with the owner of a small but excellent wine shop in Connecticut who complained that he never knows where to shelf the odd varietal. As a result, he often doesn't stock, say, the the Rhône red.

I have a similar dilemma. All of the wines in this section were excellent enough to win the highest medal at one or more top competition. Yet they're not numerous enough to make up their own sections. Therefore, I've had to lump the less common reds all together. Don't be put off by these offbeat varietals. Give them a try. You may fall in love with a type of red you've never experienced before and can get your winemonger to start stocking it.

Alicante Bouschet Often used as a blending agent, it makes a deep-purple-colored wine that tends to be high in alcohol with robust fruitiness.

Carignane A red Rhône grape capable of producing rich, spicy, earthy wines. Often used in Rhône-style blends.

Cinsault The Cinsault (often spelled Cinsaut) grape makes wines that are typically light, soft, and aromatic. Sometimes used to make rosés.

Durif An uncommon red wine grape that seems to do better in the New World than in its native France. In Australia and America, it can produce moderately tannic reds with flavors and aromas of black cherries, blackberries, and herbs.

Grenache Often used in spicy Rhône-style red blends, Grenache is also used to make light and fruity rosés.

Lemberger Mostly found in the state of Washington, this German red wine grape produces fresh and fruity, light red wines meant to be drunk young.

Mataro See Mourvèdre.

Mourvèdre A Rhône red varietal with plenty of structure, intense fruit, and blackberry perfume. Often used in Rhône-style blends. Also sometimes called Mataro in Australia and in California.

Petite Verdot Another classic Bordeaux red, Petite Verdot is fairly new to California and is usually used to make Red Meritage. It has many of the same strengths as Cabernet Sauvignon: rich color, hefty tannins, and excellent flavor concentration.

Pinotage A cross between Pinot Noir and Cinsault, this is South Africa's own wine grape, although New Zealand is beginning to plant some, and other countries may follow suit. It can produce either a Gamay-like light red, or a more serious, robust, Cabernet-style red that calls for serious aging in the bottle.

Tannat A deeply colored and tannic red wine reminiscent of Nebbiolo and grown mostly in South America.

Tempranillo Spain's answer to Cabernet Sauvignon, this grape is also grown in Argentina and to a lesser extent in California. It produces heavy reds with scents of tobacco, leather, and spices.

Alban 1995 Grenache
Region: California, Edna Valley $28
Golds/Awards: Gold (WWC-91 pts)

Callaway 1994 Mourvèdre
Region: California, Temecula $16
Golds/Awards: Gold (NW); Best of Class (NW)

Chouinard 1996 Mohr-Fry Ranches Alicante Bouschet
Region: California, Lodi $14
Golds/Awards: Gold (OC)

Did You Know...?

One British wine journalist complains that American cookbooks are better at imparting wine and food suggestions to readers. Britain's best-selling cookbook, *Complete Cookery Course*, by Delia Smith, has no mention of wine, whereas *The Joy of Cooking*, first published in 1931, has a full chapter on the subject.

Cline 1995 Ancient Vines Carignane
Region: California, Contra Costa County $18
Golds/Awards: Gold (WWC-90 pts)

Cline 1995 Ancient Vines Mourvèdre
Region: California, Contra Costa County $18
Golds/Awards: Gold (WWC-92 pts)

Cline 1996 Ancient Vines Mourvèdre
Region: California, Contra Costa $18
Golds/Awards: Gold (WC)

D'Arenburg 1996 The Twenty Eight Road Mourvèdre
Region: Australia, McLaren Vale $23
Golds/Awards: Gold (PR)

**Geyser Peak 1995 Trione Vineyards Winemaker's
Selection Petite Verdot**
Region: California, Alexander Valley $20
Golds/Awards: Gold (PR, NW, OC, CA); Best of Class (CA)

Hawthorne Mountain Vineyards 1996 Lemberger
Region: Canada, Okanagan Falls   (Can $) 17.95
Golds/Awards: Gold (NW)

Jekel 1994 Sanctuary Estate Petite Verdot
Region: California, Arroyo Seco $30
Golds/Awards: Gold (OC)

Kanonkop 1995 Pinotage
Region: South Africa, Stellenbosch $19.99
Golds/Awards: Gold (WWC-92 pts)

Mount Prior 1994 Durif
Region: Australia $28.50
Golds/Awards: Gold (WWC-90 pts)

Pagor 1996 "Vino Tinto" Tempranillo
Region: California $10
Golds/Awards: Gold (OC)

Peju Province 1994 Petite Verdot
Region: California, Napa Valley $55
Golds/Awards: Gold (WWC-91 pts)

Ridge 1995 Mataro
Region: California, Contra Costa County $20
Golds/Awards: Gold (WWC-90 pts)

Topolos 1995 Alicante Bouschet
Region: California, Sonoma County $18
Golds/Awards: Gold (WWC-93 pts)

Did You Know...?

Wanting a career in wine? You may have to wing it.
Most marketers and wine business people
come from other industries, as the
wine industry has been slow to
provide training programs for
their own professionals.

Miscellaneous Reds   **RED**

Trentadue 1995 Carignane
Region: California, Sonoma County $12
Golds/Awards: Gold (CA)

Van Roekel Vineyards 1996 Grenache
Region: California $12.95
Golds/Awards: Gold (OC)

W.B. Bridgman 1997 Lemberger
Region: Washington, Yakima Valley $8.99
Golds/Awards: Gold (SD)

Windsor 1996 Carignane
Region: California, Mendocino $9.50
Golds/Awards: Gold (PR)

Yalumba 1996 Grenache
Region: Australia $15
Golds/Awards: Gold (PR); Best of Class (PR)

Did You Know...?

"Drink a glass of wine after your soup
and steal a ruble from your doctor."
                    —old Russian proverb

NATIVE REDS AND FRENCH-AMERICAN HYBRIDS

Native American wines are not wines made by Native Americans. The term refers to the grape, not the winemaker. Nearly every region of the world has grapes that are native to it, just as most regions have all kinds of flora and fauna that originated there.

The wine grape is from the genus Vitis. The species of grape depends on where that grape originally grew, before the intervention of man. Native American grapes are different species from Vitis vinifera, called vinifera for short, the chief European grape that includes most of the wines in this book as well as most of the fine wines grown commercially in the world.

There are more than a dozen native American species. The most common red wine is the one your grandmother may have made from her backyard arbor: Concord. Hardy native grapes have an advantage over their delicate French cousins in that they can grow almost anywhere, from Florida to Minnesota. However, when you try a native American wine for the first time, get ready for a sensation you won't experience with vinifera wines. Some call it "foxy," others "musky," but it's a decidedly distinct quality that American grapes impart and one that takes a bit of getting used to.

French-American hybrids The need for grapes that could resist disease in France and the extreme temperatures in Canada and the eastern U.S. resulted in the development over the next 150 years of French-American hybrids such as Baco Noir, Chambourcin, Norton, and Foch. These are wines that combine the best qualities of both species: the elegance of European red wines, the tough pioneer hardiness of American. These reds do not have the foxiness of their American half; they are likeable, easy-to-enjoy reds.

Girardet Wine Cellars 1996 Baco Noir
Region: Oregon, Umpqua Valley $14
Golds/Awards: Gold (PR); Best of Class (PR)

Meier's Wine Cellars NV Concord
Region: Ohio $3.99
Golds/Awards: Gold (PR)

Pontchartrain Vineyards 1996 Creole Rouge Chambourcin
Region: Louisiana $15
Golds/Awards: Gold (DA)

Quails' Gate 1995 Old Vines Foch
Region: Canada, Okanagan Valley   (Can $) 18.95
Golds/Awards: Gold (WWC-91 pts)

St. James Winery 1993 Norton
Region: Missouri $14.99
Golds/Awards: Gold (NW)

St. James Winery 1994 Norton
Region: Missouri $14.99
Golds/Awards: Gold (PR); Best of Class (PR)

St. James Winery 1994 Private Reserve Norton
Region: Missouri $19.99
Golds/Awards: Gold (SD); Best of Class (SD)

St. James Winery NV Velvet Red Concord
Region: Missouri $5.99
Golds/Awards: Gold (NW, SD); Best of Class (NW)

Stone Hill NV Concord
Region: Missouri $6.50
Golds/Awards: (RI)

Stone Hill 1996 Estate Bottled Norton
Region: Missouri $18.99
Golds/Awards: Gold (LA)

Did You Know...?

The translation of *labrusca* (the native American grape) is "fox grape" because foxes and deer love to eat it off the vine. Hence the term "foxy" is often used to describe native American wines.

PETITE SIRAH

Sometimes spelled Petite Syrah, this grape is no relation to Syrah, although it was once thought to be. In fact, the experts haven't come up with a definitive accounting of its mysterious origins.

Petite Sirah has been growing in North and South America for a long time. Almost all Petite Sirah vines in California are much older than the state average, which of course is good, since the older the vine, the more concentrated the grapes.

Petite Sirah can produce red, almost black, wines that are extremely tannic but well balanced, with distinctive flavors and aromas that include black pepper. Its Rhône-like qualities make Petite Sirah an attractive blending agent for Zinfandel. But increasingly it is made into its own varietal wine that's full of character and aging potential.

I love Petite Sirah. Luckily, one can find gold medal examples of this varietal at really reasonable prices.

Food companions: Try Petite Sirah with hard cheeses, lamb, barbecued beef, venison dishes, jambalaya, pizza, or other hearty fare.

Did You Know...?
Grapes have the highest sugar level of any fruit.

Bogle 1996 Petite Sirah
Region: California $9
Golds/Awards: Gold (LA, WWC-91 pts); Best of Class (LA)

Carmen 1995 Petite Sirah
Region: Chile, Maipo Valley $13.99
Golds/Awards: Gold (WWC-90 pts)

Christopher Creek 1995 Estate Bottled Petite Sirah
Region: California, Russian River Valley $18
Golds/Awards: Gold (NW)

Christopher Creek 1996 Estate Bottled Petite Sirah
Region: California, Russian River Valley $18
Golds/Awards: Gold (OC)

Cilurzo 1996 Estate Petite Sirah
Region: California, Temecula $19.95
Golds/Awards: Gold (PR); Best of Class (PR)

Concannon 1995 Petite Sirah
Region: California $9.95
Golds/Awards: Gold (NW); Best of Class (NW)

David Bruce 1996 Petite Syrah
Region: California, Central Coast $15
Golds/Awards: Gold (PR)

David Bruce 1996 Shell Creek Vineyard Petite Syrah
Region: California, Paso Robles $18
Golds/Awards: Gold (IV, WWC-93 pts)

Guenoc 1995 Petite Sirah
Region: California $15.50
Golds/Awards: Gold (WC)

Lolonis 1995 Orpheus Private Reserve Petite Sirah
Region: California, Redwood Valley $17
Golds/Awards: Gold (SD)

Petite Sirah

RED

Mirassou 1996 Family Selection Petite Sirah
Region: California, Monterey County $11.95
Golds/Awards: Gold (LA); Best of Class (LA)

**Nichelini 1995 Estate Bottled Nichelini Vineyard
Petite Sirah**
Region: California, Napa Valley $17.50
Golds/Awards: Gold (OC)

Rosenblum 1996 Kenefick Ranch Petite Sirah
Region: California, Napa Valley $18
Golds/Awards: Gold (WC); Best of Class (WC)

Stag's Leap 1994 Petite Sirah
Region: California, Napa Valley $22
Golds/Awards: Gold (PR, WWC-90 pts); Four Star Gold (OC)

Did You Know...?

Too Much Spare Time Department: Georg Riedel,
famous for his line of Riedel wine glasses, each uniquely
shaped for a different type of wine, has applied for a
patent on his newest invention: a tiny wine-tasting glass
that holds about one tablespoon of wine. To use it, place
the glass on its side and roll it around the table to coat
its sides with the precious liquid before tasting it. The
idea is to aid the senses while avoiding any waste
whatsoever.

PINOT NOIR

Often described in poetic, sensual terms, a great Pinot Noir has subtlety, elegance, complexity, and finesse. On the palate it can be lush, broad, and seductive, with essences of raspberries, strawberries, loganberries, cherries, herbs, earth, and bouquets of fresh wildflowers such as violets.

But more than these wonderful qualities, which winemakers the world over try to achieve with their Pinot Noirs, the grape's most dominant feature is how exasperating it is to grow. Winemakers spend their entire careers wrestling with this thin-skinned, fragile grape that's susceptible to various maladies and vulnerable to frost. For these and other reasons, Pinot Noirs tend to be expensive.

Pinot Noir is made in almost every country where ambitious winemakers ply their trade. It's the sole grape of which France's red burgundy is made. California, Washington, and especially Oregon, with a climate very similar to Burgundy's, are doing wonders with this fickle grape. Canada, Australia, South Africa, and New Zealand are also attempting to master it, with Australia the real wild card, since many of its recently planted Pinot Noir vines are now coming of age.

Because Pinot Noir loses its tannins quickly, most bottles should be consumed within a couple years of the vintage, no more than seven or eight years max.

Food companions: Have Pinot Noir with swordfish, fresh tuna steak, roast chicken, veal, pork loin, cornish hens, or turkey, and game such as pheasant, rabbit, or quail. It also goes well with hard cheeses and cheddar cheese. More robust-style Pinots can accompany lamb, steak, and venison.

Adelsheim 1995 Pinot Noir
Region: Oregon $18.99
Golds/Awards: Gold (WWC-90 pts)

Alderbrook 1996 Pinot Noir
Region: California, Russian River Valley $18.75
Golds/Awards: Gold (NW)

Amity 1993 Winemaker's Reserve Pinot Noir
Region: Oregon, Willamette Valley $35
Golds/Awards: Gold (WWC-90 pts)

Anapamu 1995 Pinot Noir
Region: California, Central Coast $11.99
Golds/Awards: Gold (NW, PR)

Ata Rangi Vineyard 1996 Pinot Noir
Region: New Zealand, Martinborough $32
Golds/Awards: Gold (WS)

Au Bon Climat 95/96 Pinot Noir
Region: California, Central Coast $19
Golds/Awards: Gold (WWC-90 pts)

Did You Know...?

A mechanical harvester can do the work of sixty people.

Bartholomew Park Winery 1996 Estate Vineyards Pinot Noir
Region: California, Sonoma Valley $23
Golds/Awards: Gold (CA)

Beaulieu Vineyard 1995 Pinot Noir
Region: California, Carneros $15
Golds/Awards: Gold (WC)

Beaulieu Vineyard 1996 Pinot Noir
Region: California, Carneros $15
Golds/Awards: Gold (RI, OC); Chairman's Award (RI)

Beaux Frères 1995 Pinot Noir
Region: Oregon, Yamhill County $50
Golds/Awards: Gold (WWC-90 pts)

Benton Lane 1996 Reserve Pinot Noir
Region: Oregon $28
Golds/Awards: Gold (WWC-90 pts)

Did You Know...?

Pinot Noir is known as "the headache grape" because of its fragile character and how difficult it is to grow and to work with.

Beringer 1996 Pinot Noir
Region: California, North Coast $15
Golds/Awards: Gold (RI)

Bouchaine 1994 Reserve Pinot Noir
Region: California, Carneros $27
Golds/Awards: Gold (WWC-92 pts)

Brancott Vineyards 1996 Reserve Pinot Noir
Region: New Zealand, Marlborough $18
Golds/Awards: Gold (SY)

Cambria 1996 Julia's Vineyard Pinot Noir
Region: California $24
Golds/Awards: Gold (LA); Best of Class (LA)

Castle Vineyards 1996 Pinot Noir
Region: California, Carneros $22
Golds/Awards: Gold (NW, LA)

Castoro Cellars 1996 Bien Nacido Vineyard Reserve Pinot Noir
Region: California, Santa Barbara County $16
Golds/Awards: Gold (RI)

Chateau St. Jean 1995 Durell Vineyards Pinot Noir
Region: California, Carneros $24
Golds/Awards: Gold (NW)

Clos du Bois 1996 Pinot Noir
Region: California, Sonoma County $15
Golds/Awards: Gold (CA)

Concannon 1995 Reserve Pinot Noir
Region: California, Central Coast $14.95
Golds/Awards: Gold (LA)

Cosentino 1996 Punched Cap Fermented Pinot Noir
Region: California, Russian River Valley $50
Golds/Awards: Gold (RI)

David Bruce 1994 Estate Reserve Pinot Noir
Region: California, Santa Cruz Mountains $35
Golds/Awards: Gold (WWC-91 pts)

David Bruce 1995 Pinot Noir
Region: California, Chalone $32
Golds/Awards: Gold (NW, WWC-94 pts)

David Bruce 1995 Reserve Pinot Noir
Region: California, Russian River Valley $26
Golds/Awards: Gold (WWC-92 pts)

Davis Bynum 1995 Limited Edition Pinot Noir
Region: California, Russian River Valley $28
Golds/Awards: Gold (WWC-91 pts)

Domaine Carneros 1994 Pinot Noir
Region: California, Carneros $20
Golds/Awards: Gold (WWC-90 pts)

Domaine Drouhin 1995 Laurene Pinot Noir
Region: Oregon, Willamette Valley $45
Golds/Awards: Gold (WWC-91 pts)

Domaine St. George 1996 Premier Cuvée STG Pinot Noir
Region: California, Santa Maria Valley $10
Golds/Awards: Gold (DA, LA); Best of Class (LA)

Domaine Serene 1995 Evenstad Reserve Pinot Noir
Region: Oregon, Willamette Valley $33
Golds/Awards: Gold (WWC-93 pts)

Did You Know...?

"Where there is not wine there is no love."
—Euripides

Edmeades 1996 Pinot Noir
Region: California, Anderson Valley $20
Golds/Awards: Gold (OC)

Elkhorn Peak Cellars 1996 Pinot Noir
Region: California, Napa Valley $26
Golds/Awards: Gold (GH)

Did You Know...?

Legend has it that Christopher Columbus, on his historic sail to America, got wind of a mutiny. To nip it in the bud, he opened his finest casks of sherry and shared it with his men.

Fess Parker 1995 American Tradition Reserve Pinot Noir
Region: California, Santa Barbara County $28
Golds/Awards: Gold (WWC-90 pts)

Fess Parker 1996 American Tradition Reserve Pinot Noir
Region: California, Santa Barbara County $30
Golds/Awards: Gold (CA)

Fetzer 1995 Bien Nacido Vineyard Reserve Pinot Noir
Region: California, Santa Barbara County $24
Golds/Awards: Gold (WC)

Fetzer 1996 Bien Nacido Vineyard Reserve Pinot Noir
Region: California, Santa Barbara County $24
Golds/Awards: Gold (SD, OC)

Flora Springs 1996 Lavender Hill Vineyard Pinot Noir
Region: California $30
Golds/Awards: Gold (LA); Best of Class (LA)

Foley 1996 Santa Maria Hills Vineyard Pinot Noir
Region: California, Santa Maria Valley $25
Golds/Awards: Gold (OC)

Gallo Sonoma 1996 Pinot Noir
Region: California, Russian River Valley $10
Golds/Awards: Gold (LA)

Gary Farrell 1995 Allen Vineyard Pinot Noir
Region: California, Russian River Valley $40
Golds/Awards: Gold (WWC-90 pts)

Gary Farrell 1995 Pinot Noir
Region: California, Anderson Valley $30
Golds/Awards: Gold (WWC-90 pts)

Gary Farrell 1995 Rochioli Vineyard Pinot Noir
Region: California, Russian River Valley $50
Golds/Awards: Gold (WWC-93 pts)

Gary Farrell 1996 Pinot Noir
Region: California, Russian River Valley $22.50
Golds/Awards: Gold (SD, LA, CA)

Gary Farrell 1996 Bien Nacido Vineyard Pinot Noir
Region: California, Santa Barbara County $28
Golds/Awards: Gold (RI, SD, WC, CA); Chairman's Award
(RI); Best of Class (SD, CA); Best of California (CA)

Gehringer Brothers 1996 V.Q.A. Pinot Noir
Region: Canada, Okanagan Valley   (Can $) 12.95
Golds/Awards: Gold (NW); Best of Class (NW)

Geisen 1996 Canterbury Reserve Barrel Selection Pinot Noir
Region: New Zealand, Canterbury $25
Golds/Awards: Gold (SY)

Did You Know...?

Not surprisingly there are more styles, labels,
and producers of wine to choose from than
ever before in history.

Greenwood Ridge Vineyards 1996 Pinot Noir
Region: California, Anderson Valley $22
Golds/Awards: Gold (NW, RI, SD, WC); Best of Class (NW);
Best of Varietal (NW); Chairman's Award (RI)

Hacienda Wine Cellars 1996 Clair de Lune Pinot Noir
Region: California $6.99
Golds/Awards: Gold (NW); Best of Class (NW)

Hagafen 1996 Pinot Noir
Region: California, Napa Valley $13
Golds/Awards: Gold (RI); Chairman's Award (RI)

Handley Cellars 1995 Pinot Noir
Region: California, Anderson Valley $21
Golds/Awards: Gold (PR, NW, WC)

Handley Cellars 1995 Estate Reserve Pinot Noir
Region: California, Anderson Valley $29
Golds/Awards: Gold (PR)

Did You Know...?

"A peculiar subgenre of the English language . . . has flowered wildly in recent years, like some pulpy jungle plant. It's called Winespeak."
–Frank Prial

Hartford Court 1996 Dutton Ranch Sanchetti Vineyard Pinot Noir
Region: California, Russian River Valley $35
Golds/Awards: Gold (PR, RI); Best of Class (PR)

Hartford Court 1996 Pinot Noir
Region: California, Sonoma Coast $32
Golds/Awards: Gold (PR, NW, DA, OC, CA)

Hartford Court 1996 Arrendell Vineyard Pinot Noir
Region: California, Russian River Valley $42
Golds/Awards: Gold (DA, LA, WC)

Indigo Hills 1996 Pinot Noir
Region: California, Mendocino County $9
Golds/Awards: Gold (RI)

Ken Wright 1995 Canary Hill Vineyard Pinot Noir
Region: Oregon, Willamette Valley $24.99
Golds/Awards: Gold (WWC-90 pts)

Kendall-Jackson 1994 Grand Reserve Pinot Noir
Region: California $30
Golds/Awards: Gold (NW)

La Crema 1996 Reserve Pinot Noir
Region: California, Sonoma Coast $27
Golds/Awards: Gold (PR, CA); Best of Class (CA)

Laetitia 1996 La Colline Vineyard Pinot Noir
Region: California, San Luis Obispo County $29
Golds/Awards: Gold (OC)

Laetitia 1996 Reserve Pinot Noir
Region: California $19
Golds/Awards: Gold (PR, OC)

Lorane Valley 1995 Pinot Noir
Region: Oregon $10
Golds/Awards: Gold (EN)

MacRostie 1995 Reserve Pinot Noir
Region: California, Carneros $25
Golds/Awards: Gold (WWC-91 pts)

Martin Ray 1995 Pinot Noir
Region: California $36
Golds/Awards: Gold (WWC-90 pts)

McIlroy Wines 1996 Aquarius Ranch Pinot Noir
Region: California, Russian River Valley $18
Golds/Awards: Gold (RI)

Meridian 1995 Reserve Pinot Noir
Region: California, Santa Barbara/San Luis Obispo $20
Golds/Awards: Gold (DA, LA); Best of Class (LA)

Meridian 1995 Pinot Noir
Region: California, Santa Barbara $15.50
Golds/Awards: Gold (PR, WC, GH); Best of Class (WC)

Did You Know...?

"Drink and the world drinks with
you; swear off and you drink alone."
—Anonymous

Meridian 1996 Pinot Noir
Region: California, Santa Barbara County $15.50
Golds/Awards: Gold (LA); Best of Class (LA)

Mirassou 1996 Family Selection Pinot Noir
Region: California, Monterey $10.95
Golds/Awards: Gold (NW, SD)

Mirassou 1996 Harvest Reserve Pinot Noir
Region: California, Monterey County $15.95
Golds/Awards: Gold (RI)

Did You Know...?

Why do old wines need a lot of tannin?
Because tannin—a compound found in the seeds,
stems, and skin of grapes, as well as in oak
barrels—is a natural preservative. Without tannin,
wines that are cellared for many years would spoil.

Napa Ridge 1995 Reserve Pinot Noir
Region: California, Carneros $15
Golds/Awards: Gold (DA)

Napa Ridge 1996 Pinot Noir
Region: California, North Coast $11
Golds/Awards: Gold (NW)

Newlan 1995 Pinot Noir
Region: California, Napa Valley $19
Golds/Awards: Gold (WWC-90 pts)

Nichols 1996 Cottonwood Canyon Vineyard Pinot Noir
Region: California, Santa Barbara County $33
Golds/Awards: Gold (WWC-90 pts)

Nichols 1996 Pisoni Vineyard Pinot Noir
Region: California, Monterey County $42
Golds/Awards: Gold (WWC-91 pts)

Nichols 1996 Reserve Pinot Noir
Region: California, Central Coast $45
Golds/Awards: Gold (WWC-90 pts)

Oak Knoll 1994 Vintage Reserve Pinot Noir
Region: Oregon, Willamette Valley $34
Golds/Awards: Gold (WWC-91 pts)

Orfila 1996 Pinot Noir
Region: California, San Luis Obispo $16
Golds/Awards: Gold (NW, OC); Best of Class (NW)

Palliser Estate 1996 Pinot Noir
Region: New Zealand, Martinborough $29.99
Golds/Awards: Gold (SY)

Panther Creek 1995 Freedom Hill Vineyard Pinot Noir
Region: Oregon, Willamette Valley $27.99
Golds/Awards: Gold (WWC-90 pts)

Pepperwood Springs 1996 Romani Vineyard Pinot Noir
Region: California, Anderson Valley $30
Golds/Awards: Gold (WC)

Ponzi 1995 25th Anniversary Reserve Pinot Noir
Region: Oregon, Willamette Valley $50
Golds/Awards: Gold (WWC-90 pts)

Quatro 1995 Pinot Noir
Region: California, Sonoma County $12.99
Golds/Awards: Gold (PR)

Robert Mondavi 1995 Coastal Pinot Noir
Region: California, Central Coast $10.95
Golds/Awards: Gold (IW)

Did You Know...?

How can I make money from *my* refuse? Robert
Mondavi Winery's new gourmet-store product,
"Wine Vines for Grilling," consists of bundles of
dead vines packaged beautifully with a grape-
leaf label. It retails for $9.99.

St. Innocent 1995 Freedom Hill Vineyard Pinot Noir
Region: Oregon, Willamette Valley $24.99
Golds/Awards: Gold (WWC-91 pts)

St. Innocent 1995 O'Connor Vineyard Pinot Noir
Region: Oregon, Willamette Valley $19.99
Golds/Awards: Gold (WWC-90 pts)

Saintsbury 1995 Reserve Pinot Noir
Region: California, Carneros $28
Golds/Awards: Gold (WWC-91 pts)

Sanford 1995 Pinot Noir
Region: California, Santa Barbara County $20
Golds/Awards: Gold (WWC-90 pts)

Did You Know...?

French agronomist Claude Bourguignon, on the overly cultivated vineyard soil in France: "Many of the Côte d'Or's vineyards are more devoid of microbial life than the Sahara Desert."

Signorello 1995 Las Amigas Vineyard Pinot Noir
Region: California, Carneros $48
Golds/Awards: Gold (WWC-92 pts)

Steele 1995 Bien Nacido Vineyard Pinot Noir
Region: California, Santa Barbara County $34
Golds/Awards: Gold (WWC-91 pts)

Steele 1995 Pinot Noir
Region: California, Anderson Valley $23
Golds/Awards: Gold (WWC-90 pts)

Stonestreet 1995 Pinot Noir
Region: California, Russian River Valley $30
Golds/Awards: Gold (PR, NW, WC, WWC-90 pts); Best of
Class (PR)

Villa Mt. Eden 1996 Pinot Noir
Region: California $12
Golds/Awards: Gold (SD, CA); Best of Class (CA)

Wild Horse 1996 Pinot Noir
Region: California, Central Coast $18
Golds/Awards: Gold (RI)

Windsor 1995 Signature Series Pinot Noir
Region: California $16
Golds/Awards: Gold (CA)

Yarra Ridge 1997 Pinot Noir
Region: Australia, Yarra Valley $11.99
Golds/Awards: Gold (SY)

ZD Wines 1995 Pinot Noir
Region: California, Carneros $24
Golds/Awards: Gold (WWC-90 pts)

ZD Wines 1996 Pinot Noir
Region: California, Carneros $27
Golds/Awards: Gold (LA)

Did You Know...?

The top three countries that export
American-made wine: UK, Canada, and
Japan. Fourth is Germany, fifth Taiwan.

RED BLENDS

This is my favorite section of the book. I love red wine blends. In this section are all kinds of red blends made from Bordeaux grapes, Rhône grapes, combinations of the two, with sometimes Italian red grapes or other less common varieties thrown in for good measure. These wines are exciting, different, innovative, and always delicious—otherwise they wouldn't have won a gold medal. If you're bored with Cabernet Sauvignon, check out red blends. I guarantee you'll love them, perhaps more than single-variety wines. Serve them with foods that complement their component varietals.

Meritage, or Bordeaux-style blends Meritage is a trade-marked name coined by American wineries to solve a marketing problem. To call a wine by its varietal name, say, Cabernet Sauvignon, it must be composed of a minimum of 75 percent Cabernet Sauvignon. When that wasn't the case, high-class wineries had to call their red or white gems "table wine," or give the wine some proprietary name that gave consumers no clue as to what was in the bottle.

To use the name Meritage, red wines have to be made up of two or more of the following Bordeaux grape varieties: Cabernet Sauvignon, Merlot, Cabernet Franc, Petit Verdot, Malbec, Gros Verdot, or Carmenère.

Bordeaux-style red blends tend to be long-lived, big, chewy, full-bodied wines, and are often quite pricy.

Rhône-style blends A group of adventurous California winemakers, collectively known as the Rhône Rangers, have been trying to recreate the wonderful reds of France's Rhône Valley, using grapes such as Syrah, Carignane, Grenache, Mourvèdre, and Alicante Bouschet. These wines will often be rich and spicy, and they're usually less expensive than Bordeaux-style red blends.

Red Blends RED

Beaulieu Vineyard 1994 Reserve Tapestry (Bordeaux-style)
Region: California, Napa Valley $20
Golds/Awards: Gold (SD, WWC-90 pts)

Beringer 1994 Alluvium (Bordeaux-style)
Region: California, Knight's Valley $25
Golds/Awards: Gold (LA, OC); Best of Class (LA)

Carmenet 1993 Moon Mountain Estate (Bordeaux style)
Region: California, Sonoma Valley $27.50
Golds/Awards: Gold (WWC-91 pts)

Carmody McKnight 1995 Cadenza (Bordeaux-style)
Region: California, Paso Robles $21.50
Golds/Awards: Gold (WC)

Did You Know...?

Attention wine counterfeiters: A German sommelier with a vast knowledge of rare, old Bordeaux has developed what he considers exact recipes for rare Pétrus. For instance, he says 1961 Pétrus is fairly easy to duplicate by blending 1960 Pétrus with a younger Pomerol.

Castoro Cellars 1995 Quattordici Anni (Bordeaux-style)
Region: California, Paso Robles $17
Golds/Awards: Gold (RI, OC); Four Star Gold (OC)

Charles B. Mitchell NV Côtes du Cosumnes (Rhône-style)
Region: California $9
Golds/Awards: Gold (CA)

Charles Krug 1994 Peter Mondavi Family Generations (Bordeaux-style)
Region: California, Napa Valley $30
Golds/Awards: Gold (DA, PR, WC); Best of Class (PR)

Cloudy Cellars 1995 Bacio Divino (Mixed Reds)
Region: California $50
Golds/Awards: Gold (LA)

Concannon 1995 Raboli Field Blend (Mixed Reds)
Region: California, Livermore Valley $16.95
Golds/Awards: Gold (CA); Best of Class (CA)

Conn Creek 1994 Anthology (Bordeaux-style)
Region: California, Napa Valley $45
Golds/Awards: Gold (DA)

Cosentino 1995 "M. Coz" (Bordeaux-style)
Region: California, Napa Valley $75
Golds/Awards: Gold (OC)

Cuisine Cellars NV "Rich Red" (Mixed Reds)
Region: California $6
Golds/Awards: Gold (OC, LA); Best of Class (LA)

Cullen 1996 Cabernet Merlot
Region: Australia $40
Golds/Awards: Gold (IW)

Curtis 1996 Old Vines Heritage (Rhône-style)
Region: California $10
Golds/Awards: Gold (CA)

D'Arenberg 1996 The Ironstone Pressings Grenache-Shiraz
Region: Australia, McLaren Vale $25
Golds/Awards: Gold (BR, IV); Grand Gold Medal (BR)

De Lorimier 1995 Mosaic (Bordeaux-style)
Region: California, Alexander Valley $24
Golds/Awards: Gold (WC); Best of Class (WC)

Dominus 1994 Napanook Vineyard (Bordeaux-style)
Region: California, Napa Valley $75
Golds/Awards: Gold (WWC-95 pts)

Duckhorn 1995 Paraduxx (Italian Reds)
Region: California, Napa Valley $20
Golds/Awards: Gold (WWC-93)

Eberle Winery 1996 Côtes Du Robles (Rhône-style)
Region: California, Paso Robles $13
Golds/Awards: Gold (WC); Best of Class (WC)

Did You Know...?
What to eat with incredibly hot, spicy foods:
fairly robust, fruity red wines such as Rhône-
style reds.

Estancia 1995 Duo Reserve (Italian Reds)
Region: California, Alexander Valley $18
Golds/Awards: Gold (WWC-91 pts)

Fenestra NV True Red (Mixed Reds)
Region: California $8
Golds/Awards: Gold (OC)

Fieldbrook Valley 1995 Medallion (Bordeaux-style)
Region: California, Trinity County $21
Golds/Awards: Gold (CA); Best of Region, Best of Class (CA)

Did You Know...?

How are New World wines different from Old
World wines? A single California winery might
produce a dozen or more different types of
wine, while an established winery in
Bordeaux, for example, produces but one
type of wine (bordeaux).

Fife 1995 Max Cuvée (Rhône-style)
Region: California, Napa Valley $24
Golds/Awards: Gold (WWC-90 pts)

Geyser Peak 1995 Reserve Alexandre (Bordeaux-style)
Region: California, Alexander Valley $24.99
Golds/Awards: Gold (SD, WS, GH); Best Blended Red Wine
(WS)

Hamilton 1996 Leconfield Cabernets
Region: Australia, Coonawarra $19.50
Golds/Awards: Gold (IV)

Heron Hill NV Red Table Wine (Mixed Reds)
Region: New York, Finger Lakes $4.99
Golds/Awards: Gold (RI)

Howard Park 1995 Cabernet Sauvignon Merlot
Region: Australia $42
Golds/Awards: Gold (SY)

Jamieson's Run 1996 Coonawarra Reserve Cabernet Shiraz
Region: Australia $50
Golds/Awards: Gold (IW)

Jefferson Vineyards 1995 Meritage
Region: Virginia, Monticello $16
Golds/Awards: Gold (RI)

Did You Know...?

"The French drink their Bordeaux young, afraid that the Socialists will take it away from them. The British drink their Bordeaux old because they like to show off their dusty bottles to impress their friends. The Americans drink their Bordeaux whenever they want to because they don't know any better."
—Unknown

Justin 1995 Estate Unfiltered Shiraz/Cabernet
Region: California, Paso Robles $20
Golds/Awards: Gold (PR)

Kanonkop Estate 1995 Paul Sauer (Bordeaux-style)
Region: South Africa, Stellenbosch $26
Golds/Awards: Gold (WS)

Kathryn Kennedy Winery 1996 Lateral (Bordeaux-style)
Region: California $30
Golds/Awards: Gold (IV, LA, WC, CA); Best of Class (LA, CA)

KWV Cathedral Cellar 1995 Triptych (Bordeaux-style)
Region: South Africa, Coastal Region $12
Golds/Awards: Gold (SM)

Langtry 1995 Meritage
Region: California, North Coast $48
Golds/Awards: Gold (LA)

Langtry 1996 Meritage
Region: California, Guenoc Valley $21
Golds/Awards: Double Gold, Best of Class (CA)

Le Ducq 1992 Le Ducq 92 (Bordeaux-style)
Region: California, Napa Valley $68.99
Golds/Awards: Gold (NW, WWC-91 pts); Best of Class (NW)

Le Ducq 1993 Le Ducq 93 (Bordeaux-style)
Region: California, Napa Valley $69
Golds/Awards: Gold (RI, LA); Chairman's Award (RI)

Le Ducq 1994 Le Ducq 94 (Bordeaux-style)
Region: California, St. Helena/Napa $65
Golds/Awards: Gold (GH, WWC-92 pts)

Lindemans 1993 Limestone Ridge Shiraz-Cabernet
Region: Australia, Coonawarra $27.99
Golds/Awards: Gold (WWC-90 pts)

Lindemans 1993 Pyrus (Bordeaux-style)
Region: Australia, Coonawarra $27.85
Golds/Awards: Gold (WWC-90 pts)

Lindemans 1994 Limestone Ridge Shiraz Cabernet Sauvignon
Region: Australia, Coonawarra $27.85
Golds/Awards: Gold (SY)

Mazzocco Vineyards 1994 Matrix-Estate (Bordeaux-style)
Region: California, Dry Creek Valley $30
Golds/Awards: Gold (RI)

Did You Know...?

In France and Italy, annual per capita
consumption of wine is 22 to 24 gallons.
In the U.S. it is only 2 gallons.

Meerlust 1992 Rubicon
Region: South Africa, Stellenbosch $22
Golds/Awards: Gold (WWC-91 pts)

Murrieta's Well 1995 Estate Vineyard Vendimia (Bordeaux-style)
Region: California, Livermore Valley $28
Golds/Awards: Gold (OC)

Nevada City Winery 1994 Director's Reserve Claret (Bordeaux-style)
Region: California, Sierra Foothills $16
Golds/Awards: Gold (WC)

Niebaum-Coppola Estate 1996 Black Label Claret (Bordeaux-style)
Region: California, North Coast $17
Golds/Awards: Gold (CA); Best of Class (CA)

Norman Vineyards 1996 No Nonsense Red (Bordeaux-style)
Region: California, Paso Robles $15
Golds/Awards: Gold (LA)

Opus One 1994 (Bordeaux-style)
Region: California $90
Golds/Awards: Gold (IW, WWC-94 pts)

Did You Know...?

In 1972 Baron Philippe de Rothschild said, "All American wines taste the same. They all taste like Coca-Cola." Seven years later he entered into a partnership with California winemaker Robert Mondavi to produce Opus One.

Penfolds 1994 Bin 389 Cabernet-Shiraz
Region: Australia, South Australia $19
Golds/Awards: Gold (WWC-90 pts)

Peter Lehmann 1992 Mentor Cabernet-Malbec-Shiraz
Region: Australia, Barossa $30
Golds/Awards: Gold (WWC-92 pts)

Peter Lehmann 1995 Clancy's Gold Preference (Mixed Reds)
Region: Australia, Barossa Valley $18
Golds/Awards: Gold (SY)

Peter Lehmann 1996 Clancy's Gold Preference (Mixed Reds)
Region: Australia, South Australia $18
Golds/Awards: Gold (SY)

Red Blends   RED

Reif Estate 1995 Tesoro (Bordeaux-style)
Region: Canada, Niagara Peninsula   (Can $) 49.95
Golds/Awards: Gold (WS)

Did You Know...?

It takes three to five years from the time a grapevine is
planted until the vine produces grapes for harvest.

Richardson 1996 Synergy (Bordeaux-style)
Region: California, Sonoma Valley $20
Golds/Awards: Double Gold, Best of Class (CA)

Ridge 1995 Lytton Springs (Mixed Reds)
Region: California $27.50
Golds/Awards: Gold (IW)

Robert Craig 1995 Affinity (Bordeaux-style)
Region: California, Napa Valley $28
Golds/Awards: Gold (OC)

Robert Pepi 1995 Due Baci (Mixed Reds)
Region: California, Napa Valley $25
Golds/Awards: Gold (LA); Best of Class (LA)

Rosemount 1995 "GSM" Grenache Shiraz Mourvèdre
Region: Australia, McLaren Vale $18.95
Golds/Awards: Gold (SY)

Rosemount 1995 Mountain Blue Shiraz Cabernet Sauvignon
Region: Australia, Mudgee $30
Golds/Awards: Gold (SY, WS); Best Australian Red Wine (WS)

Rosemount 1995 Traditional Cabernet Sauvignon Merlot Petite Verdot
Region: Australia, McLaren Vale $18.95
Golds/Awards: Gold (SY)

Rosemount 1997 Diamond Label Grenache Shiraz
Region: Australia, Southeastern Region $8.50
Golds/Awards: Gold (NW); Best of Class (NW)

Rosenblum 1995 Holbrook Mitchell Trio (Bordeaux-style)
Region: California $35
Golds/Awards: Gold (LA)

Did You Know...?

Unlike other foods and beverages, alcohol goes into the bloodstream without being digested. About 20% is absorbed through the stomach lining, the rest through the walls of the intestines.

Rust en Vrede 1992 Estate Red (Bordeaux-style)
Region: South Africa, Stellenbosch $25
Golds/Awards: Gold (WWC-92 pts)

Rust en Vrede 1993 Estate Selection (Bordeaux-style)
Region: South Africa, Stellenbosch $25
Golds/Awards: Gold (WWC-91)

St. Supéry 1994 Meritage
Region: California, Napa Valley $40
Golds/Awards: Gold (SD, LA, OC, CA); Best of Class (SD, LA, CA)

St. Supéry 1996 Meritage
Region: California, Napa Valley $20
Golds/Awards: Gold (SD)

Sierra Vista 1997 Fleur de Montagne (Rhône-style)
Region: California, El Dorado $14
Golds/Awards: Gold (SD, OC, CA); Best of Class (SD, CA)

Silverlake Winery 1996 Cabernet-Merlot
Region: Washington, Columbia Valley $13.99
Golds/Awards: Gold (EN)

Sonora Winery & Port Works 1996 Vinho Tinto
Region: California, Sierra Foothills $18
Golds/Awards: (RI); Chairman's Award (RI)

Stonelake NV Caballo Loco Number 2
Region: Chile, Lontue $25
Golds/Awards: Gold (BR)

Sunstone 1995 Eros Reserve (Bordeaux-style)
Region: California $28
Golds/Awards: Gold (LA); Best of Class (LA)

Swanson Vineyards 1995 Napa Valley Estate "Alexis" (Mixed Reds)
Region: California, Napa Valley $40
Golds/Awards: Gold (WS); Double Gold, Best of Class (CA)

Thomas Coyne 1996 Quest (Rhône-style)
Region: California $10
Golds/Awards: Gold (CA); Best of Class (CA)

Vigil 1995 Valiente (Bordeaux-style)
Region: California, Napa Valley $20
Golds/Awards: Gold (NW)

Vigil 1996 Terra Vin (Rhône-style)
Region: California $10
Golds/Awards: Gold (OC)

Villa Maria 1996 Cellar Selection Cabernet Sauvignon/Merlot
Region: New Zealand, Hawkes Bay $30
Golds/Awards: Gold (IV)

Windsor 1995 Private Reserve Meritage
Region: California, Sonoma County $23.50
Golds/Awards: Gold (DA, IV)

Zaca Mesa 1996 Syrah-Mourvèdre
Region: California $18
Golds/Awards: Gold (LA)

Did You Know...?

One of the problems with successfully exporting wine to China is that China has no middle class. The wines sold there are primarily very cheap wines.

SYRAH/SHIRAZ

One of the great grapes of the Rhône, Syrah, called Shiraz in Australia, produces dark, dense, deeply flavorful red wines that hint of pepper and other exotic spices. Australian Shiraz became wildly popular with Americans in the last decade and helped to catapult that country into the international competitive world of wine. California's and more recently Washington State's Syrahs are in greater demand as well.

The Australians are fond of blending their Shiraz with Cabernet Sauvignon and other Bordeaux varietals. In California, one is more apt to see Syrah in spicy Rhône-style blends.

South Africa produces some Syrah, called Shiraz, and Argentina also grows a small amount, which they call Balsamia.

Food companions: Whatever you call it, Syrah/Shiraz is usually big and full-flavored, and therefore will marry best with foods that can stand up to its weight. Try it with rich meat stews, barbecued meat or vegetables, chili, roast goose, or duck and turkey with all of the trimmings.

Alban 1995 Reva Estate Syrah
Region: California, Eden Valley $21
Golds/Awards: Gold (WWC-90 pts)

Belvedere 1995 Syrah
Region: California, Dry Creek $24
Golds/Awards: Gold (WC)

Benziger 1995 Syrah
Region: California, Central Coast $16
Golds/Awards: Gold (RI, SD, WWC-90 pts)

Cambria 1996 Estate Bottled Tepusquet Vineyard Syrah
Region: California, Santa Maria Valley $18
Golds/Awards: Gold (OC)

Chateau Reynella 1994 Basket Pressed Shiraz
Region: Australia, McLaren Vale $20
Golds/Awards: Gold (WWC-90 pts)

Cline Cellars 1996 Syrah
Region: California, Carneros $18
Golds/Awards: Gold (WC)

Columbia Winery 1996 Syrah
Region: Washington, Yakima Valley $14
Golds/Awards: Gold (WC)

> *Did You Know...?*
>
> Syrah is considered Washington State's next big thing, perhaps outshining that state's famous Merlots.

Correas 1996 Syrah
Region: Argentina, Maipu $8.99
Golds/Awards: Gold (BR)

Curtis 1995 Ambassador's Vineyard Syrah
Region: California, Santa Ynez Valley $14
Golds/Awards: Gold (WWC-90 pts)

D'Arenberg 1996 The Dead Arm Shiraz
Region: Australia, McLaren Vale $50
Golds/Awards: Gold (IV)

Syrah/Shiraz   RED

D'Arenberg 1996 The Footbolt Old Vine Shiraz
Region: Australia, McLaren Vale $16
Golds/Awards: Gold (BR)

Deakin Estate 1997 Shiraz
Region: Australia $9.99
Golds/Awards: Gold (IW)

Did You Know...?

To be called Syrah in the U.S., a wine has to consist of at
least 75% Syrah. In Australia, a Syrah (a.k.a. Shiraz) has
to have 80% of that grape. And in France, the percentage
is 100% to be called Syrah.

Ebenezer 1994 E&E Black Pepper Shiraz
Region: Australia, Barossa Valley $69.99
Golds/Awards: Platinum (WWC-96 pts)

Ebenezer 1994 Shiraz
Region: Australia, Barossa Valley $25.99
Golds/Awards: Gold (WWC-92 pts)

Eileen Hardy 1994 Shiraz
Region: Australia, McLaren Vale/Padthaway/Clare Valley
Golds/Awards: Gold (WWC-93 pts) $54.99

Eileen Hardy 1995 Shiraz
Region: Australia, South Eastern Australia $54.99
Golds/Awards: Gold (WS, IW); Best Shiraz/Syrah (WS)

Elderton 1994 Shiraz
Region: California, Barossa Valley $17.99
Golds/Awards: Gold (WWC-93 pts)

Fairview Estate 1993 Shiraz
Region: South Africa, Paarl $14.99
Golds/Awards: Gold (WS); Best South African Red Wine (WS)

Folie à Deux 1996 Syrah
Region: California, Amador County $22
Golds/Awards: Gold (OC)

Forest Glen 1996 Shiraz
Region: California, Sonoma $10
Golds/Awards: Gold (LA)

Geyser Peak 1995 Reserve Shiraz
Region: California, Sonoma County $29.99
Golds/Awards: Gold (SD, LA, WC, WWC-90 pts)

Geyser Peak 1995 Shiraz
Region: California, Sonoma County $12.99
Golds/Awards: Gold (NW, SD); Best of Class (NW)

Geyser Peak 1996 Shiraz
Region: California, Sonoma County $12.99
Golds/Awards: Gold (NW, WC, CA); Best of Class (CA)

Goundrey 1996 Reserve Shiraz
Region: Australia, Mount Barker $22
Golds/Awards: Gold (WS)

Hart Winery 1995 Estate Bottled Syrah
Region: California, Temecula $18
Golds/Awards: Gold (PR)

Hermitage Road 1997 Shiraz
Region: Australia, South Eastern Region $12.99
Golds/Awards: Gold (RI)

Did You Know...?

Grape cultivation in China dates back 6000 years.

Hidden Cellars 1996 Syrah
Region: California, Mendocino $18
Golds/Awards: Gold (WC)

Hillstowe 1994 Buxton Shiraz
Region: Australia, McLaren Vale $19
Golds/Awards: Gold (WWC-90 pts)

Hogue 1995 Syrah
Region: Washington, Columbia Valley $15
Golds/Awards: Gold (NW)

Jim Barry 1994 "The Armaugh" Shiraz
Region: Australia, Clare Valley $76
Golds/Awards: Gold (WWC-90 pts)

Jim Barry 1995 "McCrae Wood" Shiraz
Region: Australia, South Australia $30
Golds/Awards: Gold (SY)

Did You Know...?

"What is man, when you come to think upon him, but a minutely set, ingenious machine for turning with infinite artfulness, the red wine of Shiraz into urine?"

–Isak Dinesen

Kaesler Winery 1995 Old Vine Shiraz
Region: Australia, Barossa Valley $35
Golds/Awards: Gold (NW)

Kathryn Kennedy Winery 1996 Maridon Vineyard Syrah
Region: California, Santa Cruz Mountains $40
Golds/Awards: Gold (IV, WS, LA, OC, WC); Best of Class,
Division Sweepstakes (LA, WC); Governor's Award (LA)

Lawson's 1992 Shiraz
Region: Australia, Padthaway $35
Golds/Awards: Gold (WWC-95 pts)

Maglieri 1994 Steve Maglieri Shiraz
Region: Australia, McLaren Vale $29
Golds/Awards: Gold (WWC-91 pts)

Maglieri 1995 Steve Maglieri Shiraz
Region: Australia, McLaren Vale $35
Golds/Awards: Gold (SY, WWC-90 pts)

Maglieri 1996 Shiraz
Region: Australia, McLaren Vale $21
Golds/Awards: Gold (SM, IW)

Marietta 1995 Syrah
Region: California $14.99
Golds/Awards: Gold (WWC-90 pts)

McDowell 1995 Estate Syrah
Region: California, Mendocino $16
Golds/Awards: Gold (NW, WWC-91 pts); Best of Class,
Best of Varietal (NW)

McDowell 1996 Syrah
Region: California, Mendocino $10
Golds/Awards: Gold (RI, CA); Best of Region, Best of Class
(CA)

Meridian 1996 Syrah
Region: California, Paso Robles $15
Golds/Awards: Gold (LA, OC, WC); Double Gold, Best of
Show, Best of Region, Best of California, Best of Class (CA)

Monthaven 1996 Syrah
Region: California $9.99
Golds/Awards: Gold (WC)

Nevada City Winery 1996 Syrah
Region: California, Nevada County $14
Golds/Awards: Gold (CA); Best of Class (CA)

Norman's 1995 Chais Clarendon Shiraz
Region: Australia $17.99
Golds/Awards: Gold (NW)

Norman's 1996 Chais Clarendon Shiraz
Region: Australia, McLaren Vale $17.99
Golds/Awards: Gold (IV)

Penfolds 1992 Grange Shiraz
Region: Australia, South Australia $121.50
Golds/Awards: Gold (WWC-95 pts)

Did You Know...?

Australian law enforcement officials are still trying
to figure out who counterfeited at least six bottles
of Penfolds Grange, Australia's most famous
wine. Found in March 1998, the bottles full of
dreck were labeled 1990 vintage, recognized as *Wine Spectator*'s Wine of the Year
in 1995.

Pepper Tree Wines 1996 Reserve Shiraz
Region: Australia, McLaren Vale $30
Golds/Awards: Gold (IV)

Rabbit Ridge 1994 Syrah
Region: California, Sonoma County $20
Golds/Awards: Gold (PR)

Did You Know...?

In Utah, a waiter can't offer a customer the
wine list; the customer has to *ask* for it.

Rosemount 1995 Balmoral Shiraz
Region: Australia, McLaren Vale $40
Golds/Awards: Gold (WS)

Rosemount 1995 Reserve Shiraz
Region: Australia, McLaren Vale $22.95
Golds/Awards: Gold (SY)

Rymill Winery 1995 Coonawarra Shiraz
Region: Australia, Coonawarra $16.50
Golds/Awards: Gold (SY, IW)

St. Hallett 1993 Old Block Shiraz
Region: Australia, Barossa $30.99
Golds/Awards: Gold (WWC-90 pts)

Santa Barbara Winery 1996 Syrah
Region: California, Santa Barbara County $21
Golds/Awards: Gold (RI); Chairman's Award (RI)

Sebastiani 1995 Syrah
Region: California $18
Golds/Awards: Gold (LA)

Sierra Vista 1995 Red Rock Ridge Syrah
Region: California $17
Golds/Awards: Gold (LA)

Sierra Vista 1996 Estate Bottled Syrah
Region: California, El Dorado $19
Golds/Awards: Gold (NW); Best of Class (NW)

Silver Ridge 1996 Barrel Select Syrah
Region: California $10
Golds/Awards: Gold (NW)

Stanley Brothers 1995 John Hancock Shiraz
Region: Australia, Barossa Valley $25
Golds/Awards: Gold (WWC-90 pts)

Stellenzicht 1994 Syrah
Region: South Africa, Stellenbosch $79.99
Golds/Awards: Gold (WWC-92 pts)

Swanson Vineyards 1995 Estate Bottled Syrah
Region: California, Napa Valley $40
Golds/Awards: Gold (SD, WWC-90 pts); Best of Class (SD)

Thackrey 1995 Orion Old Vines Syrah
Region: California, St. Helena $45
Golds/Awards: Platinum (WWC-97 pts)

Tim Adams Alberfeldy Shiraz
Region: Australia $17.90
Golds/Awards: Gold (IW)

Truchard 1996 Syrah
Region: California, Napa Valley $28
Golds/Awards: Gold (OC)

Did You Know...?

Unionization of grape workers has come slowly
to California, but that trend may be changing as
UFW leaders hold elections and increasingly
push for workers to organize.

Vasse Felix 1996 Shiraz
Region: Australia, Margaret River $22
Golds/Awards: Gold (SY)

Viña Errazuriz 1997 Reserve Syrah
Region: Chile $18
Golds/Awards: Gold (IW)

Wellington 1996 Alegria Vineyards Syrah
Region: California, Russian River Valley $17
Golds/Awards: Gold (OC)

Wynns Coonawarra Estate 1994 Michael Shiraz
Region: Australia $40
Golds/Awards: Gold (IW, WWC-91 pts)

Yalumba 1994 The Octavius
Region: Australia $52
Golds/Awards: Gold (IW)

Zaca Mesa Winery 1996 Chapel Vineyard Syrah
Region: California $18
Golds/Awards: Gold (LA); Best of Class, Chairman's Award (LA)

Did You Know...?

Less than half of all American adults consume alcoholic beverages in any given week, and 43 percent abstain entirely from alcohol.

ZINFANDEL

This exotic red-wine grape has taken the New World by storm. California is where most Zinfandel is cultivated these days, with Australia and South Africa new entrants in the field. Thanks to DNA testing, it's been determined that Zinfandel is actually the same as Italy's Primativo grape.

One reason this varietal has so much popular appeal is that it lends itself to any number of styles. Zinfandel can be fruity, light, Beaujolais-like, or medium bodied with definite character, or extremely rich, intensely flavored, tannic, and long-lived, like a great Cabernet Sauvignon. Some winemakers also make it into a sweet dessert wine.

Zinfandel has an easily recognizable varietal character: aromas and flavors of black pepper and brambles, with cherries, blackberries, and raspberries, and a lush, supple texture.

It is also the grape used to make White Zinfandel (which is actually pink), one of the most consumed varietals in the United States. (See the Blush Wines chapter for White Zinfandel listings.)

Food companions: Because of its well-flavored, spicy nature, serve Zin with equally sturdy dishes, such as ratatouille, anchovy and olive antipasti, sausage-stuffed veal, steak with mustard sauce, and leg of lamb marinated in garlic, onion, and rosemary. Zinfandel can hold its own next to Mexican food such as spicy burritos, and even goes well with cheesecake.

Alderbrook 1996 George's Vineyard Zinfandel
Region: California, Dry Creek Valley $24
Golds/Awards: Gold (NW)

Amador 1995 Ferrero Vineyard Zinfandel
Region: California, Shenandoah Valley $12.50
Golds/Awards: Gold (OC)

Did You Know...?

Even though there are 30,000 acres of planted
vineyards in France's Alsace region, the average
plot of land for each grower is only 3 acres.

Barefoot Cellars NV Barefoot Zinfandel
Region: California, Santa Rosa $5.99
Golds/Awards: Gold (NW); Best of Class (NW)

Benziger 1996 Zinfandel
Region: California, Sonoma County $17.99
Golds/Awards: Gold (LA); Best of Class (LA)

Beringer 1995 Appellation Collection Zinfandel
Region: California, North Coast $12
Golds/Awards: Gold (LA, CA); Best of Class (LA)

Black Rock Wineworks 1996 Zinfandel
Region: California, Lake County $14.50
Golds/Awards: Gold (NW)

Buehler Vineyards 1995 Estate Zinfandel
Region: California, Napa Valley $25
Golds/Awards: Gold (SD)

Castle Vineyards 1996 Zinfandel
Region: California, Sonoma County $17
Golds/Awards: Gold (NW)

Castoro Cellars 1996 Zinfandel
Region: California, Paso Robles $12
Golds/Awards: Gold (OC, CA); Best of Class (CA)

Castoro Cellars 1996 Tribute Estate Vineyard Zinfandel
Region: California, Paso Robles $15
Golds/Awards: Gold (WC); Best of Class (WC)

Chateau Potelle 1995 Mount Veeder Estate VGS Zinfandel
Region: California, Napa Valley $35
Golds/Awards: Gold (WWC-91 pts)

Cline 1996 Big Break Vineyard Zinfandel
Region: California, Contra Costa County $24
Golds/Awards: Platinum (WWC-97 pts)

Cline 1996 Bridgehead Vineyard Zinfandel
Region: California, Contra Costa County $24
Golds/Awards: Gold (WWC-91 pts)

Cline 1996 Live Oak Vineyard Zinfandel
Region: California, Contra Costa County $24
Golds/Awards: Gold (WWC-95 pts)

David Bruce 1995 Ranchita Canyon Vineyard Zinfandel
Region: California, Paso Robles $15
Golds/Awards: Gold (WWC-91 pts)

De Rose 1995 Cedolini Family Vineyard Old Vines Zinfandel
Region: California, Cienega Valley $17.95
Golds/Awards: Gold (OC)

Deaver Vineyards 1995 Zinfandel
Region: California, Amador County $15
Golds/Awards: Gold (OC)

DeLoach 1996 Barbieri Ranch Zinfandel
Region: California, Russian River Valley $20
Golds/Awards: Gold (WWC-94 pts)

DeLoach 1996 O.F.S. Zinfandel
Region: California, Russian River Valley $27.50
Golds/Awards: Gold (WWC-93 pts, RI); Best of Class, Best
of Category (RI)

DeLoach 1996 Saltone Ranch Zinfandel
Region: California, Russian River Valley $20
Golds/Awards: Gold (WWC-93 pts)

Did You Know...?

ALL NATIONS WELCOME EXCEPT CARRIE
(an old saloon sign)

Deux Amis 1995 Zinfandel
Region: California, Sonoma County $15
Golds/Awards: Gold (OC, WC)

Dry Creek Vineyard 1995 Reserve Zinfandel
Region: California, Sonoma County $25
Golds/Awards: Gold (LA); Best of Class (LA)

Edmeades 1996 Ciapusci Vineyard Zinfandel
Region: California, Mendocino $24
Golds/Awards: Gold (CA); Best of Class (CA)

Did You Know...?

The European parliament is studying a proposed law that would require ingredient labeling on all drinks containing more than 1.2% alcohol.

Edmeades 1996 Zinfandel
Region: California, Mendocino County $19
Golds/Awards: Gold (SD, GH, CA)

Eric Ross Winery 1996 Old Vines Zinfandel
Region: California, Russian River Valley $24
Golds/Awards: Gold (CA)

Fanucchi 1996 Fanucchi-Wood Road Vineyard Old Vines Zinfandel
Region: California, Russian River Valley $33.75
Golds/Awards: Gold (OC, WC, GH)

Folie à Deux 1996 Old Vine Zinfandel
Region: California, Amador County $18
Golds/Awards: Gold (CA)

Forchini Vineyards 1996 Estate Bottled Zinfandel
Region: California, Dry Creek Valley $16
Golds/Awards: Gold (WC)

Gallo Sonoma 1994 Frei Ranch Zinfandel
Region: California $14
Golds/Awards: Gold (IW)

Gallo Sonoma 1995 Frei Ranch Zinfandel
Region: California, Dry Creek Valley $14
Golds/Awards: Gold (BR, OC)

Gary Farrell 1996 Old Vine Selection Zinfandel
Region: California, Sonoma County $21.50
Golds/Awards: Gold (WWC-91 pts, PR, NW, SD, WC); Best
of Class (PR, SD); Best in Show (SD)

Geyser Peak 1995 Zinfandel
Region: California, Sonoma County $12.99
Golds/Awards: Gold (PR, SD); Best of Class (SD)

Granite Springs Winery 1995 Estate Bottled Zinfandel
Region: California, El Dorado $11.50
Golds/Awards: Gold (WC, CA)

Greenwood Ridge Vineyards 1996 Scherrer Vineyards Zinfandel
Region: California, Sonoma County $18
Golds/Awards: Gold (PR, RI)

Grgich Hills 1995 Zinfandel
Region: California, Sonoma County $20
Golds/Awards: Gold (IV)

Did You Know...?

Mike Grgrich decided to honor his Croatian
roots by returning to his homeland to produce
wine. He uses the Croatian spelling of his
name, Grgic on his new Croatian wine, which
sells for about $20 a bottle.

Hartford Court 1996 Fanucchi Wood Road Vineyard Zinfandel
Region: California, Russian River Valley $25
Golds/Awards: Gold (SD, PR)

Hartford Court 1996 Hartford Vineyard Zinfandel
Region: California, Russian River Valley $35
Golds/Awards: Gold (RI, WC); Double Gold (CA); Best of
Class (CA)

Hidden Cellars 1995 Hildreth Ranch Heritage Zinfandel
Region: California, Mendocino $25
Golds/Awards: Gold (NW)

Hop Kiln 1996 Primativo Zinfandel
Region: California, Sonoma County $22
Golds/Awards: Gold (WC, CA, WWC-90 pts); Best of Class
(WC)

Hop Kiln 1996 Zinfandel
Region: California, Sonoma County $16
Golds/Awards: Gold (WWC-90 pts, RI)

Did You Know...?

If you'd like to visit a virtual art gallery, check out
www.foodwine.com/food/wine/daily/depts/art.html,
where you'll find wine artists' works on display.

J. Runquist Wines 1996 "Z" Massoni Ranch Zinfandel
Region: California $18
Golds/Awards: Gold (LA)

Kendall-Jackson 1994 Grand Reserve Zinfandel
Region: California $25
Golds/Awards: Gold (NW, WS); Best Zinfandel (WS)

Kendall-Jackson 1996 Vintner's Reserve Zinfandel
Region: California $16
Golds/Awards: Gold (OC)

Kenwood 1995 Nun's Canyon Zinfandel
Region: California $20
Golds/Awards: Gold (NW, DA); Best of Class, Best of
Varietal, New World Grand Champion (NW)

La Crema 1996 Reserve Zinfandel
Region: California, Sonoma County $22
Golds/Awards: Gold (SD)

Lake Sonoma Winery 1995 Zinfandel
Region: California, Dry Creek Valley $17
Golds/Awards: Gold (WC)

Zinfandel   RED

Lambert Bridge 1996 Zinfandel
Region: California, Dry Creek Valley $20
Golds/Awards: Gold (WWC-91 pts)

Lamborn Family 1995 The French Connection Not Filtered Zinfandel
Region: California, Howell Mountain $22.50
Golds/Awards: Gold (WWC-93 pts)

Latcham Vineyards 1995 Special Reserve Estate Grown Zinfandel
Region: California, El Dorado $14
Golds/Awards: Gold (SD)

Lava Cap Winery 1996 Reserve Zinfandel
Region: California, Sierra Foothills $25
Golds/Awards: Double Gold (CA); Best of Class (CA)

Madrona 1996 Zinfandel
Region: California, El Dorado $10
Golds/Awards: Gold (CA)

Markham 1995 Zinfandel
Region: California, Napa $16
Golds/Awards: Gold (WWC-92 pts)

Martinelli 1996 Jackass Vineyard Zinfandel
Region: California, Russian River Valley $25
Golds/Awards: Platinum (WWC-96 pts)

Did You Know...?

Graves, which is an area of Bordeaux, gets its
name from the word *graves*, which means
gravel—the type of soil found in the region.

Martini & Prati 1996 Reserve Zinfandel
Region: California, Russian River Valley $18
Golds/Awards: Gold (WC, WWC-90 pts)

McIlroy Wines 1996 Porter-Bass Vineyards Zinfandel
Region: California, Russian River Valley $18
Golds/Awards: Gold (NW, CA); Best of California, Best of Class (CA)

Mirassou 1995 Harvest Reserve Zinfandel
Region: California, Santa Clara Valley $15.95
Golds/Awards: Gold (DA)

Murphy-Goode 1995 Zinfandel
Region: California, Dry Creek Valley/Alexander Valley $18
Golds/Awards: Gold (OC)

Murphy-Goode 1996 Zinfandel
Region: California, Alexander Valley $16
Golds/Awards: Gold (WC)

Navarro 1996 Zinfandel
Region: California, Mendocino $18
Golds/Awards: Gold (OC, WC)

Obester Winery 1995 Zinfandel
Region: California, Mendocino County $14.95
Golds/Awards: Gold (WC)

Parducci 1996 Old Vines Zinfandel
Region: California, Mendocino $10
Golds/Awards: Gold (DA)

Pedroncelli 1996 Mother Clone Special Vineyard Selection Zinfandel
Region: California, Dry Creek Valley $12
Golds/Awards: Gold (WWC-90 pts)

Quivira Vineyards 1996 Zinfandel
Region: California, Dry Creek Valley $17
Golds/Awards: Gold (RI)

Did You Know...?

Ever since the famous V for victory on the label of Mouton-Rothschild, Phillippe de Rothschild has commissioned a different artist to design his labels each year. Some famous artists include:
Salvador Dali (1958); Henry Moore (1964); Joàn Miró (1969); Mark Chagall (1970); Pablo Picasso (1973); Robert Motherwell (1974); and Andy Warhol (1975).

Ravenswood 1996 Dickerson Zinfandel
Region: California, Napa Valley $24
Golds/Awards: Gold (WWC-91 pts)

Ravenswood 1996 Monte Rosso Zinfandel
Region: California, Sonoma Valley $24
Golds/Awards: Gold (WWC-95 pts)

Ravenswood 1996 Old Hill Vineyard Zinfandel
Region: California, Sonoma Valley $26
Golds/Awards: Gold (WWC-91 pts)

Ravenswood 1996 Wood Road Belloni Zinfandel
Region: California, Russian River Valley $24
Golds/Awards: Gold (WWC-94 pts)

Red Rock Winery 1994 Zinfandel
Region: California $8
Golds/Awards: Gold (NW)

Did You Know...?

"Although man is already ninety percent water,
the Prohibitionists are not yet satisfied."
—John Kendrick Bangs

Ridge 1995 Geyserville Zinfandel
Region: California, Sonoma County $22
Golds/Awards: Gold (WWC-92 pts)

Ridge 1995 Pagani Ranch Late-Picked 100 Year Old Vines Zinfandel
Region: California, Sonoma Valley $22
Golds/Awards: Gold (WWC-91 pts)

Ridge 1996 Dusi Ranch Zinfandel
Region: California, Paso Robles $25
Golds/Awards: Gold (WWC-95 pts)

Ridge 1996 Lytton Springs Zinfandel
Region: California, Dry Creek Valley $25
Golds/Awards: Gold (WWC-92 pts)

Rocking Horse 1996 Lamborn Vineyard Zinfandel
Region: California, Howell Mountain　　　　　　$18
Golds/Awards: Gold (WWC-94 pts)

Did You Know...?

One way to get a great wine every time is to find a
producer who's top rated for one varietal, such as
Zinfandel. If that label's Zins consistently win golds
—whether they're $10 or $30—you'll never be
disappointed with any Zin from that producer.

Rosenblum 1996 Annette's Reserve Vineyard Zinfandel
Region: California, Redwood Valley　　　　　$20
Golds/Awards: Gold (WWC-95 pts)

Rosenblum 1996 Harris Kratka Vineyard Zinfandel
Region: California, Alexander Valley　　　　$22
Golds/Awards: Gold (OC, WWC-91 pts)

Rosenblum 1996 Pato Vineyard Zinfandel
Region: California, Contra Costa　　　　　$19
Golds/Awards: Gold (PR)

Rosenblum 1996 Richard Sauret Vineyard Zinfandel
Region: California, Paso Robles　　　　　$17
Golds/Awards: Gold (WWC-90 pts, PR, OC)

Rosenblum 1996 Rockpile Vineyard Zinfandel
Region: California, Dry Creek Valley　　　　$22
Golds/Awards: Gold (WWC-91 pts)

Rosenblum 1996 Samsel Vineyard Maggie's Reserve Zinfandel
Region: California, Sonoma Valley　　　　　$28
Golds/Awards: Gold (WWC-95 pts, LA, WC); Best of Class (LA)

Rosenblum 1996 White Cottage Vineyard Zinfandel
Region: California, Howell Mountain　　　　$21
Golds/Awards: Gold (WWC-95 pts)

Rosenblum NV Vintner's Cuvée XVI Zinfandel
Region: California　　　　　　　　　$9.50
Golds/Awards: Gold (LA)

St. Francis 1996 Old Vines Zinfandel
Region: California, Sonoma County $20
Golds/Awards: Gold (WWC-94 pts)

St. Francis 1996 Reserve Pagani Vineyard Zinfandel
Region: California, Sonoma Valley $28
Golds/Awards: Gold (WWC-95 pts)

Sebastiani 1995 Domenici Zinfandel
Region: California, Sonoma County $24
Golds/Awards: Gold (NW, OC); Best of Class (NW)

Sierra Vista 1996 Herbert Vineyard Zinfandel
Region: California, El Dorado $15
Golds/Awards: Gold (WC)

Sierra Vista 1996 Reeves Vineyard Zinfandel
Region: California, El Dorado $15
Golds/Awards: Gold (WWC-93 pts)

Did You Know...?

The 1997 wine grape harvest was the biggest in California history.

Sonora Winery & Port Works 1996 Story Vineyard Zinfandel
Region: California, Amador County $18
Golds/Awards: Gold (GH)

Sparrow Lane 1996 Reserve Beatty Ranch Zinfandel
Region: California, Howell Mountain $25
Golds/Awards: Gold (WWC-90 pts)

Steele 1996 Catfish Vineyard Zinfandel
Region: California, Clear Lake $18
Golds/Awards: Gold (WWC-95 pts)

Steele 1996 Du Pratt Vineyard Zinfandel
Region: California, Mendocino $20
Golds/Awards: Gold (WWC-93 pts)

Steele 1996 Pacini Vineyard Zinfandel
Region: California, Mendocino $16
Golds/Awards: Gold (WWC-92 pts)

Storybook Mountain 1995 Eastern Exposures Zinfandel
Region: California, Napa Valley $19.50
Golds/Awards: Gold (WWC-90 pts)

Truchard 1996 Zinfandel
Region: California, Carneros $18
Golds/Awards: Gold (WWC-90 pts)

Turley 1996 Hayne Vineyard Zinfandel
Region: California, Napa Valley $35
Golds/Awards: Gold (WWC-95 pts)

Turley 1996 Old Vines Zinfandel
Region: California $30
Golds/Awards: Gold (WWC-92 pts)

V. Sattui 1995 Sears-Black Vineyard Zinfandel
Region: California, Howell Mountain $18
Golds/Awards: Double Gold (CA); Best of Region, Best of Class (CA)

V. Sattui Winery 1995 Howell Mountain Zinfandel
Region: California, Napa Valley $18
Golds/Awards: Gold (IV)

Valley of the Moon 1996 Zinfandel
Region: California, Sonoma Valley $25
Golds/Awards: Gold (WWC-90 pts)

Did You Know...?

Estate-bottled means that the wine was made, produced, and bottled at the vineyard.

Villa Mt. Eden 1995 Monte Rosso Vineyard Grand Reserve Zinfandel
Region: California, Sonoma Valley $20
Golds/Awards: Gold (GH)

Windsor 1995 Zinfandel
Region: California, Alexander Valley $14.50
Golds/Awards: Gold (DA)

Did You Know...?

"Many a Miss would not be a Missus,
If Liquor did not add spark to her kisses."
—Bill Tennenbaum

Windsor 1996 Private Reserve Old Vines Zinfandel
Region: California $13.50
Golds/Awards: Gold (LA)

Windsor 1996 Zinfandel
Region: California, Sonoma County $9.75
Golds/Awards: Gold (LA); Best of Class (LA)

York Mountain Winery 1996 Zinfandel
Region: California, San Luis Obispo $12
Golds/Awards: Gold (WC)

White Wines

Chardonnay
Chenin Blanc
Gewurztraminer
Miscellaneous Varietal Whites
Native Whites & French-American Hybrids
Pinot Blanc
Pinot Gris
Riesling
Sauvignon Blanc
Semillon
Viognier
White Blends

CHARDONNAY

This is the white vinifera grape of France's white burgundy and champagne as well as American sparkling wine. Chardonnay is by far the most popular white wine produced in the New World. It's in such demand worldwide that it has the dubious distinction of being the variety of which the most cuttings are smuggled—in places like New Zealand, South Africa, and Australia, where rigid quarantine laws are enforced.

Chardonnay is easy to grow and adapts well to cool regions. That's why you see great Chardonnays from places like Canada and Washington State. This varietal ages well, and more than other whites, the interesting aromas and flavors derived from oak barrel fermentation and aging assume a key role in its personality.

There are two predominant Chardonnay styles. The first is fresh, fruity, and lightly oaked; the second is toasty, spicy, buttery, and big. Either way, most Chardonnay is fairly fruity, with plenty of balancing acidity, and has a flavor and bouquet that may include apple, pineapple, peaches, tangerine, and lime; cinnamon and clove spices; and buttery, vanilla, smoky, nutty, or grassy hints.

Food companions: Oysters, lobster, salmon in cream sauce or Hollandaise sauce, seviche, clam chowder—these distinctly rich and flavorful seafood and shellfish dishes will nicely complement your Chardonnay. Chardonnay also goes well with spicy Thai, ham, pasta in butter sauces, cream soups, soft cheeses, and fruit-filled tarts.

Anapamu 1996 Chardonnay
Region: California, Central Coast $12
Golds/Awards: Gold (NW)

Apex 1996 Chardonnay
Region: Washington, Columbia Valley $17.99
Golds/Awards: Gold (PR)

Arrowood 1995 Cuvée Michel Berthoud Chardonnay
Region: California, Sonoma County $32
Golds/Awards: Gold (WWC-92 pts)

Au Bon Climat 1995 "Le Bouge" Bien Nacido Vineyard Chardonnay
Region: California, Santa Barbara County $26.99
Golds/Awards: Gold (WWC-92 pts)

Au Bon Climat 1995 Reserve Talley Chardonnay
Region: California, Arroyo Grande Valley $26.99
Golds/Awards: Gold (WWC-90 pts)

Did You Know...?

Spiritual grapes: Trefethen Estate's 1996
Chardonnay was blessed at harvest by local
Catholic, Protestant, Jewish, and Buddhist
spiritual leaders.

Baileyana 1996 Chardonnay
Region: California, Edna Valley $15
Golds/Awards: Gold (LA, CA); Best of California, Best of Class (CA)

Bargetto 1996 Chardonnay
Region: California, Santa Cruz Mountains $18
Golds/Awards: Gold (WC)

Baywood 1996 Monterey Vineyard Select Chardonnay
Region: California $19
Golds/Awards: Gold (WC, NW)

Beaucanon 1996 Jacques de Coninck Chardonnay
Region: California, Napa Valley $28
Golds/Awards: Gold (WWC-90 pts)

Belvedere 1996 Chardonnay
Region: California, Russian River Valley $16
Golds/Awards: Gold (OC)

Benziger 1996 Chardonnay
Region: California, Carneros $13
Golds/Awards: Gold (OC)

Benziger 1996 Reserve Carneros Chardonnay
Region: California $29.99
Golds/Awards: Gold (NW); Best of Class (NW)

Beringer 1995 Private Reserve Chardonnay
Region: California, Napa Valley $30
Golds/Awards: Gold (WWC-92 pts)

Did You Know...?

Does Chardonnay go well with tofu and mung sprouts? To view the newest diet pyramid for vegetarians, which includes alcohol, see www.wineinstitute.org.

Bogle 1996 Chardonnay
Region: California $8
Golds/Awards: Gold (PR)

Bogle 1997 Chardonnay
Region: California $8
Golds/Awards: Gold (CA); Best of Class (CA)

Brancott Vineyards 1996 Ormond Estate Chardonnay
Region: New Zealand, Gisborne $22
Golds/Awards: Gold (SY)

Brancott Vineyards 1997 Reserve Chardonnay
Region: New Zealand, Marlborough $17
Golds/Awards: Gold (WS)

Buehler Vineyards 1996 Chardonnay
Region: California, Russian River Valley $15
Golds/Awards: Gold (DA, OC)

C.J. Pask 1996 Hawkes Bay Reserve Chardonnay
Region: New Zealand, Hawkes Bay $25
Golds/Awards: Gold (SY)

Chardonnay

Cambria 1996 Estate Bottled Reserve Chardonnay
Region: California, Santa Maria Valley $36
Golds/Awards: Double Gold (CA); Best of Class (CA)

Canepa 1997 Private Reserve Chardonnay
Region: Chile, Rancagua $12.99
Golds/Awards: Gold (WS)

Canyon Road 1995 Reserve Chardonnay
Region: California, Russian River Valley $18
Golds/Awards: Gold (RI)

Canyon Road 1997 Chardonnay
Region: California $7.99
Golds/Awards: Gold (NW, SD, WC); Best of Class (NW, WC)

Carta Vieja 1997 Reserve Chardonnay
Region: Chile, Maule Valley $9
Golds/Awards: Gold (BR)

Casa LaPostolle 1995 Cuvée Alexandre Chardonnay
Region: Chile, Casablanca Valley $15
Golds/Awards: Gold (WWC-90 pts)

Castle Vineyards 1996 Chardonnay
Region: California, Sonoma Valley $16
Golds/Awards: Gold (WC)

Chalone 1995 Chardonnay
Region: California, Chalone $27
Golds/Awards: Gold (WWC-91 pts)

Did You Know...?

What is meant by a wine's "style"? Two Chardonnays, for example, can be very different. How ripe the grapes are at harvest, whether the juice is fermented in stainless steel or oak, how long the wine is aged, what other grapes are used in the blend, how long the wine is aged in the bottle before it's sold—all of these contribute to a wine's individual style.

Chamonix 1995 Reserve Chardonnay
Region: South Africa, Franschhoek $15
Golds/Awards: Gold (WWC-92 pts)

Chandelle of Sonoma 1996 Pan American Dixie Chardonnay
Region: California, Sonoma County $11.95
Golds/Awards: Gold (NW)

Chateau La Joya 1997 Gran Reserva Chardonnay
Region: Chile $12.99
Golds/Awards: Gold (VN, VI)

Chateau St. Jean 1994 Robert Young Vineyard Reserve Chardonnay
Region: California, Alexander Valley $50/magnum
Golds/Awards: Gold (PR)

Chateau St. Jean 1996 Belle Terre Vineyards Chardonnay
Region: California, Alexander Valley $21.50
Golds/Awards: Gold (OC)

Chateau St. Jean 1996 Chardonnay
Region: California, Sonoma County $13
Golds/Awards: Gold (GH)

Did You Know...?

Rome's great vintages had amazing longevity. The
famous Opimian, from the year 121 BC, was being
drunk and raved about when it was 125 years old.

Chateau Ste. Michelle 1996 Cold Creek Vineyard Chardonnay
Region: Washington, Columbia Valley $24.99
Golds/Awards: Gold (DA)

Chateau Souverain 1995 Winemaker's Reserve Chardonnay
Region: California, Russian River Valley $20
Golds/Awards: Gold (WWC-90 pts)

Chateau Souverain 1996 Chardonnay
Region: California, Sonoma County $14
Golds/Awards: Gold (PR)

Chardonnay

Chateau Souverain 1996 Winemaker's Reserve Barrel Fermented Chardonnay
Region: California, Russian River Valley $20
Golds/Awards: Gold (OC)

Cloninger Cellars 1996 Estate Bottled Chardonnay
Region: California, Monterey $11
Golds/Awards: Gold (CA); Best of Class (CA)

Did You Know...?

To avoid palate fatigue, go to bed! According to Robert Parker, "it is imperative to get a good night's rest prior to a long day of tasting." Your mouth and tongue need sleep too.

Clos du Bois 1996 Flintwood Chardonnay
Region: California, Dry Creek Valley $17
Golds/Awards: Gold (NW)

Clos du Bois 1996 Special Selection Chardonnay
Region: California, Alexander Valley $15
Golds/Awards: Gold (NW)

Clos du Val 1996 Carneros Chardonnay
Region: California, Napa Valley $16
Golds/Awards: Gold (BR)

Clos LaChance 1995 Chardonnay
Region: California, Santa Cruz Mountains $18
Golds/Awards: Gold (WWC-91 pts)

Cobblestone 1996 Chardonnay
Region: California, Monterey County $22.50
Golds/Awards: Gold (WWC-90 pts)

Columbia Crest 1996 Chardonnay
Region: Washington, Columbia Valley $9
Golds/Awards: Gold (WC)

Columbia Crest 1996 Estate Series Chardonnay
Region: Washington $15
Golds/Awards: Gold (WC); Best of Class (WC)

Did You Know...?

"The less I behave like Whistler's
mother the night before, the more
I look like her the morning after."
—Tallulah Bankhead

Columbia Crest 1996 Reserve Chardonnay
Region: Washington $16.99
Golds/Awards: Gold (PR)

Columbia Winery 1995 Otis Vineyard Chardonnay
Region: Washington, Yakima Valley $22
Golds/Awards: Gold (WWC-90 pts)

Concannon 1996 Chardonnay
Region: California, Central Coast $9.95
Golds/Awards: Gold (NW)

Concannon 1996 Reserve Chardonnay
Region: California, Livermore Valley $15.95
Golds/Awards: Gold (NW)

Cooper-Garrod 1996 Chardonnay
Region: California, Santa Cruz Mountains $18
Golds/Awards: Gold (LA)

Cooper's Creek 1996 Swamp Reserve Chardonnay
Region: New Zealand $26.99
Golds/Awards: Gold (IW)

Cooper's Creek 1997 Hawkes Bay Chardonnay
Region: New Zealand, Hawkes Bay $17.98
Golds/Awards: Gold (SY)

Corbans Wines 1996 Private Bin Oaked Chardonnay
Region: New Zealand $13.99
Golds/Awards: Gold (IW)

Corbett Canyon 1997 Chardonnay
Region: California, Santa Barbara County $9
Golds/Awards: Gold (CA)

Chardonnay

Cronin 1995 Chardonnay
Region: California, Santa Cruz Mountains $20
Golds/Awards: Gold (WWC-91 pts)

D'Arenberg 1997 The Olive Grove Chardonnay
Region: Australia, McLaren Vale $15
Golds/Awards: Gold (BR, IW)

De Bortoli 1996 Chardonnay
Region: Australia, Yarra Valley $21
Golds/Awards: Gold (IW)

De Lorimier 1996 Estate Bottled Chardonnay
Region: California, Alexander Valley $16
Golds/Awards: Gold (NW)

Dehlinger 1995 Chardonnay
Region: California, Russian River Valley $18
Golds/Awards: Gold (WWC-90 pts)

DeLoach 1996 O.F.S. Chardonnay
Region: California, Russian River Valley $27.50
Golds/Awards: Gold (WWC-90 pts, BR, SD)

DeLoach 1996 Sonoma Cuvée Chardonnay
Region: California, Sonoma County $13
Golds/Awards: Gold (NW)

Dry Creek Vineyard 1996 Barrel Fermented Chardonnay
Region: California, Sonoma County $20
Golds/Awards: Gold (NW)

Did You Know...?

According to the Wine Market Council, the reason 21- to 39-year-olds prefer beer to wine is that they perceive wine as being too complicated to understand, they see it as a special-occasion beverage, and they don't understand how and when to drink it.

Chardonnay

Dry Creek Vineyard 1996 Reserve Chardonnay
Region: California, Sonoma County $20
Golds/Awards: Gold (RI, WC, GH); Best of Class (WC)

Dry Creek Vineyard 1997 Chardonnay
Region: California, Sonoma County $16
Golds/Awards: Gold (LA)

Dunnewood 1996 Chardonnay
Region: California, Carneros $7.99
Golds/Awards: Gold (PR)

Eberle Winery 1997 Chardonnay
Region: California, Paso Robles $14
Golds/Awards: Gold (LA)

Echelon 1997 Chardonnay
Region: California, Central Coast $11
Golds/Awards: Gold (CA)

Ehlers Grove 1996 Winery Reserve Chardonnay
Region: California, Sonoma County $25
Golds/Awards: Gold (CA); Best of Region, Best of Class (CA)

Eikendal 1997 Chardonnay
South Africa, Stellenbosch $17.99
Golds/Awards: Gold (WWC-90, VL); Champion White (VL)

El Molino 1995 Chardonnay
Region: California, Napa Valley $37.99
Golds/Awards: Gold (WWC-92 pts)

Eos Estate Winery 1996 Estate Bottled Chardonnay
Region: California, Paso Robles $14.99
Golds/Awards: Gold (RI)

Did You Know...?

Money launderers have discovered the world of fine wines. Drug dealers, needing places to get rid of large sums of cash, purchase ultrafine wines and then turn around and sell them. Trading in fine wine, called "layering," is an illegal form of money cleaning.

Chardonnay

Errazuriz 1997 Chardonnay
Region: Chile, Casablanca Valley $9
Golds/Awards: Gold (VI)

Estancia 1996 Pinnacles Chardonnay
Region: California, Monterey County $11
Golds/Awards: Gold (OC)

Did You Know...?

American oak—not French—is the oak of
choice for sherry makers in Spain and elsewhere.

Etchart 1997 Cafayate Chardonnay
Region: Argentina $11.99
Golds/Awards: Gold (SY)

Etchart 1997 Rio de Plata Chardonnay
Region: Argentina $6.99
Golds/Awards: Gold (VL)

Ferrari Carano 1995 Chardonnay
Region: California, Alexander Valley $22
Golds/Awards: Gold (WWC-90 pts)

Fess Parker 1996 American Tradition Reserve Chardonnay
Region: California, Santa Barbara County $22
Golds/Awards: Gold (CA)

Fetzer 1997 Sundial Chardonnay
Region: California $8.99
Golds/Awards: Gold (NW)

Fisher 1995 Whitney's Vineyard Chardonnay
Region: California, Sonoma County $26
Golds/Awards: Gold (WWC-91 pts)

Flichman 1997 Chardonnay
Region: Argentina $9.95
Golds/Awards: Gold (VN)

Folie à Deux 1996 Chardonnay
Region: California $14
Golds/Awards: Gold (OC)

Chardonnay

Freemark Abbey 1994 Carpy Ranch Chardonnay
Region: California, Napa Valley $20.49
Golds/Awards: Gold (WWC-90 pts)

Gainey 1995 Limited Selection Chardonnay
Region: California, Santa Barbara County $25
Golds/Awards: Gold (WWC-95 pts)

Did You Know...?

Alcohol is an excellent preservative. That's why high-
alcohol wines such as sherry can keep for months even
after being opened.

Gallo Sonoma 1994 Laguna Ranch Chardonnay
Region: California, Northern Sonoma $16
Golds/Awards: Gold (BR)

Gallo Sonoma 1995 Estate Chardonnay
Region: California, Northern Sonoma $35
Golds/Awards: Gold (WWC-92 pts, OC, WS); Best
Chardonnay (WS)

Gallo Sonoma 1995 Laguna Ranch Vineyard Chardonnay
Region: California, Russian River Valley $18
Golds/Awards: Gold (WWC-90 pts)

Gallo Sonoma 1996 Estate Chardonnay
Region: California, Russian River Valley $39.99
Golds/Awards: Gold (BR)

Gallo Sonoma 1996 Laguna Ranch Chardonnay
Region: California $16
Golds/Awards: Gold (IW, VI); Grand Gold Medal (VI)

Gallo Sonoma 1996 Stefani Vineyard Chardonnay
Region: California, Dry Creek Valley $16
Golds/Awards: Gold (WC)

Gary Farrell 1996 Allen Vineyard Chardonnay
Region: California, Russian River Valley $28
Golds/Awards: Gold (WWC-90 pts, PR, RI); Best of Class,
Best Chardonnay (PR)

Chardonnay

WHITE

Geyser Peak 1995 Reserve Chardonnay
Region: California, Alexander Valley $23
Golds/Awards: Gold (LA)

Geyser Peak 1997 Chardonnay
Region: California, Sonoma County $14
Golds/Awards: Gold (BR, OC)

Glen Ellen 1996 Expressions Chardonnay
Region: California, Sonoma County $10
Golds/Awards: Gold (LA, WC)

Gloria Ferrer Champagne Caves 1995 Chardonnay
Region: California, Carneros $19
Golds/Awards: Gold (PR, NW)

Gloria Ferrer Champagne Caves 1996 Chardonnay
Region: California, Carneros $19
Golds/Awards: Gold (WC)

Gordon Brothers 1997 Chardonnay
Region: Washington, Columbia Valley $15.49
Golds/Awards: Gold (EN)

Grove Mill 1996 Chardonnay
Region: New Zealand, Marlborough $20
Golds/Awards: Gold (SY)

Guenoc 1996 Chardonnay
Region: California, North Coast $15.50
Golds/Awards: Gold (DA)

Did You Know...?

The battleground between environmentalists and
vineyard developers is heating up in California. The
former say that the boom in the wine business
is resulting in insensitive land development.
Flooding or insufficient water supply; the
intrusion on creek, river, and woodland habitat;
land erosion; and water pollution from chemical
run-off are some of the issues environmentalists
are peeved about.

Chardonnay

Guenoc 1997 Chardonnay
Region: California, North Coast $15.50
Golds/Awards: Gold (LA)

Gundlach-Bundschu 1996 Barrel Fermented Sangiacomo Ranch Chardonnay
Region: California $16
Golds/Awards: Gold (NW)

Handley Cellars 1996 Estate Grown Chardonnay
Region: California, Anderson Valley $16
Golds/Awards: Gold (OC)

Handley Cellars 1996 Handley Vineyard Chardonnay
Region: California, Dry Creek Valley $16
Golds/Awards: Gold (RI)

Hardys 1996 Padthaway Chardonnay
Region: Australia $12.99
Golds/Awards: Gold (IW)

Hartford Court 1996 Seascape Vineyard Chardonnay
Region: California $35
Golds/Awards: Gold (LA)

Henry of Pelham 1995 Barrel Fermented Chardonnay
Region: Canada, Niagara Peninsula $16.50
Golds/Awards: Gold (WS)

Hidden Cellars 1996 Heritage Chardonnay
Region: California, Mendocino $25
Golds/Awards: Gold (NW); Best of Class (NW)

Husch 1996 Chardonnay
Region: California, Mendocino $12.50
Golds/Awards: Gold (RI); Chairman's Award (RI)

Did You Know...?

One hundred years ago everyone owned a corkscrew, since everything from perfume to horse liniment was kept in a bottle with a cork stopper. Ladies carried corkscrews in their purses.

Chardonnay WHITE

Jacob's Creek 1997 Chardonnay
Region: Australia, South Eastern Australia $8.99
Golds/Awards: Gold (SY)

Jarvis 1995 Chardonnay
Region: California, Napa Valley $36
Golds/Awards: Gold (WWC-90 pts)

Did You Know...?

A vintage date (such as 1996) on a label means
that at least 95% of the wine in that bottle
was grown in 1996.

Jory 1996 Lion Oaks Ranch Selected Clone Chardonnay
Region: California, Santa Clara Valley $25
Golds/Awards: Gold (WWC-90 pts)

Kendall-Jackson 1996 Camelot Vineyard Chardonnay
Region: California, Santa Maria Valley $20
Golds/Awards: Gold (NW, IV, OC); Best of Class, Best of
Varietal (NW)

Kistler Vineyards 1995 Vine Hill Ranch Chardonnay
Region: California, Russian River Valley $50
Golds/Awards: Gold (OC)

La Crema 1996 Reserve Chardonnay
Region: California, Sonoma Coast $27
Golds/Awards: Gold (LA)

**Lake Sonoma 1996 Heck Family Cellar Selection
Chardonnay**
Region: California, Russian River Valley $15
Golds/Awards: Gold (SD)

Landmark 1996 Overlook Chardonnay
Region: California, Sonoma County $20
Golds/Awards: Gold (WWC-90 pts)

Leasingham 1996 Chardonnay
Region: Australia $14
Golds/Awards: Gold (IW)

Lin Court Vineyards 1996 Chardonnay
Region: California, Santa Barbara County $16
Golds/Awards: Gold (LA)

Lindemans 1997 Padthaway Chardonnay
Region: Australia $12
Golds/Awards: Gold (RI); Chairman's Award (RI)

> ### Did You Know...?
> No other wine has been named Best Buy in
> *Wine Spectator* more times than Lindemans
> Bin 65 Chardonnay.

Louis M. Martini 1995 Reserve Chardonnay
Region: California, Russian River Valley $18
Golds/Awards: Gold (LA)

Madrona 1996 Estate Chardonnay
Region: California, El Dorado $12
Golds/Awards: Gold (OC)

Maglieri 1996 Chardonnay
Region: Australia, McLaren Vale $16
Golds/Awards: Gold (SY)

Magnotta 1994 Gran Riserva Chardonnay
Region: Canada, Niagara Peninsula   (Can $) 23.95
Golds/Awards: Gold (IV)

Magnotta 1994 Lenko Vineyards Chardonnay
Region: Canada   (Can $) 9.95
Golds/Awards: Gold (VL)

Marcelina 1995 Chardonnay
Region: California, Napa Valley $18
Golds/Awards: Gold (PR, RI); Best of Class (PR)

Mark West 1995 Reserve Chardonnay
Region: California, Russian River Valley $20
Golds/Awards: Gold (WWC-90 pts)

Mark West 1996 Chardonnay
Region: California, Russian River Valley $15
Golds/Awards: Gold (WC)

McIlroy Wines 1996 Aquarius Ranch Chardonnay
Region: California, Russian River Valley $18
Golds/Awards: Gold (LA); Best of Class (LA, CA), Division
Sweepstakes Award (LA), Double Gold (CA)

Mer et Soleil 1995 Chardonnay
Region: California, Central Coast $35
Golds/Awards: Gold (WWC-93 pts)

Meridian 1996 Coastal Reserve Chardonnay
Region: California, Edna Valley $16
Golds/Awards: Gold (SD, WC); Best of Class (SD)

Merryvale 1995 Reserve Chardonnay
Region: California, Napa Valley $30
Golds/Awards: Gold (WWC-90 pts)

Merryvale 1996 Startmont Chardonnay
Region: California, Napa Valley $18
Golds/Awards: Gold (NW)

Mirassou 1996 Harvest Reserve Chardonnay
Region: California, Monterey $15.95
Golds/Awards: Gold (PR)

Mirassou 1996 Showcase Selection Chardonnay
Region: California, Monterey $28
Golds/Awards: Gold (GH, CA)

Did You Know...?

Because organic farming requires handwork
for tasks such as weed removal and deleafing,
organic growers generally spend more time in
the vineyards than their conventional agricultural
counterparts. Because of this constant scrutiny, the
vines are often in better condition.

Mission Hill 1995 Grand Reserve Barrel Select Chardonnay
Region: Canada, Okanagan Valley   (Can $) 17.95
Golds/Awards: Gold (WS)

Mission Hill 1996 Grand Reserve Chardonnay
Region: Canada, Okanagan Valley   (Can $) 17.95
Golds/Awards: Gold (IV)

Did You Know...?

"The hangover is something to occupy the head that wasn't used the night before."
—Anonymous

Monthaven 1996 Chardonnay
Region: California, Monterey County $15.99
Golds/Awards: Gold (SD, LA, OC, WC); Four Star Gold (OC)

Monticello 1994 Corley Reserve Chardonnay
Region: California, Napa Valley $26
Golds/Awards: Gold (WWC-91 pts)

Morgan 1995 Reserve Chardonnay
Region: California, Monterey $25
Golds/Awards: Gold (WWC-91 pts)

Morton Estate 1996 Hawkes Bay Chardonnay
Region: New Zealand, Hawkes Bay $10.99
Golds/Awards: Gold (IW)

Napa Creek Winery 1997 Chardonnay
Region: California, Lodi $8.99
Golds/Awards: Gold (LA)

Napa Ridge 1996 Chardonnay
Region: California, North Coast $9
Golds/Awards: Gold (WC)

Orfila 1995 Ambassador's Reserve Chardonnay
Region: California, San Diego County $14.95
Golds/Awards: Gold (NW)

Orlando 1997 St. Hilary Chardonnay
Region: Australia $22
Golds/Awards: Gold (IW)

Page Mill 1996 Bien Nacido Vineyard Chardonnay
Region: California, Santa Maria Valley $18
Golds/Awards: Gold (WWC-90 pts)

Chardonnay

Parducci 1996 Bighorn Ranch Reserve Chardonnay
Region: California, Carneros/Napa Valley $20
Golds/Awards: Gold (PR, NW)

Pedroncelli 1996 Chardonnay
Region: California, Dry Creek Valley $10
Golds/Awards: Gold (WC)

Pedroncelli 1996 F. Johnson Vineyards Chardonnay
Region: California, Dry Creek Valley $12.50
Golds/Awards: Gold (NW, RI); Chairman's Award (RI)

Penfolds 1996 Adelaide Hills Chardonnay
Region: Australia, South Australia $24
Golds/Awards: Gold (SY)

Penfolds 1996 The Valleys Chardonnay
Region: Australia, South Australia $12
Golds/Awards: Gold (RI); Chairman's Award (RI)

> Did You Know...?
>
> Southcorp, Australia's largest wine company, which owns the brands Penfolds, Lindemans, Wynns Coonawarra Estate, and Seaview, is spending $135 million in direct investment over the next five years to double its red wine production.

Pezzi King 1996 Chardonnay
Region: California, Sonoma County $17
Golds/Awards: Gold (OC)

Pine Ridge 1996 Dijon Clones Chardonnay
Region: California, Stags Leap District $35
Golds/Awards: Gold (WWC-92 pts)

Pintler Cellar 1996 Chardonnay
Region: Idaho $10.99
Golds/Awards: Gold (EN)

R.H. Phillips 1996 Estate Bottled "Toasted Head" Chardonnay
Region: California, Dunnigan Hills $12
Golds/Awards: Gold (OC)

Raymond Vineyard 1996 Raymond Estate Chardonnay
Region: California, Monterey $13
Golds/Awards: Gold (WC)

Raymond Vineyard 1996 Raymond Generations Chardonnay
Region: California $27
Golds/Awards: Gold (LA); Best of Class (LA)

Ridge 1995 Chardonnay
Region: California, Santa Cruz Mountains $22.50
Golds/Awards: Gold (WWC-90 pts)

Robert Mondavi 1995 Reserve Chardonnay
Region: California, Napa Valley $32
Golds/Awards: Gold (WWC-91 pts)

Rombauer 1995 Chardonnay
Region: California, Carneros $23.75
Golds/Awards: Gold (WWC-90 pts)

Rosemount 1994 Roxburgh Chardonnay
Region: Australia, Hunter Valley $35
Golds/Awards: Gold (WWC-90 pts)

S. Anderson Vineyard 1996 Estate Bottled Chardonnay
Region: California, Stag's Leap District $22
Golds/Awards: Gold (SD)

Ste. Chapelle 1996 Barrel Fermented Chardonnay
Region: Idaho $9.89
Golds/Awards: Gold (EN)

Did You Know...?

The American Center for Wine, Food, and the Arts, scheduled to open in Napa in 2001, is designed to bring together students, scholars, winemakers, writers, visual and performing artists, chefs, and other food/wine experts to explore and celebrate the relationship between food and art.

Chardonnay

Saint Clair 1996 Chardonnay
Region: New Zealand, Marlborough $15
Golds/Awards: Gold (WWC-90 pts)

Did You Know...?

Dr. Louis Pasteur defined the process of
fermentation as *anaerobic,* meaning life without
air, since yeast do not require oxygen to survive.

St. Clement 1996 Abbotts Vineyard Chardonnay
Region: California, Carneros $20
Golds/Awards: Gold (OC)

Sanford 1995 Barrel Select Chardonnay
Region: California, Santa Barbara County $30
Golds/Awards: Gold (WWC-90 pts)

Sanford 1995 Sanford and Benedict Vineyard Chardonnay
Region: California, Santa Barbara County $24
Golds/Awards: Gold (WWC-93 pts)

Santa Barbara Winery 1996 Chardonnay
Region: California, Santa Barbara County $15
Golds/Awards: Gold (LA)

Santa Barbara Winery 1996 Reserve Chardonnay
Region: California, Santa Ynez Valley $25
Golds/Awards: Gold (LA, CA)

Santa Julia 1996 Oak Reserve Chardonnay
Region: Argentina, Mendoza $8.50
Golds/Awards: Gold (WWC-90 pts, SM)

Santa Julia 1997 Chardonnay
Region: Argentina $6.99
Golds/Awards: Gold (VN)

Seaview 1996 Edwards & Chaffey Chardonnay
Region: Australia, McLaren Vale $25
Golds/Awards: Gold (SY)

Sebastiani 1995 Dutton Ranch Chardonnay
Region: California, Russian River Valley $25
Golds/Awards: Gold (WWC-91 pts)

Chardonnay

Seifried Estate 1996 Nelson Chardonnay
Region: New Zealand, South Island $16.99
Golds/Awards: Gold (WS)

Sequoia Grove 1996 Chardonnay
Region: California, Carneros/Napa Valley $18
Golds/Awards: Gold (BR)

Did You Know...?

A PhD candidate from University of California at Davis tested soil samples from a number of different vineyards and found soil from organic vineyards more resistant to phylloxera, the deadly insect that has wiped out most of the world's grapevines at one time or another.

Seven Peaks 1996 Chardonnay
Region: California $12.99
Golds/Awards: Gold (PR, RI, OC); Chairman's Award (RI)

Shafer 1995 Red Shoulder Ranch Chardonnay
Region: California, Carneros $30
Golds/Awards: Gold (WWC-90 pts)

Signorello 1995 Founder's Reserve Chardonnay
Region: California, Napa Valley $48
Golds/Awards: Gold (WWC-94 pts)

Silver Ridge 1996 Barrel Fermented Chardonnay
Region: California $10
Golds/Awards: Gold (WC)

Simi 1994 Reserve Chardonnay
Region: California, Sonoma County $30
Golds/Awards: Gold (WWC-91 pts)

Sonoma-Loeb 1996 Private Reserve Chardonnay
Region: California, Sonoma County $30
Golds/Awards: Gold (WWC-90 pts)

Stag's Leap 1994 Barrel Fermented Chardonnay
Region: California $10
Golds/Awards: Gold (OC)

Stag's Leap 1995 Beckstoffer Ranch Chardonnay
Region: California, Napa Valley $28
Golds/Awards: Gold (WWC-93 pts)

Stag's Leap 1995 Chardonnay
Region: California, Napa Valley $24
Golds/Awards: Gold (WWC-91 pts)

Stag's Leap 1995 Reserve Chardonnay
Region: California, Napa Valley $37
Golds/Awards: Gold (WWC-92 pts)

Stag's Leap 1996 Chardonnay
Region: California, Napa Valley $21
Golds/Awards: Gold (PR, WC)

Steele 1995 Bien Nacido Vineyard Chardonnay
Region: California, Santa Barbara County $27.99
Golds/Awards: Gold (WWC-90 pts)

Steele 1995 Du Pratt Vineyard Chardonnay
Region: California, Mendocino $29.99
Golds/Awards: Gold (WWC-91 pts)

Steele 1995 Sangiacomo Vineyard Chardonnay
Region: California, Carneros $27.99
Golds/Awards: Gold (WWC-90 pts)

Stone Creek 1997 Chardonnay
Region: California $6.89
Golds/Awards: Gold (LA)

Strewn Winery 1996 Barrel Aged Chardonnay
Region: Canada, Niagara Peninsula (Can $) 14
Golds/Awards: Gold (SM)

Did You Know...?

The abundance of cork-stopped bottles in the 1800s
inspired one company to devise tiny wire corkscrews
that fit around your finger, designed to take a little cork
out of a medicine bottle. Twenty-five were linked
together, sold for 10 cents, and imprinted with the
slogan "Don't swear"—presumably because you could
now find a corkscrew when you needed one.

Chardonnay

Sylvester Winery 1996 Kiara Reserve Chardonnay
Region: California, Paso Robles $12
Golds/Awards: Gold (WC)

Did You Know...?

"The best cure for drunkenness is while sober
to see a drunken man."
                                        —Chinese proverb

Talbott 1995 Sleepy Hollow Vineyard Chardonnay
Region: California, Monterey $30
Golds/Awards: Gold (WWC-90 pts)

Tasman Bay 1996 Chardonnay
Region: New Zealand, Marlborough $14
Golds/Awards: Gold (SY)

Temecula Crest 1997 Chardonnay
Region: California, Temecula $15
Golds/Awards: Gold (CA); Best of Class (CA)

Thomas Fogarty 1995 Estate Reserve Chardonnay
Region: California, Santa Cruz Mountains $27.50
Golds/Awards: Gold (WWC-91 pts)

Thomas Fogarty 1996 Santa Cruz Mountains Chardonnay
Region: California $19
Golds/Awards: Gold (NW); Best of Class (NW)

Trellis Vineyards 1997 Chardonnay
Region: California, Russian River Valley $8.50
Golds/Awards: Gold (LA)

V. Sattui Winery 1996 Barrel Fermented Chardonnay
Region: California, Napa Valley $16.75
Golds/Awards: Gold (NW, PR)

Venezia 1995 Beaterra Vineyards Chardonnay
Region: California, Alexander Valley $20
Golds/Awards: Gold (NW, CA)

Venezia 1996 Regusci Vineyard Chardonnay
Region: California, Napa Valley $20
Golds/Awards: Gold (NW)

Villa Mt. Eden 1996 Bien Nacido Vineyards Grand Reserve Chardonnay
Region: California, Santa Maria Valley $18
Golds/Awards: Gold (RI); Chairman's Award (RI)

Villa Mt. Eden 1996 Chardonnay
Region: California $11
Golds/Awards: Gold (PR)

Viña Calina 1996 Seleccion de las Lomas Chardonnay
Region: Chile, Central Valley $16
Golds/Awards: Gold (RI); Best of Class, Best of Category (RI)

Viña Santa Carolina 1996 Reserva Chardonnay
Chile, Maipo Valley $7.99
Golds/Awards: Gold (RI)

Did You Know...?

Saintsbury's, Britain's major wine store, conducted a survey that found that even among "heavy wine drinkers 70% do not know the region, and 75% do not know the grape the wine is made from."

Viña Tarapaca 1997 Reserva Chardonnay
Region: Chile, Maipo Valley $10
Golds/Awards: Gold (LA)

Viu Manent 1997 Chardonnay
Region: Chile, Colchagua Valley $8
Golds/Awards: Gold (BR)

Weinstock Cellars 1996 Chardonnay
Region: California $10.99
Golds/Awards: Gold (WC)

Wente Vineyards 1995 Herman Wente Reserve Chardonnay
Region: California, Livermore Valley $22
Golds/Awards: Gold (SD)

Wild Horse 1996 Chardonnay
Region: California, Central Coast $14
Golds/Awards: Gold (OC)

William Hill Winery 1996 Reserve Chardonnay
Region: California, Napa Valley $20
Golds/Awards: Gold (DA)

Windemere Winery 1996 MacGregor Vineyards Chardonnay
Region: California, Edna Valley $18
Golds/Awards: Gold (CA)

Windsor 1996 Chardonnay
Region: California, Calaveras County $10
Golds/Awards: Gold (PR, OC)

Windsor 1996 Estate Bottled Private Reserve Chardonnay
Region: California, Russian River Valley $20
Golds/Awards: Gold (SD); Best of Class (SD)

Windsor 1997 Private Reserve Chardonnay
Region: California, North Coast $14
Golds/Awards: Gold (NW); Best of Class, Best of Varietal (NW)

Wolf Blass 1997 President's Selection Chardonnay
Region: Australia, McLaren Vale $15
Golds/Awards: Gold (RI)

Yarra Ridge 1997 Chardonnay
Region: Australia $11.99
Golds/Awards: Gold (RI)

ZD Wines 1996 Chardonnay
Region: California $25
Golds/Awards: Gold (LA); Best of Class (LA)

Did You Know...?

If an American wine has a certain federally recognized viticultural area on the label, such as Napa Valley, then at least 85% of the grapes had to have been grown in Napa Valley.

CHENIN BLANC

ere's a grape that's been largely ignored in the New World. However, that trend is changing as consumers are beginning to look for simple, appealing white wines at reasonable prices. Often blended with other whites, Chenin Blanc is a crowd pleaser coming into its own in places like California, Washington State, and Chile.

Chenin Blanc is made in two basic styles. The drier of the two is Chardonnay-like, taking on oak-barrel flavors and aromas (spicy, roasted, or vanilla). The second is sweeter, marked by delicate hints of flowers, melons, pears, and honey. Because this grape produces buds earlier and ripens later than most, either style will usually have lots of natural clean, crisp acidity and plenty of fruit, which means it can age well.

Food companions: When you think of Chenin Blanc, think summer: August picnics with antipasto, raw clams or oysters, crudité, guacamole and chips, fresh fruit, pasta salad, and chicken. This wine also goes well with spicy Thai, Szechuan, and Mexican dishes.

Alexander Valley Vineyards 1996 Dry Chenin Blanc
Region: California, Northern Sonoma $9
Golds/Awards: Gold (GH)

Chalone 1994 Reserve Chenin Blanc
Region: California, Chalone $16
Golds/Awards: Gold (WWC-91 pts)

Chappellet 1995 Old Vine Cuvée Dry Chenin Blanc
Region: California, Napa Valley $12
Golds/Awards: Gold (WWC-90 pts)

Columbia Winery 1995 Chenin Blanc
Region: Washington, Yakima Valley $5.99
Golds/Awards: Gold (WWC-90 pts)

Dry Creek Vineyard 1996 Clarksburg Dry Chenin Blanc
Region: California $8
Golds/Awards: Gold (NW); Best of Class (NW)

Fantaisie 1996 Chenin Blanc
Region: California, Napa Valley $8
Golds/Awards: Gold (NW)

Hogue 1997 Chenin Blanc
Region: Washington, Columbia Valley $7
Golds/Awards: Gold (LA)

Husch 1997 La Ribera Vineyards Chenin Blanc
Region: California, Mendocino $8.50
Golds/Awards: Gold (LA, CA); Best of Class (CA)

Did You Know...?

The Duke and Duchess of Windsor had hundreds of
bottles of wine, as well as claret jugs, sherry glasses,
decanters, and other priceless collectibles. After Wallis
Windsor's death in 1986, Mohamed Al Fayed, owner of
Harrod's and father of Dodi, Princess Di's ill-
fated boyfriend, acquired the contents of the
Windsor villa in Paris. He sold their lifetime
collection at auction in just nine days for $23
million—the proceeds going to the Dodi Fayed
International Charitable foundation.

Did You Know...?

Happy squid: In November of 1997 a Boston-bound
French freighter was hit by an unexpected 75-foot wave
that split the hull of the 937-foot ship in two. Among the
precious cargo were rare Armagnacs worth $700/bottle
and 100,000 other bottles of French wine.

Navarro 1997 Chenin Blanc
Region: California, Mendocino $9.50
Golds/Awards: Gold (LA, OC)

Stellenzicht 1996 Chenin Blanc
Region: South Africa, Stellenbosch $29.99
Golds/Awards: Gold (WWC-90 pts)

**Ventana Vineyards 1997 Barrel Fermented Estate Bottled
Chenin Blanc**
Region: California, Monterey $10
Golds/Awards: Gold (RI, WC, CA); Best of Class (WC, CA)

Windsor 1996 Chenin Blanc
Region: California $7.50
Golds/Awards: Gold (CA); Best of Class (CA)

GEWURZTRAMINER

The name is pronounced *guh-WERZ-truh-meener*, and in German *gewürz* means spicy. Words commonly used to describe this wine's flavors and bouquet include clove, nutmeg, lychee nut, carnations, and wildflowers. A great Gewurztraminer will indeed be spicy, with a heady perfume and slight sweetness. This pink-skinned grape makes whites that are exotic, deeply colored, and fuller bodied than almost any other white.

Australia has had a lot of success with this grape, where it's called Traminer. New Zealand is also producing fine examples, as well as the American Northwest and California.

Food companions: Serve it with pork sausages, foie gras, steamed vegetables, Indian curries, Oriental cuisine—especially mouth-searing Thai—crab, scallops, or trout. After a meal Gewurz goes well with cheesecake and fresh fruit.

Gewurztraminer

Adler Fels 1996 Gewurztraminer
Region: California, Sonoma County $11
Golds/Awards: Gold (WWC-90 pts)

Adler Fels 1997 Gewurztraminer
Region: California, Sonoma County $11
Golds/Awards: Gold (WWC-90 pts)

**Alderbrook 1997 McIlroy Vineyard Barrel Fermented
Gewurztraminer**
Region: California, Russian River Valley $12
Golds/Awards: Gold (OC)

Alderbrook 1997 Saralee's Vineyard Gewurztraminer
Region: California, Russian River Valley $11
Golds/Awards: Gold (CA)

Alexander Valley Vineyards 1997 Wetzel Family Selection
Region: California, North Coast $9
Golds/Awards: Gold (CA)

Bargetto 1995 Gewurztraminer
Region: California, Monterey County $10
Golds/Awards: Gold (WWC-90 pts)

Bayview Cellars 1997 Gewurztraminer
Region: California $8.50
Golds/Awards: Gold (CA)

Did You Know...?

An unusual tasting took place recently at VINEXPO
in Bordeaux. Celebrated wine experts from all over the
world were hooked up to heart monitors to determine
emotional response levels. A 1989 French
Gewurztraminer, described as "spectacular,"
"magnificent," "sumptuous," and
"explosive" by various tasters, also
elicited accelerated rhythms,
indicating uncontrolled
emotion gone haywire.

Beringer 1996 Gewurztraminer
Region: California $7
Golds/Awards: Gold (PR); Best of Class (PR)

Brancott Vineyards 1996 Patutahi Estate Gewurztraminer
Region: New Zealand, Gisborne $22
Golds/Awards: Gold (SY, WWC-90 pts)

Did You Know...?

Kosher wines are being made in Germany for the first time since the Nazi regime. A producer called Schenkel has made a red and a white kosher wine under the Nagile label. *Nagile* is Hebrew for "joy."

Chateau St. Jean 1997 Gewurztraminer
Region: California, Sonoma County $9.50
Golds/Awards: Gold (LA, CA); Best of Class (LA)

Cosentino 1996 Gewurztraminer
Region: California, Napa Valley $14
Golds/Awards: Gold (WWC-91 pts)

DeLoach 1997 Early Harvest Gewurztraminer
Region: California, Russian River Valley $12
Golds/Awards: Gold (RI)

Edmeades 1996 Gewurztraminer
Region: California, Anderson Valley $16
Golds/Awards: Gold (PR)

Fetzer 1997 Gewurztraminer
Region: California $6.99
Golds/Awards: Double Gold (CA); Best of Class (CA)

Gan Eden 1996 Gewurztraminer
Region: California, Monterey/Mendocino $12
Golds/Awards: Gold (OC)

Geyser Peak 1997 Gewurztraminer
Region: California $7.50
Golds/Awards: Gold (NW)

Gundlach-Bundschu 1997 Rhinefarm Vineyards Estate Bottled Gewurztraminer
Region: California, Sonoma Valley $12
Golds/Awards: Gold (SD, CA); Best of Class (CA)

Hoodsport 1997 Select Premium Gewurztraminer
Region: Washington, Yakima Valley $8.99
Golds/Awards: Gold (SD, NW); Best of Class, Best of Varietal (NW)

Husch 1997 Estate Bottled Gewurztraminer
Region: California, Anderson Valley $11
Golds/Awards: Gold (SD)

Kendall-Jackson 1996 Vintner's Reserve Gewurztraminer
Region: California $10
Golds/Awards: Four Star Gold (OC)

Louis M. Martini 1996 Gewurztraminer
Region: California, Russian River Valley $12
Golds/Awards: Gold (RI); Chairman's Award (RI)

M.G. Vallejo 1996 Gewurztraminer
Region: California, Sonoma $6
Golds/Awards: Gold (NW)

Mark West 1997 Reserve Gewurztraminer
Region: California, Russian River Valley $15
Golds/Awards: Gold (OC)

Meridian 1997 Gewurztraminer
Region: California, Santa Barbara County $8
Golds/Awards: Gold (CA); Best of California, Best of Class (CA)

Did You Know...?

"You say man learned first to build a fire and then to ferment his liquor. Had he but reversed the process we should have no need of flint and tinder to this day."
—Anonymous

Mill Creek 1996 Estate Bottled Gewurztraminer
Region: California, Dry Creek Valley $10
Golds/Awards: Four Star Gold (OC)

Navarro 1995 Gewurztraminer
Region: California, Anderson Valley $14
Golds/Awards: Gold (WWC-90 pts)

Prejean Winery 1996 Dry Gewurztraminer
Region: New York, Finger Lakes $12
Golds/Awards: Gold (PR)

Standing Stone 1996 Gewurztraminer
Region: New York, Finger Lakes $10.99
Golds/Awards: Gold (RI)

Did You Know...?

Christmas Day, 1980, is known as the Christmas Day Massacre in Upstate New York. On that day the temperature dropped 50 degrees in one day, resulting in major damage to the grapevines, which can ordinarily cope with temperature changes, but not ones that happen that fast.

Storrs 1996 Viento Vineyard Gewurztraminer
Region: California, Monterey $12
Golds/Awards: Gold (OC)

Thomas Fogarty 1997 Gewurztraminer
Region: California, Monterey $12.50
Golds/Awards: Gold (OC)

Ventana 1997 Estate Bottled Gewurztraminer
Region: California, Monterey $10
Golds/Awards: Gold (RI)

MISCELLANEOUS VARIETAL WHITES

New World wine producers are beginning to take more chances with white varietals, knowing that consumers are ready to step away from the Chardonnay routine. In this section are some less common, and in some cases unusual, varietal whites named "best" by the experts.

Cortese An Italian white grape that produces crisp, uncomplicated, agreeable, fresh white wines that nicely complement fresh fish. The word *cortese* means "courteous" in Italian.

French Columbard Also spelled Colombard, this varietal is a pleasantly crisp and lively white.

Malvasia Bianca Widely planted in Italy, but rare in the New World, Malvasia is a grape with ancient origins. Malvasia Bianca is a white wine made from the Malvasia grape, and can be deeply colored, high in alcohol, and often slightly sweet.

Marsanne Increasingly popular, Marsanne is a deeply colored white with full body and often heavy, almond-like aromas.

Palomino Best known for being the major grape used in Spanish sherry, Palomino is also grown in California, Argentina, Australia, and New Zealand, where it produces a light-bodied white wine.

Roussanne This is an elegant Rhône varietal, often blended with Marsanne, that is known for its mysterious aroma of herb tea and its refreshing acidity.

Torrontés This white grape indigenous to Spain is gaining popularity throughout South America, particularly Argentina. It produces whites with assertive acidity and wonderful aromas reminiscent of Muscat. Makes a wonderful aperitif when served icy cold.

Miscellaneous Whites

Castelletto 1996 Cortese
Region: California, Temecula $16
Golds/Awards: Gold (SD, LA, DA, CA, WWC-93 pts); Best
of Class (CA)

Cline 1996 Marsanne
Region: California, Los Carneros $20
Golds/Awards: Gold (WWC-91 pts)

Concannon 1996 Marsanne
Region: California, Santa Clara Valley $14.95
Golds/Awards: Gold (LA); Best of Class (LA)

Etchart 1997 Torrontés
Region: Argentina, Cafayate $7.99
Golds/Awards: Gold (VN, SM)

Mount Palomar 1997 Rey Sol Rousanne
Region: California, Temecula $18
Golds/Awards: Gold (RI); Chairman's Award (RI)

Robert Pepi 1996 Malvasia Bianca
Region: California, Central Coast $14
Golds/Awards: Gold (PR)

Rosenblum 1996 Fleur de Hoof Palomino
Region: California, Contra Costa $8
Golds/Awards: Gold (NW, OC); Best of Class (NW)

Stony Ridge NV Malvasia Bianca
Region: California $12
Golds/Awards: Gold (OC)

Windsor 1997 French Columbard
Region: California, Sonoma County $6.75
Golds/Awards: Gold (OC); Double Gold, Best of Class (CA)

Zaca Mesa Winery 1996 Zaca Vineyards Roussanne
Region: California, Santa Barbara County $16.50
Golds/Awards: Gold (CA); Best of Class (CA)

Did You Know...?

"Girls and vineyards are hard to guard."
—Portuguese proverb

NATIVE WHITES AND
FRENCH-AMERICAN HYBRIDS

Native American species of white grapes such as Delaware can produce delicious wines that are easy to enjoy with local cuisine. They have the added advantage of being genetically suited to grow in places such as Missouri, where so-called fine wine grapes perish.

French-American hybrids In the cooler winemaking regions with shorter growing seasons, such as Canada and upstate New York, winemakers needed to find grapes that would withstand the harsh winters yet ones that wouldn't produce wines with the "foxy" flavor characteristics associated with native American species.

Ingenious scientists, beginning in the late 1900s and continuing to the present, have been developing French-American hybrids in order to find vines that combine the hardiness and disease resistance of American varieties with the flavor and elegance of French varieties. Some particularly successful results are Seyval Blanc and Vidal Blanc—both widely grown in New York and Canada to produce delicious white wines, icewines, and botrytized dessert wines.

Augusta Winery 1997 Seyval Blanc
Region: Missouri $7.03
Golds/Awards: Gold (NW); Best of Class (NW)

Augusta Winery 1997 Vignoles
Region: Missouri $8.43
Golds/Awards: Gold (RI)

Did You Know...?

Malcolm Forbes acquired a 1787 bottle of Château Lafite for $156,450—the largest amount ever paid for a bottle of wine. The wine supposedly belonged to Thomas Jefferson.

Botham 1996 American Dry Seyval Blanc
Region: Wisconsin $8
Golds/Awards: Gold (NW)

Ferrante Wine Farm 1996 Barrel Fermented Seyval
Region: Ohio, Lake Erie $9.99
Golds/Awards: Gold (SD)

Ferrante Wine Farm 1997 Catawba
Region: Ohio, Lake Erie $5.99
Golds/Awards: Gold (LA); Best of Class (LA)

Ferrante Wine Farm 1997 Vidal Blanc
Region: Ohio, Lake Erie $7.49
Golds/Awards: Gold (LA); Best of Class (LA)

Goose Watch 1997 Melody
Region: New York $7.50
Golds/Awards: Gold (LA)

Phillips Farms Vineyards 1997 Highway 12 Vineyards Symphony
Region: California, Lodi $4.99
Golds/Awards: Gold (CA); Best of Region, Best of Class (CA)

Pillitteri Estates 1995 V.Q.A. Ontario Semi-Dry Vidal
Region: Canada   (Can $) 6.95
Golds/Awards: Gold (PR); Best of Class (PR)

Pontchartrain 1996 American Beau Soleil Seyval-Vidal Blanc
Region: Louisiana $9.25
Golds/Awards: Gold (RI)

St. James Winery NV Country White
Region: Missouri $5.99
Golds/Awards: Gold (SD); Best of Class (SD)

St. James Winery 1997 Vintner's Reserve Seyval Blanc
Region: Missouri $9.99
Golds/Awards: Gold (NW, PR)

St. James Winery 1997 Vintner's Reserve Vignoles
Region: Missouri $12.99
Golds/Awards: Gold (PR, NW, RI); Best of Class (NW)

St. Julian 1997 Sweet Reserve Seyval Blanc
Region: Michigan $6.50
Golds/Awards: Gold (LA); Best of Class (LA)

Did You Know...?

"Boys should abstain from the use of
wine until their eighteenth year, for
it is wrong to add fire to fire."
                                    —Plato

Stone Hill NV Missouri Golden Rhine
Region: Missouri $6.79
Golds/Awards: Gold (RI)

Stone Hill 1996 Seyval
Region: Missouri $11.29
Golds/Awards: Gold (SD); Best of Class (SD)

Stone Hill 1996 Steinberg White Wine
Region: Missouri $8.29
Golds/Awards: Gold (RI); Chairman's Award (RI)

Stone Hill 1997 Estate Bottled Hermann Vidal Blanc
Region: Missouri $9.29
Golds/Awards: Gold (SD)

Stone Hill 1997 Hermann Vignoles
Region: Missouri $11.29
Golds/Awards: Gold (RI, LA)

Native & Hybrid Whites

Swedish Hill 1996 Cayuga White
Region: New York, Finger Lakes $5.99
Golds/Awards: Gold (NW)

Swedish Hill 1996 Delaware
Region: New York, Finger Lakes $7.99
Golds/Awards: Gold (PR, NW)

Swedish Hill 1996 Vidal Blanc
Region: New York, Finger Lakes $7.99
Golds/Awards: Gold (PR, NW)

Did You Know...?
New York's Hudson Valley has the oldest
continuously active winery in the U.S.—
Brotherhood Winery, first vintage 1839.

Swedish Hill 1997 Cayuga White
Region: New York, Finger Lakes Region $5.99
Golds/Awards: Gold (RI); Chairman's Award (RI)

Swedish Hill 1997 Vignoles
Region: New York $8.99
Golds/Awards: Gold (LA); Best of Class (LA)

Wollersheim Winery 1997 Prairie Fumé
Region: Wisconsin $8
Golds/Awards: Gold (LA)

PINOT BLANC

P inot Blanc, widely planted in France, is a mutation of Pinot Gris, and bears some resemblance to Chardonnay. In fact, in California some wineries use the same winemaking techniques on Pinot Blanc that they use for Chardonnay, and end up with a wine that is similar in some respects, although without as much fruit concentration. Another style of Pinot Blanc is subtly fruity and light, with crisp acidity. Pinot Blanc is also used to make California sparkling wines. Older vines of New World Pinot Blanc may actually be Melon, a white wine of Burgundian origins, and sometimes the two names are used interchangeably.

Food companions: Try Pinot Blanc with clams, oysters, crudité, smoked fish, prosciutto and melon appetizers, and pasta with cream sauce.

Did You Know...?

Wine writer Kevin Zraly witnessed firsthand the
Burgundy winemaker's obsession with his own
vineyard's particular soil. After a five-day rain,
Zraly observed the workers at the bottom
of the slopes with pails and shovels—
collecting the soil that had run off to
return to the vineyard!

Chalone 1993 Reserve Pinot Blanc
Region: California, Chalone $26
Golds/Awards: Gold (WWC-92 pts)

Chalone 1994 Reserve Pinot Blanc
Region: California, Chalone $26
Golds/Awards: Gold (WWC-91 pts)

Fetzer 1995 Bien Nacido Vineyard Reserve Pinot Blanc
Region: California $20
Golds/Awards: Gold (NW); Best of Class (NW)

**Hester Creek Estate Winery 1996 Grand Reserve
Pinot Blanc**
Region: Canada, Okanagan Valley   (Can $) 12.95
Golds/Awards: Gold (PR)

J. Lohr 1995 October Night Pinot Blanc
Region: California, Monterey $14
Golds/Awards: Gold (WWC-91 pts)

Laetitia 1996 Reserve Pinot Blanc
Region: California $28
Golds/Awards: Gold (PR, OC)

Mirassou 1995 Harvest Reserve Pinot Blanc
Region: California, Monterey County $15.95
Golds/Awards: Gold (WWC-90 pts)

Mirassou 1996 Family Selection White Burgundy
Region: California, Monterey County $10.95
Golds/Awards: Gold (SD); Best of Class (SD)

Pinot Blanc

Palmer 1996 Estate Pinot Blanc
Region: New York, North Fork Long Island $11.99
Golds/Awards: Gold (DA)

Paraiso Springs 1997 Reserve Pinot Blanc
Region: California, Santa Lucia Highlands $22.50
Golds/Awards: Gold (CA)

Summerhill Estate Winery 1996 Pinot Blanc
Region: Canada, British Columbia   (Can $) 12.95
Golds/Awards: Gold (NW); Best of Class (NW)

Thornton 1996 Limited Bottling Pinot Blanc
Region: California, South Coast $16
Golds/Awards: Gold (SD)

Villa Mt. Eden 1996 Bien Nacido Vineyard Grand Reserve Pinot Blanc
Region: California, Santa Maria Valley $20
Golds/Awards: Gold (OC)

Wild Horse 1997 Pinot Blanc
Region: California, Monterey County $13
Golds/Awards: Gold (CA); Four Star Gold (OC); Best of Region, Best of Class (CA)

Willakenzie 1997 Pinot Blanc
Region: Oregon, Willamette Valley $14
Golds/Awards: Gold (EN)

Did You Know...?

Q: What's the winegrower's favorite bug?
A: The ladybug, which eats mealybugs, aphids, leafhoppers, and all sorts of other harmful pests that attack grapes and grapevines.

PINOT GRIS

From beautiful pink-grey grapes, Pinot Gris is a white wine that's found widely in the New World, particularly Oregon and New Zealand. A typical Pinot Gris is full bodied yet soft with gentle perfumes. It's also sometimes called Pinot Grigio.

Food companions: Pinot Gris will nicely complement quiche, smoked salmon, clam chowder, red snapper, mussels, and Chinese food.

Pinot Gris

Cooper Mountain 1997 Estate Bottled Pinot Gris
Region: Oregon, Willamette Valley $12.75
Golds/Awards: Gold (LA)

Handley Cellars 1997 Pinot Gris
Region: California, Anderson Valley $18
Golds/Awards: Gold (RI); Chairman's Award (RI)

Henry Estate 1997 Pinot Gris
Region: Oregon $13
Golds/Awards: Gold (EN)

Ivan Tamas 1996 Pinot Grigio
Region: California, Central Coast $8.95
Golds/Awards: Gold (SD); Best of Class (SD)

King Estate 1996 Pinot Gris
Region: Oregon $13
Golds/Awards: Gold (WWC-90 pts, LA); Best of Class (LA)

King Estate 1996 Reserve Pinot Gris
Region: Oregon $18
Golds/Awards: Gold (RI)

Lavelle 1996 Winter's Hill Vineyard Pinot Gris
Region: Oregon $13
Golds/Awards: Gold (DA)

Mission Hill 1996 Grand Reserve Barrel Select Pinot Gris
Region: Canada   (Can $) 14.95
Golds/Awards: Gold (IW)

Oak Knoll 1996 Vintage Reserve Pinot Gris
Region: Oregon, Willamette Valley $17
Golds/Awards: Gold (WWC-93 pts)

Willamette Valley Vineyards 1996 Pinot Gris
Region: Oregon $12.50
Golds/Awards: Gold (SD, GH)

Did You Know...?
The word "Reserve" has no legal meaning.

RIESLING

I n Oregon it's White Riesling. In Australia it's Rhine Riesling. In California it's Johannisberg Riesling, or sometimes just Riesling. Regardless, they're all one and the same.

Riesling is a grape variety of German origin that makes wines in two basic styles: dry to off-dry, and lusciously sweet. The reason for the latter is that it is often harvested late and allowed to be infected with the "noble rot," also known as *Botrytis cinerea*, which produces juice that's highly concentrated and sweet, fragrant, with apricot and peach overtones. (Late Harvest Rieslings are listed in the Dessert and Fortified Wines chapter.) The drier versions are fresh, flowery, and delicate, with hints of apples and pears. What they both have in common is their surprisingly inexpensive price.

Food companions: What you eat with your Riesling depends on the style of the wine. The medium-dry versions go well with cold meats, oysters, pasta salads, roasted turkey or chicken, mild Thai cuisine, perch, broiled salmon, sea bass, and even sushi. The sweeter ones can accompany hard cheeses, prosciutto, fresh fruit, and cheesecake.

Riesling

Amity 1995 Dry Riesling
Region: Oregon $9
Golds/Awards: Gold (WWC-90 pts)

Amity 1996 Riesling
Region: Oregon $9
Golds/Awards: Gold (WC); Best of Class (WC)

Argyle 1995 Dry Reserve Riesling
Region: Oregon, Willamette Valley $12
Golds/Awards: Gold (WWC-90 pts)

Baily 1997 Mother's Vineyard Riesling
Region: California, Temecula $8.95
Golds/Awards: Gold (OC)

Beringer 1996 Johannisberg Riesling
Region: California $7
Golds/Awards: Gold (NW)

Did You Know...?

A handful of top California wineries, which
include Clos du Bois, Beringer, Kendall-Jackson,
Robert Mondavi, and Sebastiani, are joining
forces to find the perfect alternative to cork.
If they succeed, we may be popping polyethylene
rather than cork in the future.

Chateau St. Jean 1997 Riesling
Region: California, Sonoma County $9.50
Golds/Awards: Gold (LA, OC); Best of Class (LA)

Chateau Ste. Michelle 1997 Johannisberg Riesling
Region: Washington, Columbia Valley $8
Golds/Awards: Gold (WC)

Concannon 1997 Limited Bottling Johannisberg Riesling
Region: California, Arroyo Seco $7.95
Golds/Awards: Double Gold (CA); Best of Class (CA)

Fetzer 1997 Riesling
Region: California $7.99
Golds/Awards: (RI, PR, LA); Double Gold (CA); Best of
Class, Grand Champion, Best White Wine (PR)

Dr. Konstantin Frank 1996 Semi-Dry Johannisberg Riesling
Region: New York, Finger Lakes $9.95
Golds/Awards: Gold (NW)

Gainey Vineyard 1997 Riesling
Region: California, Santa Ynez Valley $10
Golds/Awards: Four Star Gold (OC)

Greenwood Ridge 1997 Estate Bottled Riesling
Region: California, Mendocino $10.50
Golds/Awards: Gold (CA); Best of Class (CA)

Grove Mill 1996 Riesling
Region: New Zealand, Marlborough $14
Golds/Awards: Gold (WWC-90 pts)

Did You Know...?

Wine-producing regions aren't always warm.
For example, Germany, which is renowned
for its white wines, is on the same latitude
as Nova Scotia.

Hagafen 1997 Johannisberg Riesling
Region: California, Napa Valley $10
Golds/Awards: Gold (PR)

Hawthorne Mountain 1996 V.Q.A. Riesling
Region: Canada, Okanagan Valley   (Can $) 7.95
Golds/Awards: Gold (PR, RI); Chairman's Award (RI)

Henschke 1996 Julius Riesling
Region: Australia, Eden Valley $17.99
Golds/Awards: Gold (WWC-90 pts)

Heron Hill 1995 Estate Bottled Johannisberg Riesling
Region: New York, Finger Lakes $8.49
Golds/Awards: Gold (SD)

Heron Hill 1996 Ingle Vineyard Riesling
Region: New York, Finger Lakes $8.99
Golds/Awards: Gold (LA); Best of Class (LA)

Hillebrand Estates 1996 Trius Riesling
Region: Canada   (Can $) 19.95
Golds/Awards: Gold (IW)

Hogue 1997 Johannisberg Riesling
Region: Washington $7
Golds/Awards: Gold (WC)

Kendall-Jackson 1996 Vintner's Reserve Johannisberg Riesling
Region: California $11
Golds/Awards: Gold (SD, LA)

Lamoreaux Landing 1996 Semi-Dry Riesling
Region: New York, Finger Lakes $10
Golds/Awards: Gold (RI)

Mirassou 1996 Fifth Generation Family Selection Johannisberg Riesling
Region: California, Monterey County $7.50
Golds/Awards: Gold (WWC-90 pts)

Navarro 1996 Cluster Select Riesling
Region: California, Anderson Valley $35
Golds/Awards: Gold (WC)

Paraiso Springs 1995 Johannisberg Riesling
Region: California, Santa Lucia Highlands $9
Golds/Awards: Gold (WWC-92 pts)

Paul Thomas 1997 Johannisberg Riesling
Region: Washington $5.99
Golds/Awards: Gold (SD); Best of Class (SD)

Penfolds 1997 Rawsons Retreat Bin 202 Riesling
Region: Australia $7
Golds/Awards: Gold (IW)

Did You Know...?

The U.S. Bureau of Alcohol, Tobacco, and Firearms will no longer allow the word "Johannisberg" to appear on Riesling labels.

Renaissance 1996 Estate Bottled Riesling
Region: California, North Yuba
Golds/Awards: Gold (OC)
$9.99

Rusack Vineyards 1996 Lucas Select Riesling
Region: California
Golds/Awards: Double Gold (CA); Best of Class (CA)
$12.50

Selaks 1997 Riesling
Region: New Zealand, Marlborough
Golds/Awards: Gold (SY)
$12.99

Smith-Madrone 1997 Riesling
Region: California, Napa Valley
Golds/Awards: Gold (CA); Best of Class (CA)
$11

Stony Ridge 1997 Johannisberg Riesling
Region: California, Monterey County
Golds/Awards: Gold (CA)
$9

Swedish Hill 1997 Riesling
Region: New York, Finger Lakes
Golds/Awards: Gold (RI, SD)
$8.99

Temecula Crest 1997 Riesling
Region: California, Temecula
Golds/Awards: Gold (RI); Four Star Gold (OC)
$9.95

Unionville Vineyard 1997 Windfall Riesling
Region: New Jersey
Golds/Awards: Gold (RI); Chairman's Award (RI)
$7.99

Washington Hills 1997 Dry Riesling
Region: Washington, Columbia Valley
Golds/Awards: Gold (WC)
$5.99

Worden 1997 Cascade Collection Riesling
Region: Washington
Golds/Awards: Gold (LA)
$6.99

Did You Know...?

What is "corkiness"? Natural cork is increasingly
subject to cork taint, which imparts a moldy flavor
to wine that smells something like wet cardboard.

SAUVIGNON BLANC

This variety is responsible for some of the most distinctive and popular white wines of the world. It is grown virtually everywhere, with New Zealand, Australia, California, and South Africa the New World leaders, Washington and South America following.

What is most distinctive about wines made from Sauvignon Blanc is their crispness and their uniquely sharp aromas. Terms commonly used to describe this wine are grassy, musky, herbaceous, green fruits, nettles, and gooseberries.

The wine has lively acidity, making it a great match with Semillon, with which it is frequently blended and called White Meritage (a Bordeaux-style white blend).

Dry versions of Sauvignon Blanc are sometimes called Fumé Blanc, a term coined in the sixties by Robert Mondavi, who wanted to distinguish his dry Sauvignon Blanc from the popular jug wines of the time.

Food companions: Serve this wine chilled with all sorts of seafood and shellfish dinners, including raw oysters, Thai food, traditional white meat, chicken teriyaki, sushi and sashimi, tomato dishes, vegetarian Greek dishes, pesto, salad niçoise, or rich sauces such as hollandaise.

Adler Fels 1996 Organically Grown Grapes Fumé Blanc
Region: California, Sonoma County $10.50
Golds/Awards: Gold (SD)

Audubon Cellars 1997 Juliana Vineyards Sauvignon Blanc
Region: California, Napa Valley $11
Golds/Awards: Gold (OC)

Bellefleur Vineyards 1996 Sauvignon Blanc
Region: California $11
Golds/Awards: Gold (PR, NW, RI); Best of Class (NW);
Chairman's Award (RI)

Benziger 1996 Fumé Blanc
Region: California, Sonoma County $10
Golds/Awards: Gold (WWC-90 pts)

Beringer 1996 Sauvignon Blanc
Region: California, Napa Valley $9
Golds/Awards: Gold (WWC-90 pts)

Beringer 1997 Founder's Estate Sauvignon Blanc
Region: California $8.99
Golds/Awards: Gold (CA); Best of Class (CA)

Boeger 1997 Estate Bottled Sauvignon Blanc
Region: California, El Dorado $9.50
Golds/Awards: Gold (OC, CA); Best of Region, Best of
Class (CA)

Brancott Vineyards 1997 Reserve Sauvignon Blanc
Region: New Zealand, Marlborough $17
Golds/Awards: Gold (SY)

Brutocao 1996 Estate Bottled Sauvignon Blanc
Region: California, Mendocino $10.50
Golds/Awards: Gold (DA)

Did You Know...?

How do Argentineans drink their Sauvignon
Blanc? With rustic vegetable dishes, grilled
sliced beef in garlic sauce, and with *humitas*—
creamy corn mash served in a hollowed-out
squash with onion and tomato.

Cain 1996 Musque Ventana Vineyard Sauvignon Blanc
Region: California, Monterey $16
Golds/Awards: Gold (WWC-94 pts)

Cakebread 1996 Sauvignon Blanc
Region: California, Napa Valley $14
Golds/Awards: Gold (WWC-90 pts)

Did You Know...?

According to Robert Parker, "provocative"
foods to avoid that can alter the palate before a
serious tasting include hot spices, chocolate,
fresh garlic, and watercress.

Callaway 1997 Sauvignon Blanc
Region: California, Temecula $8
Golds/Awards: Gold (PR, NW)

Canyon Road 1997 Sauvignon Blanc
Region: California $6.99
Golds/Awards: Gold (NW, DA, SD, WC, GH); Best of Class
(SD, WC)

Chalk Hill 1996 Sauvignon Blanc
Region: California, Sonoma County $19
Golds/Awards: Gold (WWC-93 pts)

Chateau Los Boldos 1997 Sauvignon Blanc
Region: Chile $8.99
Golds/Awards: Gold (VN)

Chateau Souverain 1997 Sauvignon Blanc
Region: California, Alexander Valley $8.50
Golds/Awards: Gold (LA)

Cloudy Bay 1996 Sauvignon Blanc
Region: New Zealand, Marlborough $14
Golds/Awards: Gold (WWC-90 pts)

De Lorimier 1997 Estate Bottled Sauvignon Blanc
Region: California, Alexander Valley $10
Golds/Awards: Gold (SD)

Sauvignon Blanc

De Redcliffe 1996 Reserve Sauvignon Blanc
Region: New Zealand, Marlborough $16
Golds/Awards: Gold (WWC-91 pts)

Eos Estate Winery 1997 Sauvignon Blanc
Region: California, Paso Robles $12
Golds/Awards: Gold (CA); Best of Class (CA)

Estancia 1996 Pinnacles Fumé Blanc
Region: California, Monterey County $10
Golds/Awards: Gold (WWC-94 pts)

Did You Know...?

Biodynamic viticulture operates on the principle that the more micro-organisms there are in the soil, the more these will act as predators of and competitors with unwanted, harmful micro-organisms.

Fallbrook 1996 Sauvignon Blanc
Region: California $7
Golds/Awards: Gold (NW); Best of Class, Best of Varietal, Best New World Sauvignon Blanc (NW)

Fetzer 1996 Echo Ridge Sauvignon Blanc
Region: California $7.99
Golds/Awards: Gold (RI, LA); Best of Class (LA)

Filsinger 1997 Fumé Blanc
Region: California, Temecula $6
Golds/Awards: Gold (CA); Best of Class (CA)

Foley Estates 1996 Sauvignon Blanc
Region: California, Santa Barbara County $14
Golds/Awards: Gold (WWC-93 pts)

Fountain Grove 1996 Sauvignon Blanc
Region: California $9
Golds/Awards: Gold (OC)

Gan Eden 1995 Sauvignon Blanc
Region: California $10
Golds/Awards: Gold (SD)

Gary Farrell 1997 Sauvignon Blanc
Region: California, Russian River Valley $15
Golds/Awards: Gold (RI)

Geyser Peak 1997 Sauvignon Blanc
Region: California, Sonoma County $8.50
Golds/Awards: Gold (PR, DA, WC)

Greenwood Ridge 1997 Sauvignon Blanc
Region: California, Mendocino County $11
Golds/Awards: Gold (CA); Best of Class (CA)

Grgich Hills 1996 Fumé Blanc
Region: California, Napa Valley $16
Golds/Awards: Gold (RI, SD); Best of Class, Best in Show (SD)

Grove Mill 1996 Sauvignon Blanc
Region: New Zealand, Marlborough $17
Golds/Awards: Gold (WWC-93 pts)

Grove Mill 1997 Sauvignon Blanc
Region: New Zealand, Marlborough $18
Golds/Awards: Gold (SY)

Handley Cellars 1996 Sauvignon Blanc
Region: California, Dry Creek Valley $13
Golds/Awards: Gold (PR, NW, LA); Best of Class (PR, LA)

Hanna Winery 1996 Sauvignon Blanc
Region: California, Russian River Valley $11
Golds/Awards: Gold (PR)

Did You Know...?

A Colorado school principal took a group of seventh and eighth graders to France for a one-week lesson in French culture. Their experience included a three-hour Parisian meal, where they sampled escargots, duck, and were allowed to taste *thimblefuls* of wine—all in the context of an educational presentation on French cuisine, culture, and lifestyle. Upon his return, the teacher was demoted and recommended for transfer by his superintendent.

Hogue 1997 Fumé Blanc
Region: Washington, Columbia Valley $7.95
Golds/Awards: Gold (EN)

Indigo Hills 1996 Sauvignon Blanc
Region: California, Mendocino County $8
Golds/Awards: Gold (SD)

Jory Winery 1996 Sauvignon Blanc
Region: New Mexico $15
Golds/Awards: Gold (NW)

Did You Know...?

New Mexico bills itself as the oldest wine region in the
United States. Two Franciscan priests
planted "mission grapes" at Senecú,
a Piro Indian pueblo near present-
day Socorro, New Mexico. The
monks at Senecú began producing
sacramental wine in 1633.

Kenwood 1997 Sauvignon Blanc
Region: California, Sonoma County $10
Golds/Awards: Gold (OC, WC); Best of Class (WC)

Lakespring 1996 Sauvignon Blanc
Region: California $8
Golds/Awards: Gold (OC)

Lincoln 1997 Sauvignon Blanc
Region: New Zealand, Marlborough $14.99
Golds/Awards: Gold (SY)

Lolonis 1997 Organically Grown Grapes Fumé Blanc
Region: California, Mendocino $11
Golds/Awards: Gold (OC)

Matanzas Creek 1996 Sauvignon Blanc
Region: California, Sonoma County $18
Golds/Awards: Gold (WWC-91 pts)

Maurice Car'rie 1996 Sauvignon Blanc
Region: California, Temecula $6.95
Golds/Awards: Gold (RI)

Sauvignon Blanc

Miguel Torres 1997 Santa Digna Sauvignon Blanc
Region: Chile $7.99
Golds/Awards: Gold (VN)

Murphy-Goode 1996 The Deuce Fumé II
Region: California, Alexander Valley $24
Golds/Awards: Gold (WWC-93 pts)

Murphy-Goode 1996 The Reserve Fumé
Region: California, Alexander Valley $16.50
Golds/Awards: Gold (WWC-92 pts)

Murphy-Goode 1997 Fumé Blanc
Region: California, Sonoma County $11.50
Golds/Awards: Gold (SD)

Nautilus 1997 Sauvignon Blanc
Region: New Zealand, Marlborough $13.99
Golds/Awards: Gold (SY)

Navarro 1996 Sauvignon Blanc
Region: California, Mendocino $12.50
Golds/Awards: Gold (PR)

Neil Ellis 1997 Sauvignon Blanc
Region: South Africa, Groenekloof $12
Golds/Awards: Gold (WWC-90)

Palliser Estate 1997 Estate Sauvignon Blanc
Region: New Zealand $19
Golds/Awards: Gold (IW)

Peter Michael 1996 L'Apres-Midi Sauvignon Blanc
Region: California, Napa County $20
Golds/Awards: Gold (WWC-91 pts)

Did You Know...?

The first patent for a corkscrew was taken out in 1795 by Samuel Henshall of Birmingham, England. The screw, known familiarly as "the worm," was actually used as far back as the 1630s for cleaning and loading firearms.

Robert Mondavi 1995 To-Kalon Vineyard I Block Fumé Blanc
Region: California, Napa Valley $50
Golds/Awards: Gold (WWC-92 pts)

Did You Know...?

Investing . . . fun? No stuffy boardrooms for Mondavi shareholders, who have their annual meeting at the Oakville winery, where they taste Mondavi wines, meet the winemakers, and enjoy a gourmet lunch. And joining "Partner's Circle," regardless of how many shares you own, brings you newsletters, discounts on Mondavi wines, invitations to exclusive shareholder events, and more.

Rodney Strong 1997 Charlotte's Home Sauvignon Blanc
Region: California, Northern Sonoma $10
Golds/Awards: Gold (RI)

St. Supéry 1997 Dollarhide Ranch Sauvignon Blanc
Region: California, Napa Valley $10.55
Golds/Awards: Gold (WWC-91 pts, PR, DA, CA); Best of Class (CA)

Selaks 1997 Sauvignon Blanc
Region: New Zealand, Marlborough $12.99
Golds/Awards: Gold (SY)

Sierra Vista 1997 Estate Bottled Sauvignon Blanc
Region: California, El Dorado $8.50
Golds/Awards: Gold (NW)

Stellenzicht 1996 Sauvignon Blanc
Region: South Africa, Stellenbosch $17.99
Golds/Awards: Gold (WWC-90 pts)

Taltarni 1997 Victoria Estate Grown Sauvignon Blanc
Region: Australia, Victoria $14.50
Golds/Awards: Gold (NW, PR); Best of Class (NW)

Temecula Crest 1997 Sauvignon Blanc
Region: California, Temecula $9.95
Golds/Awards: Gold (LA)

Trellis Vineyards 1997 Special Selection Sauvignon Blanc
Region: California $8.99
Golds/Awards: Gold (WC)

V. Sattui 1996 Suzanne's Vineyard Sauvignon Blanc
Region: California, Napa Valley $12.75
Golds/Awards: Gold (PR)

Vavasour 1996 Sauvignon Blanc
Region: New Zealand, Marlborough $19
Golds/Awards: Gold (WWC-90 pts)

Vavasour 1996 Single Vineyard Sauvignon Blanc
Region: New Zealand, Marlborough $25
Golds/Awards: Gold (WWC-93 pts)

Villa Maria 1997 Clifford Bay Reserve Sauvignon Blanc
Region: New Zealand, Marlborough $38
Golds/Awards: Gold (SY)

Viu Manent 1997 Sauvignon Blanc
Region: Chile, Colchagua Valley $10
Golds/Awards: Gold (VI)

Voss 1997 Sauvignon Blanc
Region: California, Napa Valley $12.50
Golds/Awards: Gold (WS, CA, WWC-95 pts); Best Sauvignon
Blanc (WS); Best of Class, Best of California (CA)

Windsor 1996 Middle Ridge Vineyards Fumé Blanc
Region: California, Mendocino County $11
Golds/Awards: Gold (RI)

Did You Know...?

"The best use of bad wine is to drive
away poor relations."
                    —French proverb

SEMILLON

This is an excellent, high-yielding grape that produces classy and distinctive white wines that are low in acidity. Because of its weight and plentifulness, Semillon is frequently used as a blending wine, to add background to Chardonnay (called Semchard), or to add weight and fruit to Sauvignon Blanc in White Meritage, or Bordeaux-style blends.

Susceptible to botrytis, Semillon is often made into rich, sweet dessert wines (listed in the Dessert and Fortified Wines chapter).

California, Washington, and Australia are making wonderful (and often inexpensive) Semillon, as are Chile and Argentina.

Food companions: Crisp, fresh, green Semillons go well with shellfish and Pacific Rim cuisine. Richer Semillons complement oily fish and tomato-based sauces.

Semillon

Barnard Griffin 1997 Semillon
Region: Washington, Columbia Valley $9.95
Golds/Awards: Gold (EN)

Basedow 1996 Semillon
Region: Australia, Barossa Valley $9.99
Golds/Awards: Gold (SY)

Henschke 1996 Louis Semillon
Region: Australia, Eden Valley $21
Golds/Awards: Gold (WWC-90 pts)

Hogue 1996 Semillon
Region: Washington, Columbia Valley $8
Golds/Awards: Gold (RI); Chairman's Award (RI)

Indian Springs Vineyards 1997 Semillon
Region: California, Nevada County $10.50
Golds/Awards: Gold (OC)

Kendall-Jackson 1996 Vintner's Reserve Semillon
Region: California $12
Golds/Awards: Gold (LA); Best of Class (LA)

Morris 1996 Semillon
Region: Australia, South Eastern Australia $14
Golds/Awards: Gold (SY)

Rosenblum 1996 Semillon
Region: California, Sonoma Valley $14
Golds/Awards: Gold (WWC-90 pts)

Stellenzicht 1996 Reserve Semillon
Region: South Africa, Stellenbosch $16
Golds/Awards: Gold (WWC-91 pts)

Stellenzicht 1997 Reserve Semillon
Region: South Africa, Stellenbosch $27.95
Golds/Awards: Gold (WS); Best S. African Dry White (WS)

Washington Hills Cellars 1996 Semillon
Region: Washington, Columbia Valley $7.99
Golds/Awards: Gold (EN); Grand Prize (EN)

Did You Know...?

"Beer is made by men, wine by God!"
—Martin Luther

VIOGNIER

There's nothing quite so humbling as bumbling through French words with a leftover midwestern accent. So for your enlightenment, the pronunciation is *vee-on-YAY*.

This Rhône white wine grape is difficult to grow and rather rare. In recent years it's captured the imagination of California as well as Australian winemakers, who love its unusual spicy flavors and its aromas of violets, peaches, and apricots. It makes an excellent Riesling-like white wine, but it can also be vinified in the style of an oaky Chardonnay. With American consumers looking for Chardonnay alternatives, Viognier's fortunes will no doubt steadily rise.

Food companions: Quiche, striped bass, truffles, Chinese dishes spiced with ginger, Indian food, crab, and lobster all pair nicely with Viognier.

Viognier

Alban 1996 Viognier
Region: California, Central Coast $20
Golds/Awards: Gold (WWC-90 pts)

Bonterra 1996 Viognier
Region: California, North Coast $23
Golds/Awards: Gold (WWC-90 pts)

Eberle 1996 Fralich Vineyard Viognier
Region: California, Paso Robles $20
Golds/Awards: Gold (WWC-91 pts)

Edna Valley 1997 Fralich Vineyard Viognier
Region: California $18
Golds/Awards: Gold (LA)

Fess Parker 1996 Viognier
Region: California, Santa Barbara County $22
Golds/Awards: Gold (WWC-91 pts)

Hart Winery 1996 Estate Bottled Viognier
Region: California, Temecula $20
Golds/Awards: Gold (LA); Best of Class (LA)

Hawley Wines 1997 Viognier
Region: California, Dry Creek Valley $24
Golds/Awards: Gold (CA); Best of Class (CA)

Horton 1995 Viognier
Region: Virginia $20
Golds/Awards: Gold (WWC-92 pts)

Joseph Phelps 1996 Vin du Mistral Viognier
Region: California, Napa Valley $28
Golds/Awards: Gold (WWC-91 pts)

Kendall-Jackson 1995 Grand Reserve Viognier
Region: California $25
Golds/Awards: Gold (WWC-90 pts)

Did You Know...?

"What is the definition of a good wine? It should start and end with a smile." —William Sokolin

Viognier WHITE

McDowell 1996 Viognier
Region: California, Mendocino $16
Golds/Awards: Gold (NW); Best of Class, Best of Varietal (NW)

Perry Creek Vineyards 1997 El Dorado Estate Viognier
Region: California $15
Golds/Awards: Gold (LA)

Preston 1997 Estate Bottled Barrel Fermented Viognier
Region: California, Dry Creek Valley $20
Golds/Awards: Gold (SD, LA); Best of Class (SD)

R.H. Phillips 1997 Estate Bottled Viognier
Region: California, Dunnigan Hills $12
Golds/Awards: Gold (CA); Best of Class (CA)

Renwood 1996 Viognier
Region: California, Amador County $21.95
Golds/Awards: Gold (WWC-90 pts)

Rosenblum 1997 Viognier
Region: California, Santa Barbara County $15
Golds/Awards: Gold (WWC-91 pts)

Sunstone 1996 Viognier
Region: California, Santa Barbara County $32
Golds/Awards: Gold (WWC-90 pts)

Thomas Coyne 1997 Viognier
Region: California $15
Golds/Awards: Gold (OC, CA); Best of Class (CA)

Venezia 1997 Sonoma Moment Viognier
Region: California, Alexander Valley $19.99
Golds/Awards: Gold (RI, WC); Best of Class, Sweepstakes
White (WC)

Did You Know...?

Alcohol is a naturally occurring substance in
much that we consume—including low levels
in fruit juice and even Coca-Cola.

WHITE BLENDS

Most wines are blends. After all, it's the winemaker's way of balancing out and enhancing certain characteristics in the varietal that's used as a base. But in the U.S., if the base wine, red or white, is made of less than 75 percent of that grape, the resulting wine cannot take the varietal name.

Some wineries give these blended wines fancy proprietary names; others simply give them a hyphenated name, the result of a balanced and happy marriage.

Either way, you're likely to find high-quality, delicious, but sometimes expensive wines in this section. To me, at least, Semillon-Chardonnay seems more interesting than either of these varietals alone. It so happens that I'm not the only one in the wine world who likes this trend, which is prevalent throughout the New World. The Australians, in particular, love blended wines—and love giving them unpretentious names derived from their constituent parts. To discover what foods will best complement white blends, find out which grape comprises the largest percentage of the wine, and refer to that varietal's section of this book.

Meritage or Bordeaux-style blends To use the trademarked name *Meritage,* an American wine must be composed only of specific grapes that grow in the Bordeaux region of France. For white wines these include Sauvignon Blanc, Semillon, and Muscadelle.

Semchard A classic combination of Semillon and Chardonnay.

Archery Summit 1996 Vireton Blanc des Collines Rouges (Mixed Whites)
Region: Oregon $21
Golds/Awards: Gold (WWC-90 pts)

Carmenet 1995 Paragon Vineyard White Meritage
Region: California, Edna Valley $15
Golds/Awards: Gold (WWC-92 pts)

Did You Know...?

Since laws in the U.S. don't prohibit the creative blending of grape varietals, as they do in France, California winemakers have the freedom to be innovative with their white and red blends.

Benziger 1995 Tribute White (Bordeaux-style)
Region: California, Sonoma Mountain $17
Golds/Awards: Gold (WWC-91 pts)

Cardinale 1996 Royale (Bordeaux-style)
Region: California $20
Golds/Awards: Gold (WWC-91 pts)

Fantaisie 1996 Menage à Trois White Wine (Mixed Whites)
Region: California $8
Golds/Awards: Gold (NW); Best of Class (NW)

Handley 1997 Brightlighter White (Mixed Whites)
Region: California, Anderson Valley $8.75
Golds/Awards: Gold (CA); Best of Class (CA)

Kendall-Jackson 1995 Grand Reserve White Meritage
Region: California $25
Golds/Awards: Gold (NW); Best of Class and Varietal (NW)

Kingston Estate 1997 Semillon Sauvignon Blanc
Region: Australia $7.99
Golds/Awards: Gold (IW)

Merryvale 1996 Vignette (Bordeaux-style)
Region: California, Napa Valley $22
Golds/Awards: Gold (WWC-93 pts)

Mount Palomar 1996 Rey Sol Le Mediterrane Blanc (Rhône-style)
Region: California, Temecula $16
Golds/Awards: Gold (DA, OC)

Mount Palomar 1997 Rey Sol Le Mediterrane Blanc (Rhône-style)
Region: California, Temecula $16
Golds/Awards: Gold (RI); Chairman's Award (RI)

Rosemount 1997 Diamond Label Semillon/Chardonnay
Region: Australia, Southeastern Region $8
Golds/Awards: Gold (NW); Best of Class and Varietal (NW)

St. Supéry 1996 White Meritage
Region: California, Napa Valley $20
Golds/Awards: Gold (OC, LA, RI)

Venezia 1996 Barrel Fermented Bianca Nuovo Mondo (Bordeaux-style)
Region: California, Alexander Valley $19.99
Golds/Awards: Gold (OC)

Washington Hills 1996 Semillion/Chardonnay
Region: Washington, Columbia Valley $7.99
Golds/Awards: Gold (NW)

Yorkville Cellars 1995 Randle Hill Vineyard Eleanor of Aquitaine (Bordeaux-style)
Region: California, Mendocino $16
Golds/Awards: Gold (WWC-93 pts)

Did You Know...?

A well-known French winery, Château Giscours, is under investigation for allegedly doctoring their 1995 vintage Bordeaux with milk, tartartic acid, wood chips, and grapes from a different appellation—all of which are either frowned upon or illegal in France. This very wine was rated 92 out of a possible 100 by *Wine Spectator,* America's most snobby wine mag.

Blush Wines

White Zinfandel
Other Rosés

BLUSH WINES

Don't listen to wine bullies. There's no reason to blush, and nothing politically incorrect, naïve, or unsophisticated about pink wines. There are plenty of terrific examples of blush wines, especially the ones on this section, which were stupendous enough to win gold medals from some of the greatest world wine experts.

White Zinfandel Despite its name, White Zinfandel is actually pink. Made from Zinfandel grapes, the juice is left in contact with the skins just long enough to tint the juice. (Wine gets its color from the pigment in the grape skins.)

White Zinfandel became wildly popular in the last few years, and California is the biggest New World producer. The wines are fresh and fruity, on the sweet side, but with enough acidity to balance out the sugar. Some White Zins have a bit of spritziness. Others have some Riesling or Muscat blended in to add more balance and character.

Wine snobs don't take this wine seriously. However, the fact that it's light, fruit-filled, and lively—and made to be drunk young—gives it a lot of popular appeal, especially for people who wouldn't otherwise drink wine.

Food companions: Rosés marry well with light foods such as vegetable hors d'oeuvres, shrimp cocktail, or picnic fare. The darker, fruitier ones can also be enjoyed alongside couscous, roast pork, grilled tuna, and red snapper.

Adam Puchta Winery NV Riefenstahler
Region: Missouri $7.25
Golds/Awards: Gold (RI, SD)

Augusta Winery NV River Valley Blush
Region: Missouri $7
Golds/Awards: Gold (PR)

Barefoot Cellars NV Barefoot White Zinfandel
Region: California $4.99
Golds/Awards: Gold (SD, CA); Best of California, Best of
Class (CA)

Baron Herzog 1997 White Zinfandel
Region: California $7.49
Golds/Awards: Gold (RI)

Beaulieu Vineyard 1996 Signet Collection Pinot Noir Vin Gris
Region: California, Napa Valley $7.95
Golds/Awards: Gold (WWC-92 pts)

Beringer 1997 White Zinfandel
Region: California $6
Golds/Awards: Gold (NW); Best of Class, Best of Varietal (NW)

Blossom Hill 1996 White Zinfandel
Region: California $4.49
Golds/Awards: Gold (NW, OC)

Concannon 1996 Righteously Rosé
Region: California $8.95
Golds/Awards: Gold (WWC-90 pts)

Corbett Canyon 1997 Coastal Classic White Zinfandel
Region: California, Arroyo Grande $4.99
Golds/Awards: Gold (NW); Best of Class (NW)

Did You Know...?

A great vintage wine will bring less
pleasure than a lesser vintage if both wines
are consumed young. A blockbuster vintage
wine may take several years to mature into
something that's enjoyable, while a lesser wine
may be delicious immediately.

Cuthills Vineyard 1997 Autumn Blush Foch de Channel
Region: Nebraska $12
Golds/Awards: Gold (NW); Best of Class (NW)

DeLoach 1997 White Zinfandel
Region: California, Sonoma County $8
Golds/Awards: Gold (NW); Best of Class (NW)

Fetzer 1996 White Zinfandel
Region: California $6.99
Golds/Awards: Gold (NW)

Fetzer 1997 White Zinfandel
Region: California $5.99
Golds/Awards: Gold (OC)

Glen Ellen 1996 Proprietor's Reserve White Zinfandel
Region: California $5
Golds/Awards: Gold (RI)

Goose Watch Winery 1996 Rosé of Isabella
Region: New York, Finger Lakes $7.50
Golds/Awards: Gold (PR)

Hart Winery 1997 Collins Ranch Grenache Rosé
Region: California, Cucamonga Valley $9
Golds/Awards: Gold (PR, NW, RI, SD, OC); Best of Class
(PR, NW, RI, SD); Best of Category (RI); Best of Varietal,
Best New World Blush Wine (NW)

Heron Hill NV Bluff Point Blush
Region: New York, Finger Lakes $4.99
Golds/Awards: Gold (RI)

Did You Know...?

What does the condition of the label on an old bottle of
wine have to do with what's inside the bottle? Some
would say that a moldy label is a good
sign—that the wine's been cellared
properly in a cool, damp place. But Asian
investors don't care; they consider bottle
and label condition high priority
when investing in old wines.

Did You Know...?

Lakewood Vineyards calls their 1996 Delaware the "White Zin" alternative. Indeed, their Delaware went head to head with a large field of White Zinfandels at the National Orange Show (PR) and took the only gold.

Lakewood Vineyards 1996 Delaware
Region: New York, Finger Lakes $5.49
Golds/Awards: Gold (PR)

Les Vieux Cepages 1995 Ronfleur
Region: California $6.99
Golds/Awards: Gold (WWC-90 pts)

Maurice Car'rie 1997 White Zinfandel
Region: California, Temecula $5.95
Golds/Awards: Gold (NW)

Meier's Wine Cellars NV Pink Catawba
Region: Ohio $3.99
Golds/Awards: Gold (PR)

Paraiso Springs 1995 Baby Blush
Region: California, Monterey County $12.50
Golds/Awards: Gold (WWC-93 pts)

Paraiso Springs 1997 Baby Blush Rides Again
Region: California, Monterey County $15
Golds/Awards: Gold (WWC-93 pts)

St. James Winery NV Pink Catawba
Region: Missouri $6.99
Golds/Awards: Gold (NW, RI)

Stone Hill NV Pink Catawba
Region: Missouri $6.79
Golds/Awards: Gold (NW, RI)

Swanson Vineyards 1997 Rosé of Sangiovese
Region: California, Napa Valley $14
Golds/Awards: Gold (LA, WWC-91 pts, RI); Best of Class, Division Sweepstakes Award (LA); Chairman's Award (RI)

Sylvester Winery 1996 Kiara Reserve White Zinfandel
Region: California, Paso Robles $6
Golds/Awards: Gold (SD); Best of Class (SD)

V. Sattui Winery 1997 White Zinfandel
Region: California $7.75
Golds/Awards: Gold (LA)

Van Roekel Vineyards 1997 Estate Bottled Rosé of Syrah
Region: California, Temecula $9.95
Golds/Awards: Gold (RI, SD); Chairman's Award (RI)

Weinstock Cellars 1997 White Zinfandel
Region: California $6.49
Golds/Awards: Gold (RI)

Windsor 1997 Rosé du Soleil
Region: California, Russian River Valley $11
Golds/Awards: Gold (RI)

Wollersheim Winery 1997 Prairie Blush
Region: Wisconsin $7
Golds/Awards: Gold (SD)

Did You Know...?

Many wine producers and merchants are inadvertently aiding counterfeiters through such policies as relabeling and recorking. As a service to collectors, some Bordeaux wineries will recondition old bottles by providing a new cork or a new label and capsule. In recorking, bottles are often topped up with wine if the levels are too low. This makes it hard for experts later on to determine the wine's authenticity.

Sparkling Wines

Champagne-style
Miscellaneous Sparklers

SPARKLING WINES

Open up any wine and food magazine around holiday time and you're bound to read about sparkling wines. They'll also tell you that sparkling wines shouldn't be reserved for special occasions. I couldn't agree more. There are delicious sparkling wines in this chapter that, once you've tried them, you'll want to keep on hand for spontaneous gleeful moments.

There are lots of sparkling wines being made outside of France's Champagne district. California, the Pacific Northwest, and Australia are the New World leaders. Sparkling wine may be made from Chardonnay, Pinot Noir, Pinot Blanc, Pinot Gris, Riesling, Muscat, Symphony, and others, including native American grapes such as Catawba.

The main difference between traditional champagne-style wines and other sparkling wines has to do with the vinification method used. See Appendix 3 for an explanation of *méthode champenoise,* or the champagne style.

Blanc de Blancs (also written Blanc de Blanc) In French this means, literally, "white from whites" and refers to wines that are made exclusively from white grapes. Many Blanc de Blancs sparklers are blends of different varieties, with Chardonnay the key component.

Blanc de Noirs (also written Blanc de Noir) These are light-colored sparkling wines (the translation is "white from blacks") made from black-skinned (red wine) grapes by fermenting the crushed grapes or grape juice, known as the must, without the skins, and therefore without the pigment that gives wine its ruby hues.

Brut France has laws that govern the maximum amount of residual sugar a champagne may have and still be labeled Brut. In America and elsewhere a Brut is merely a very dry sparkling wine.

Food companions: Sparkling wines are perhaps the most enjoyable wines to serve with food merely because it is so rarely done, and your guests will be pleasantly surprised. Although champagne-style sparklers are stunning consumed on their own—without any food whatsoever—they are also good alongside caviar, oysters, smoked salmon, and lobster salad.

Did You Know...?

The pressure in a bottle of champagne is about 90 pounds per square inch (about three times the pressure in an automobile tire).

Baywood 1992 Brut
Region: California, Napa Valley $19
Golds/Awards: Gold (LA)

Baywood 1993 Blanc de Noir
Region: California, Napa Valley $19
Golds/Awards: Gold (NW); Best of Class (NW)

Baywood 1993 Brut
Region: California, Napa Valley $19
Golds/Awards: Gold (CA)

Cook's NV Spumante
Region: New York $4.49
Golds/Awards: Gold (NW); Best of Class (NW)

Domaine Carneros 1993 Sparkling Brut
Region: California, Carneros $17.95
Golds/Awards: Gold (DA)

Glenora 1989 20th Anniv. Méthode Champenoise Cuvée
Region: New York $24.99
Golds/Awards: Gold (WWC-90 pts)

Gloria Ferrer Champagne Caves NV Blanc de Noirs
Region: California, Carneros $15
Golds/Awards: Gold (DA)

Gloria Ferrer Champagne Caves 1988 Late Disgorged Brut Cuvée
Region: California, Carneros $25
Golds/Awards: Gold (WWC-92 pts)

Gloria Ferrer Champagne Caves 1989 Late Disgorged Cuvée Brut
Region: California $27
Golds/Awards: Gold (NW, PR); Best of Class, Best Sparkling Wine (PR)

Gloria Ferrer 1989 Royal Cuvée Brut
Region: California, Carneros $19
Golds/Awards: Gold (WWC-91 pts)

Goose Watch Winery NV Golden Spumante
Region: New York, Finger Lakes $9.50
Golds/Awards: Gold (PR, SD); Best of Class (SD)

Handley Cellars 1993 Brut
Region: California, Anderson Valley $22
Golds/Awards: Gold (LA); Best of Class (LA)

Hester Creek 1996 Blanc de Noir
Region: Canada, British Columbia $9.95
Golds/Awards: Gold (NW); Best of Class, Best of Varietal (NW)

Iron Horse 1990 Blanc de Blancs
Region: California, Sonoma County $45
Golds/Awards: Gold (WWC-92 pts)

Iron Horse 1992 Estate Bottled "Russian Cuvée"
Region: California, Sonoma County $23.50
Golds/Awards: Gold (OC)

Jordan 1994 J
Region: California, Sonoma County $28
Golds/Awards: Gold (LA, OC, CA)

Korbel NV Méthode Champenoise Rouge Champagne
Region: California, Sonoma County $11.99
Golds/Awards: Gold (NW)

Korbel NV Méthode Champenoise Chardonnay Champagne
Region: California $12.99
Golds/Awards: Gold (NW)

Did You Know...?

Korbel is the official sponsor of New Year's
celebrations in Times Square beginning in
1999 and continuing through 2007.

Laetitia NV Select Brut
Region: California, San Luis Obispo $13.99
Golds/Awards: Gold (LA)

Laetitia 1993 Elegance Rosé
Region: California $23
Golds/Awards: Gold (PR, LA, OC); Best of Class (LA)

Did You Know...?

Never put champagne in your freezer to quickly chill it before company comes. It can freeze and explode in as little as 15 minutes. In a bucket of ice and water, it will chill in about 20 minutes.

Magnotta 1995 Sparkling Vidal Icewine
Region: Canada, Niagara Peninsula   (Can $) 34.95
Golds/Awards: Gold (BR)

Magnotta 1996 Sparkling Vidal Icewine
Region: Canada, Niagara Peninsula   (Can $) 34.95
Golds/Awards: Gold (IV, VI)

Mirassou 1991 Sparkling Brut
Region: California, Monterey $22.75
Golds/Awards: Gold (NW)

Mumm Napa NV Cuvée Blanc de Noirs
Region: California, Napa Valley $15.95
Golds/Awards: Gold (SD)

Mumm Napa NV Cuvée Prestige Brut
Region: California, Napa Valley $15.95
Golds/Awards: Gold (SD)

Mumm Napa NV Cuvée Blanc De Blancs
Region: California, Napa Valley $19
Golds/Awards: Gold (NW); Double Gold (CA); Best of Class (CA)

Oasis NV Brut
Region: Virginia $12.50/375 ml
Golds/Awards: Gold (WWC-92 pts)

Robert & Hunter 1992 Extended Tirage Brut de Noirs
Region: California, Sonoma Valley $25
Golds/Awards: Gold (NW, WC)

Roederer Estate 1991 L'Ermitage Brut
Region: California, Anderson Valley $33
Golds/Awards: Gold (WWC-93 pts)

S. Anderson Vineyard 1993 Brut
Region: California, Napa Valley $25
Golds/Awards: Gold (PR)

St. James Winery NV Sparkling Blush
Region: Missouri $6.99
Golds/Awards: Gold (PR)

Scharffenberger NV Méthode Champenoise Brut
Region: California, Mendocino County $16.25
Golds/Awards: Gold (OC, WWC-90 pts)

Schramsberg 1993 Blanc de Blancs
Region: California, Napa Valley $19.99
Golds/Awards: Gold (WWC-92 pts)

Did You Know...?

The emergence of fine sparkling wine in the U.S. can be traced, some say, to Chinese premier Chou En-lai's visit to the Nixon White House. When he was toasted with Schramsberg, it caused such a fizz that European and American investors jumped into the California sparkling wine game, giving American bubbly a new presence in the marketplace.

Seaview 1993 Pinot Noir–Chardonnay Brut
Region: Australia, South Eastern Australia $13.50
Golds/Awards: Gold (WWC-91 pts)

Seppelt 1993 Harper's Range Sparkling Shiraz
Region: Australia, South Eastern Australia $18
Golds/Awards: Gold (WWC-90 pts)

Sumac Ridge 1993 Stellar's Jay Brut Sparkling Wine
Region: Canada, British Columbia   (Can $) 19.95
Golds/Awards: Gold (NW); Best of Class (NW)

Sutter Home NV Fre-Spumante
Region: California $5.99
Golds/Awards: Gold (SD)

Swedish Hill NV Blanc de Blanc
Region: New York, Finger Lakes $10.99
Golds/Awards: Gold (PR)

Thornton 1990 Brut Reserve Sparkling Wine
Region: California, Temecula $32
Golds/Awards: Gold (NW, SD); Best of Class (NW, SD);
Best of Varietal, Best New World Champagne/Sparkling
Wine (NW); Best in Show (SD)

V. Sattui Winery 1994 Blanc de Noirs
Region: California, Napa Valley $16.75
Golds/Awards: Gold (WC)

Westport Riv. 1993 Méthode Champenoise RJR Cuvée Brut
Region: Massachusetts $24.95
Golds/Awards: Gold (NW)

Windsor 1994 Brut Méthode Champenoise
Region: California, Sonoma County $13
Golds/Awards: Gold (RI, LA); Chairman's Award (RI)

Windsor 1994 Private Reserve Blanc de Noirs
Region: California, Sonoma County $14
Golds/Awards: Gold (RI, WC, SD); Double Gold (CA); Best
of Class (RI, WC, CA, SD); Best of Category (RI)

Did You Know...?

Market watchers say that December 31, 1999,
will be one of the biggest nights ever in terms of
champagne and sparkling wine consumption.
They also say the shortage of such new-
millennium bubbly will cause prices to pop
sky high. Stock up now!

Dessert and Fortified Wines

Icewine
Miscellaneous Sweet Wines
Muscat
Port
Sherry

DESSERT AND FORTIFIED WINES

I f you haven't discovered the incredible world of sweet and/or fortified wines, now's your chance. Try some wines you wouldn't ordinarily buy. They add intrigue to a dinner party with friends, and many aren't too expensive, since a tiny glass is all one usually needs.

For an explanation of the terms *late harvest* and *botrytized*, see Appendix 3.

Icewine (also known as Eiswein) One of the best things about researching and writing this book was discovering icewine. Now I tell all my friends about it. It's surprising how many Americans have never heard of icewine, especially given that our northern neighbor, Canada, has surpassed Germany in world recognition of this exotic wine. This is a very sweet dessert wine made from an interesting process. The grapes are allowed to freeze right on the vine, producing a high concentration of sugar in the juice when pressed. A handful of North American wineries, particularly New York and Canadian, make this treasured wine. Try it as dessert, or with sweets such as cakes, fruit tarts or pies, and flan.

Muscat Muscat is a family of grapes that's been around for centuries. There are at least four varieties of Muscat, ranging in hues, thus producing wines that vary from pale golden to dark, dark brown. Some Muscats have nicknames that reflect their hue, hence Orange Muscat, Black Muscat, and so on. Muscat Alexandria and Muscat Canelli are but two Muscat varieties. Muscat grapes are known for their incredibly perfumed berries. New World varieties include off-dry sipping wines and sweet late harvest styles that often have a distinctive spicy aroma. Depending on the wine, of course, Muscat is ideal as an aperitif. Try it with hard cheese, foie gras, or with prosciutto and melon. For dessert it complements fruit pies and puddings.

Port Port is a fortified wine that can be made from any grape variety. Portugal is where the world's most famous ports hail from, but South Africa, California, and Australia

are the New World leaders in producing outstanding ports as well.

Here's the process: red wine grapes are crushed and begin to ferment in the usual way. After two to four days, the partially fermented grape juice has about 6 percent alcohol and about 10 percent residual sugar, which is quite sweet. At this point, the grape juice is run off into containers holding 154-proof neutral wine spirits. The spirits act to stop the fermenting process, and what's left is very flavorful, very sweet wine with around 20 percent alcohol.

There are two main types of port: wood-aged and vintage ports. Wood-aged ports are ready to drink when bottled, and are made from many different vintages, added during the aging process to achieve a continuity of style. Ruby port is one type of wood-aged port that's dark red, young, fruity, and flavorful, and aged for three to four years on average before it's bottled. Tawny port is the other wood-aged port, and it's aged for eight to ten years. As a result, it's lighter in color, and more mellow and subdued.

Vintage ports, on the other hand, are made from a single vintage, and they're bottled after about two years, but it takes from ten to twenty years or more of bottle age before they reach maturity. Therefore, vintge ports may be produced only two or three times in a decade.

Port is great after dinner or before bed with a good book.

Sherry Australia, South Africa, and California are the New World regions producing sherry, a fortified wine made from white grapes, that, when made in that traditional way, gets its distinctive flavors from a yeast called *flor* that forms on the top of the wine as it's fermenting. California "sherry" often refers to fortified wines, usually sweet ones, that have been baked, aged, or artificially infused with yeast to create a product similar in flavor to Spanish sherry. Sherry can be served alongside smoked salmon, salted nuts, or grilled fish.

Augusta Winery 1997 Ice Wine
Region: Missouri $11.99/375 ml
Golds/Awards: Gold (NW)

Cedar Creek 1995 Reserve Chardonnay Icewine
Region: Canada, Okanagan Valley   (Can $) 41.95
Golds/Awards: Gold (WWC-90 pts)

Colio Estate Wines 1996 V.Q.A. Vidal Icewine
Region: Canada, Ontario   (Can $) 41.95/375 ml
Golds/Awards: Gold (IV)

Gehringer Brothers 1997 Riesling Ice Wine
Region: Canada, Okanagan Valley   (Can $) 43
Golds/Awards: Gold (IV)

Hillebrand Estates 1996 V.Q.A. Showcase Barrel Fermented Zabek Vineyard Vidal Icewine
Region: Canada, Niagara Peninsula $89.95
Golds/Awards: Gold (IV)

Did You Know...?

"I was convinced forty years ago—and the conviction remains to this day—that in wine tasting and wine talk there is an enormous amount of humbug."

—T.G. Shaw

Inniskillin Wines 1996 Ehrenfelser Ice Wine
Region: Canada, Okanagan Valley $54.95
Golds/Awards: Gold (PR)

Jackson-Triggs 1996 Proprietor's Grand Reserve Riesling Ice Wine
Region: Canada, Okanagan Valley   (Can $) 49.95
Golds/Awards: Gold (NW, IW)

Jackson-Triggs 1996 Proprietor's Reserve Vidal Ice Wine
Region: Canada, Niagara Peninsula   (Can $) 49.95
Golds/Awards: Gold (IV)

Konzelmann 1996 Riesling Traminer Icewine
Region: Canada, Niagara Peninsula   (Can $) 57.75
Golds/Awards: Gold (IV)

Konzelmann 1996 Vidal Icewine
Region: Canada, Niagara Peninsula $45.95
Golds/Awards: Gold (IV, WWC-90 pts)

Did You Know...?

Because of the phylloxera louse, many
vineyards in California had to be replanted.
Unfortunately, young vines are more vulnerable to the new scourge—Pierce's Disease—than
old vines. In California, somewhere between 35%
and 40% of all vineyards in the North Coast are new.

Magnotta 1995 Limited Edition Vidal Icewine
Region: Canada, Niagara Peninsula $39.95/375 ml
Golds/Awards: Gold (BR, GH)

Magnotta 1996 Limited Edition Vidal Icewine
Region: Canada, Niagara Peninsula $39.95/375 ml
Golds/Awards: Gold (WWC-90 pts)

Peller NV V.Q.A. Vidal Icewine
Region: Canada, Niagara Peninsula $39.95/375 ml
Golds/Awards: Gold (VI); Grand Gold Medal (VI)

Pillitteri Estates 1996 Vidal Icewine
Region: Canada   (Can $) 27.95
Golds/Awards: Gold (IW)

Reif Estate 1996 V.Q.A. Vidal Icewine
Region: Canada, Niagara Peninsula   (Can $) 46.95
Golds/Awards: Gold (VI, WWC-91 pts)

Reif Estate 1996 Riesling Ice Wine
Region: Canada   (Can $) 52.95/375 ml
Golds/Awards: Gold (IW)

Stoney Ridge 1995 Gewurztraminer Icewine
Region: Canada, Niagara Peninsula   (Can $) 49.95
Golds/Awards: Gold (WWC-90 pts)

Stoney Ridge 1996 Gewurztraminer Ice Wine
Region: Canada, Niagara Peninsula   (Can $) 49.95
Golds/Awards: Gold (WS)

Stoney Ridge 1996 Riesling-Traminer Icewine
Region: Canada, Niagara Peninsula   (Can $) 25
Golds/Awards: Gold (WWC-90 pts)

Strewn 1996 Vidal Icewine
Region: Canada, Niagara Peninsula   (Can $) 31.50
Golds/Awards: Gold (WWC-90 pts)

Sumac Ridge 1996 V.Q.A. Pinot Blanc Ice Wine
Region: Canada, Okanagan Valley   (Can $) 49.95/375 ml
Golds/Awards: Gold (PR, IV, LA, WC, WWC-94 pts); Best
of Class (PR)

Summerhill Estate Winery 1996 Riesling Icewine
Region: Canada, British Columbia   (Can $) 68/375 ml
Golds/Awards: Gold (NW)

Tinhorn Creek Vineyards 1996 Kerner Icewine
Region: Canada, Okanagan Valley   (Can $) 39.50
Golds/Awards: Gold (LA); Best of Class, Division Sweep-
stakes Award (LA)

Did You Know...?

A silver corkscrew that belonged to George III was
auctioned off at Christie's for $16,824.

Alderbrook 1997 Tredici
Region: California, Russian River Valley $10
Golds/Awards: Gold (SD)

Beringer 1994 Nightingale Private Reserve Botrytized Sauvignon Blanc/Semillon
Region: California, Napa Valley $22/375 ml
Golds/Awards: Gold (WWC-95 pts)

Breitenbach Wine Cellars NV American Frost Fires
Region: Ohio $7.00
Golds/Awards: Gold (RI, SD)

Did You Know...?

"I see where they now propose to stop cigarettes first and then profanity. They are going to have a rough time with that profanity, cause a'long as there is a prohibitionist living there will be profanity."

—Will Rogers

Calona 1995 Private Reserve Late Harvest Botrytis Affected Ehrenfelser
Region: Canada   (Can $) 21/375 ml
Golds/Awards: Gold (WWC-90 pts)

Castle Vineyards 1997 Late Harvest White Riesling
Region: Canada $16
Golds/Awards: Gold (LA)

Chappellet 1995 Moelleux
Region: California, Napa Valley $35/375 ml
Golds/Awards: Gold (WWC-95 pts)

Chateau St. Jean 1994 Belle Terre Special Select Late Harvest Johannisberg Riesling
Region: California, Alexander Valley $25/375 ml
Golds/Awards: Gold (SD, NW, LA); Best of Class, Best in Show, Best of Class (LA)

Cilurzo 1997 Estate Bottled Late Harvest Petite Sirah
Region: California, Temecula $19.95
Golds/Awards: Gold (OC)

Miscellaneous Sweet DESSERT & FORTIFIED

De Bortoli 1994 "Noble One" Australian Botrytis Semillon
Region: Australia, New South Wales $19.99
Golds/Awards: Gold (SY)

De Bortoli 1995 "Noble One" Australian Botrytis Semillon
Region: Australia, New South Wales $19.99
Golds/Awards: Gold (SY)

Did You Know...?

Botryrtis cinerea is a mold that grows on some grapes under special conditions. This "noble rot," as it's called, attacks the grapes, causing them to shrivel, thus leaving a rich, concentrated pulp inside the grape, which yields super sweet, alcoholic, nectarlike dessert wines.

Dolce 1995 Late Harvest Semillon
Region: California, Napa Valley $60/375 ml
Golds/Awards: Platinum (WWC-97 pts); Gold (OC)

Elderton 1996 Golden Semillon
Region: Australia $17/375 ml
Golds/Awards: Gold (IW)

Elk Cove 1996 Ultima Riesling
Region: Oregon, Willamette Valley $25/375 ml
Golds/Awards: Gold (WWC-94 pts)

Geyser Peak 1996 Late Harvest Riesling
Region: California, Russian River Valley $16
Golds/Awards: Gold (IV)

Geyser Peak 1997 Preston Ranch Late Harvest Riesling
Region: California, Russian River Valley $16/375 ml
Golds/Awards: Gold (RI, WWC-95 pts); Double Gold (CA);
Best of California, Best of Class (CA)

Greenwood Ridge 1996 Estate Bottled Late Harvest Riesling
Region: California, Anderson Valley $18
Golds/Awards: Gold (RI, WC); Best of Class (WC)

Grgich Hills 1994 Late Harvest Violetta
Region: California, Napa Valley $35/375 ml
Golds/Awards: Gold (WS, WWC-94 pts)

Miscellaneous Sweet DESSERT & FORTIFIED

Herzog Wine Cellars 1996 Late Harvest Riesling
Region: California, Monterey $15.99
Golds/Awards: Gold (NW)

Hogue 1997 Late Harvest White Riesling
Region: Washington, Columbia Valley $8
Golds/Awards: Gold (SD)

Husch 1997 Estate Bottled Late Harvest Gewurztraminer
Region: California, Anderson Valley $14
Golds/Awards: Four Star Gold (OC); Double Gold (CA);
Best of Class (CA)

**Jekel 1996 Gravelstone Vineyard Late Harvest
Johannisberg Riesling**
Region: California, Monterey County $25/375 ml
Golds/Awards: Gold (WWC-93 pts, NW)

**Joseph Filippi NV Winemaker's Reserve Limited Release
"Angelica Elena"**
Region: California, Cucamonga Valley $10
Golds/Awards: Gold (OC)

Joseph Filippi NV Winemaker's Reserve "Fondante Ciello"
Region: California $18
Golds/Awards: Gold (OC)

Magnotta NV Passito Del Santo
Region: Canada   (Can $) 8.50
Golds/Awards: Gold (LA, IV)

Magnotta 1996 Late Harvest Vidal
Region: Canada   (Can $) 9.95
Golds/Awards: Gold (VL)

Mirassou 1996 Reserve Late Harvest Riesling
Region: California, Monterey $15.95
Golds/Awards: Gold (NW)

Did You Know...?

"The soft extractive note of an aged cork being
withdrawn has the true sound of a man opening
his heart."

—William Samuel Benwell

Did You Know...?

Thomas Jefferson had 200 acres of wine planted at his home in Monticello in Virginia.

Navarro 1996 Cluster Select Late Harvest White Riesling
Region: California, Mendocino $19.50
Golds/Awards: Gold (PR,NW,RI,LA,OC); Best of Class (NW,LA)

Navarro 1996 Late Harvest White Riesling
Region: California $9.75
Golds/Awards: Gold (LA); Best of Class (LA)

Navarro 1997 Cluster Select Late Harvest Gewurztraminer
Region: California, Mendocino $25
Golds/Awards: Gold (OC)

Navarro 1997 Late Harvest Sweet Gewurztraminer
Region: California, Mendocino $9.75
Golds/Awards: Gold (OC)

Neethlingshof 1996 Noble Late Harvest White Riesling
Region: South Africa, Stellenbosch $19.50/375 ml
Golds/Awards: Gold (WWC-94 pts)

Neethlingshof 1997 Weisser Late Harvest Noble Riesling
Region: South Africa, Stellenbosch $29.99/375 ml
Golds/Awards: Gold (WS)

San Antonio NV Marsala "Almondoro"
Region: California $6
Golds/Awards: Gold (OC)

Silvan Ridge 1995 Late Harvest Early Muscat/Huxel Rebe
Region: Oregon $16/375 ml
Golds/Awards: Gold (WWC-90 pts)

Stone Hill 1997 Hermann Late Harvest Vignoles
Region: Missouri $16.99
Golds/Awards: Gold (RI); Chairman's Award (RI)

Stoney Ridge Cellars 1996 Puddicombe Vineyard Select Late Harvest Vidal
Region: Canada, Niagara Peninsula   (Can $) 19.95
Golds/Awards: Gold (WS, WWC-91 pts)

Thirty Bench 1995 Botrytis Riesling
Region: Canada, Niagara Peninsula   (Can $) 18.95
Golds/Awards: Gold (WS)

Viano Vineyards 1995 Late Harvest Reserve Selection Zinfandel
Region: California, Contra Costa County $13
Golds/Awards: Double Gold (CA); Best of Class (CA)

Vineland Estates 1996 St. Urban Select Late Harvest Vidal
Region: Canada, Ontario   (Can $) 21.50
Golds/Awards: Gold (IV)

Voss Vineyards 1996 Botrytis Sauvignon Blanc
Region: California, Napa Valley $18.50
Golds/Awards: Double Gold (CA); Best of Class (CA)

Windsor 1997 Murphy Ranch Special Selection Late Harvest Sauvignon Blanc
Region: California, Alexander Valley $28.50
Golds/Awards: Gold (PR, RI); Best of Class, Best of Category (RI)

Did You Know...?

"Sobriety's a real turn-on for me. You can see what you're doing." —Peter O'Toole

Did You Know...?

"Prohibition has made nothing but trouble."
—Al Capone

Arciero Winery 1996 Estate Bottled Muscat Canelli
Region: California, Paso Robles $12
Golds/Awards: Gold (NW, CA); Best of Class (CA)

Callaway 1996 Muscat Canelli
Region: California, Temecula $9.50
Golds/Awards: Gold (NW); Best of Class (NW)

Callaway 1997 Muscat Canelli
Region: California, Temecula $9.50
Golds/Awards: Gold (OC)

Gan Eden 1997 Black Muscat
Region: California, San Joaquin County $12
Golds/Awards: Gold (RI, SD, WC); Chairman's Award (RI);
Best of Class (SD, WC)

Joseph Zakon 1997 Muscatini
Region: California $9.99
Golds/Awards: Gold (OC)

Kendall-Jackson 1996 Vintner's Reserve Muscat
Region: California $11
Golds/Awards: Gold (RI); Chairman's Award (RI)

Messina Hof 1996 Late Harvest "Glory" Muscat Canelli
Region: Texas $16.99
Golds/Awards: Gold (DA)

Morris Old Premium Liqueur Muscat
Region: Australia, Rutherglen $25
Golds/Awards: Gold (SY)

Perry Creek 1997 Muscat Canelli
Region: California, El Dorado $8
Golds/Awards: Gold (RI)

Quady 1996 Elysium (Black Muscat)
Region: California $16
Golds/Awards: Gold (WWC-95 pts, NW); Best of Varietal (NW)

Quady 1996 Essensia (Orange Muscat)
Region: California $13.50
Golds/Awards: Gold (WWC-93 pts, PR, OC); Best of Class (PR)

Quady 1997 Electra
Region: California $8.50
Golds/Awards: Gold (NW)

Quady 1997 Elysium (Black Muscat)
Region: California $13.50
Golds/Awards: Gold (OC, RI, CA); Chairman's Award (RI);
Best of Class (CA)

Shenandoah 1997 20th Year Anniversary Black Muscat
Region: California, Amador County $12
Golds/Awards: Gold (OC)

Sutter Home 1996 Moscato
Region: California $5.95
Golds/Awards: Gold (NW)

Thornton 1996 Limited Bottling Moscato
Region: California, South Coast $12
Golds/Awards: Gold (SD)

Windsor 1996 Murphy Ranch Late Harvest Muscat Canelli
Region: California, Alexander Valley $12.50
Golds/Awards: Gold (NW, RI, CA); Best of Class (CA)

Yalumba NV Victoria Muscat
Region: Australia $15.99
Golds/Awards: Gold (PR)

Yalumba Museum Show Reserve Muscat
Region: Australia, Rutherglen $15.99/375 ml
Golds/Awards: Platinum (WWC-97 pts)

Did You Know...?

A bottle of 1886 Far Niente sweet Muscat was recently
found in a wine cellar by accident. The label has a
drawing of a young woman in a hammock,
perhaps by Winslow Homer, the nephew of
Far Niente founder John Benson. It's the
oldest bottle of California wine in existence.

Beringer 1994 Port of Cabernet Sauvignon
Region: California, Napa Valley $20
Golds/Awards: Gold (PR, NW, OC)

Cedar Mountain 1995 Vintage Port
Region: California, Amador County $19.50
Golds/Awards: Gold (WWC-90 pts)

Cedar Mountain 1996 Vintage Port
Region: California, Amador County $19.50
Golds/Awards: Gold (WWC-92 pts)

Chateau Reynella Old Cave Tawny Port
Region: Australia, McLaren Vale $15
Golds/Awards: Gold (WWC-92 pts)

Ficklin 1988 Vintage Port
Region: California $25
Golds/Awards: Gold (WWC-91 pts)

Ficklin Aged 10 Year Tawny Port
Region: California $24
Golds/Awards: Gold (WWC-92 pts, LA, OC)

Geyser Peak 1995 Henry's Reserve Shiraz Port
Region: California $15
Golds/Awards: Gold (LA); Best of Class (LA)

Guenoc 1994 Vintage Port
Region: California $25
Golds/Awards: Gold (SD); Best of Class (SD)

Justin 1996 Obtuse (Port)
Region: California, Paso Robles $22.50
Golds/Awards: Double Gold (CA); Best of Class (CA)

Did You Know...?

Because port has to sit around for so many years in casks that get opened to the air, evaporation is a problem. Some 20,000 bottles of port evaporate every year in Portugal alone.

Did You Know...?

Today's Madeira wines are "cooked" and purposely exposed to oxygen to simulate the first Madeira, which got its unusual flavor while being shipped through the hot tropics on its way between Europe, Africa, and the Americas in the 18th century.

Latcham 1995 Select Port
Region: California, El Dorado $15
Golds/Awards: Gold (LA)

Lonz Winery American Ruby Rich Port
Region: Ohio $8
Golds/Awards: Gold (LA)

Oakstone NV Merlot Port
Region: California, El Dorado $16
Golds/Awards: Gold (OC)

Penfolds "Club Reserve" Tawny Port
Region: Australia, South Australia $11
Golds/Awards: Gold (SY)

Prager Winery & Port Works 1993 "Aria"
Region: California, Napa Valley $32.50
Golds/Awards: Gold (OC)

Prager Winery & Port Works 1993 "Royal Escort" Petite Sirah Port
Region: California, Napa Valley $38.50
Golds/Awards: Gold (NW)

Prager Winery & Port Works NV "Noble Companion" Ten Year Old Tawny Port
Region: California, Napa Valley $45
Golds/Awards: Gold (OC)

Quady NV Batch 88 Starboard Port
Region: California $20.50
Golds/Awards: Gold (NW, PR)

Did You Know...?

The British are known for their love of port. It's traditional upon the birth of a child to buy a pipe (700 bottles) of port to put away for the brat's 21st birthday—the age of maturity for a fine port.

Quady 1993 LBV Port
Region: California, Amador County $12
Golds/Awards: Gold (CA, WWC-91 pts); Best of Class (CA)

Quady 1990 Starboard Port
Region: California, Amador County $21.50
Golds/Awards: Gold (WWC-93 pts)

Seppelt Trafford Tawny Port
Region: Australia, Barossa Valley $11
Golds/Awards: Gold (WWC-91 pts)

Sheffield Cellars NV Livingston Tawny Port
Region: California $3.99
Golds/Awards: Gold (NW)

Sonora Winery & Port Works 1994 Vintage Port
Region: California, Sierra Foothills $16
Golds/Awards: Gold (RI, WC); Chairman's Award (RI)

Stone Hill 1994 Estate Bottled Norton Port
Region: Missouri $23.99
Golds/Awards: Gold (NW)

Taylor Wine Cellars NV Tawny Port
Region: New York $3.99
Golds/Awards: Gold (SD)

Trentadue 1994 Estate Petite Sirah Port
Region: California, Alexander Valley $20
Golds/Awards: Gold (NW)

Twin Hills Winery NV Zinfandel Port
Region: California, Paso Robles $25
Golds/Awards: Gold (OC)

Widmer's Wine Cellars NV Special Selection Ruby Port
Region: New York $3.99
Golds/Awards: Gold (SD)

Windsor NV Private Reserve Rare Port
Region: California $13
Golds/Awards: Gold (OC)

Yalumba Galway Pipe Tawny Port
Region: Australia $23.99
Golds/Awards: Gold (WWC-90 pts)

Yalumba NV Clock Tower Port
Region: Australia, South Australia $10
Golds/Awards: Gold (NW); Best of Class, Best of Varietal (NW)

Did You Know...?

Definition of *drunk:* When a man feels
sophisticated, but can't pronounce it.
                    —Irish saying

Christian Brothers NV Cream Sherry
Region: California $4.99/750 ml
Golds/Awards: Gold (NW)

Christian Brothers NV Dry Sherry
Region: California $4.99/750 ml
Golds/Awards: Gold (NW, OC)

Galleano Winery NV Barrel Aged "Crema" Sherry
Region: California, Cucamonga Valley $16.95
Golds/Awards: Gold (OC)

Lonz Winery NV Three Islands Madeira
Region: Ohio $8
Golds/Awards: Gold (PR, NW)

Rancho de Philo NV Triple Cream Mission Sherry
Region: California, Cucamonga Valley $12.50
Golds/Awards: Gold (NW)

St. Julian NV Solera Cream Sherry
Region: Michigan $12
Golds/Awards: Gold (PR)

Sheffield Cellars NV Livingston Cream Sherry
Region: California $3.99
Golds/Awards: Gold (NW, CA, WC); Best of Region, Best of Class (CA)

Did You Know...?

Ever wondered why flan is so popular in Spain? Since egg whites are used to clarify Spain's world-famous sherry (i.e., rid it of sediment), there are *lots* of yolks left over to make the rich dessert.

APPENDIX 1

Best Bargain Wines

Yes, you can buy top-rated wines that won't cost you a fortune! My radio listeners are always surprised when I tell them that many bottles in *Best Wines!* are $15 and under.

More than once I've been asked to explain how one Cabernet could be $12 while another is $40, and what the qualitative differences are between the two. The full answer is long-winded, and has to do with where the grapes are grown and by whom, which juice is chosen for the batch, how much of it there is, and how the wines are made (vinification methods) and/or blended. An expensive price tag often reflects actual time and money that's gone into growing and creating a special wine, one that's meant to be cellared for a few years.

Yet a winemaker who can use his or her resources and expertise to make a delicious $12 bottle gets my vote. I like to buy under-$15 bottles for my own personal consumption, but to splurge on more expensive wines for special occasions with friends. The way I see it, there's nothing wrong with seeking bargain wines for myself as long as they're gold medal winners.

If you're a white wine lover, you're in luck: Whites in general are less expensive than reds. You'll find many wonderful bargain whites in the list below. Red wines tend to be pricier, so if you can find an inexpensive Cabernet Sauvignon, say, or a Pinot Noir that's also a gold medal winner, run—don't walk—to the nearest ATM so you can buy up a case. Believe me, these bargain gems won't last long on store shelves.

When shopping for inexpensive party wines, you'll find lots of good deals from Chile, Argentina, and South Africa.

Native American and French-American hybrids aren't included below since they're not in great demand. These are wines that will almost always be inexpensive. Too, I did not list dessert or fortified wines. Generally served in tiny glasses, these special-occasion wines will last and last—so they're good buys at almost any price.

Every wine below is an undisputed "best buy" that you'll want to bring to parties, turn your friends on to, or just keep for yourself and feel smug about. Happy shopping!

BEAUJOLAIS-STYLE REDS

Amity 1997 Gamay Noir, OR, $9

Beringer 1996 Gamay Beaujolais, CA, $8

Gallo Sonoma 1995 Barelli Creek Vineyard Valdiguié, CA, $12

Glen Ellen 1996 Proprietor's Reserve Gamay Beaujolais, CA, $5

Gundlach-Bundschu 1997 Rhinefarm Vineyards Gamay Beaujolais, CA, $9

J. Lohr 1997 Estate Wildflower Valdiguié, CA, $7.50

Navarro 1996 Napa Gamay, CA, $12

Weinstock Cellars 1997 Gamay, CA, $5.99

V. Sattui 1997 Gamay Rouge, CA, $12.75

CABERNET SAUVIGNON

Beaucanon 1995 Cabernet Sauvignon, CA, $14

Beaulieu Vineyard 1995 Cabernet Sauvignon, CA, $9.99

Bogle 1996 Cabernet Sauvignon, CA, $9

Bonterra 1995 Organically Grown Grapes Cabernet Sauvignon, CA, $15

Byington 1994 Twin Mountains Cabernet Sauvignon, CA, $14.50

Caballero de la Cepa 1993 Mendoza Reserve Cabernet Sauvignon, Argentina, $9.95

Calina 1996 Valle Central Cabernet Sauvignon, Chile, $9

Callaway 1995 Cabernet Sauvignon, CA, $11

Carmen 1996 Cabernet Sauvignon, Chile, $6.99

Chateau La Joya 1997 Cabernet Sauvignon, Chile, $8.99

Chateau Los Boldos 1996 Vielles Vignes Cabernet Sauvignon, Chile, $8.99

Clos Malverne 1994 Cabernet Sauvignon, South Africa, $14.99

Clos Malverne 1995 Cabernet Sauvignon, South Africa, $14.99

Deer Valley 1995 Cabernet Sauvignon, CA, $4.99

Dunnewood 1995 Cabernet Sauvignon, CA, $8.50

Etchart 1995 Cafayate Cabernet Sauvignon, Argentina, $6.99

Etchart 1995 Rio de Plata Cabernet Sauvignon, Argentina, $6.99

Etchart 1996 Rio de Plata Cabernet Sauvignon, Argentina, $6.99

Fenestra 1994 Cabernet Sauvignon, CA, $13.50

Fetzer 1995 Valley Oaks Cabernet Sauvignon, CA, $8.99

Flichman 1995 Cabernet Sauvignon, Argentina, $6.95

Foxridge 1996 Cabernet Sauvignon, Chile, $10

Geyser Peak 1995 Cabernet Sauvignon, CA, $15

Hillebrand Estates 1995 V.Q.A. Cabernet Sauvignon, Canada, $9.95

J. Lohr 1995 Cypress Cabernet Sauvignon, CA, $8.75

J. Lohr 1995 Seven Oaks Cabernet Sauvignon, CA, $14

KWV Cathedral Cellar 1995 Cabernet Sauvignon, South Africa, $12

La Garza 1996 Cabernet Sauvignon, OR, $15

Laborie Estate 1996 Cabernet Sauvignon, South Africa, $14

Lakespring 1994 Cabernet Sauvignon, CA, $10

Meridian 1995 Cabernet Sauvignon, CA, $12

Miguel Torres 1996 Santa Digna Cabernet Sauvignon, Chile, $8.99

Monthaven 1995 Cabernet Sauvignon, CA, $9.99

Napa Ridge 1994 Reserve Cabernet Sauvignon, CA, $15

Napa Ridge 1996 Oak Barrel Cabernet Sauvignon, CA, $10

Pedroncelli 1995 Three Vineyards Cabernet Sauvignon, CA, $11.50

Pedroncelli 1996 Vintage Selection Cabernet Sauvignon, CA, $10

Raymond 1995 Raymond Estates Cabernet Sauvignon, CA, $13

Renaissance 1995 Cabernet Sauvignon, CA, $13.99

Rodney Strong 1995 Cabernet Sauvignon, CA, $13

Rutherford Ranch 1994 Cabernet Sauvignon, CA, $10

St. Francis 1995 Cabernet Sauvignon, CA, $12

Ste. Chapelle 1995 Cabernet Sauvignon, ID, $11.50

Santa Ana 1996 Cabernet Sauvignon, Argentina, $5.99

Sea Ridge 1995 Barrel Fermented Cabernet Sauvignon, CA, $10

Silverado Hill Cellars 1995 Premium Black Label Cabernet Sauvignon, CA, $15

Sterling 1995 Cabernet Sauvignon, CA, $14

Stevenot 1995 Cabernet Sauvignon, CA, $15

Stonelake 1996 Reserva Cabernet Sauvignon, Chile, $13

Swartland 1994 Cabernet Sauvignon, South Africa, $9.99

Tittarelli 1994 Cabernet Sauvignon, Argentina, $8.99

Trellis 1996 Cabernet Sauvignon, CA, $13.99

Viña Tarapaca 1992 Gran Reserva Cabernet Sauvignon, Chile, $15

Viña Tarapaca 1996 Cabernet Sauvignon, Chile, $7

Weinstock Cellars 1996 Cabernet Sauvignon, CA, $10.99

Windsor 1995 Preference Vineyard Cabernet Sauvignon, CA, $13

Wyndham Estates 1996 Bin 444 Cabernet Sauvignon, Australia, $12.99

Wynns 1994 Coonawarra Estate Cabernet Sauvignon, Australia, $13.99

CHARDONNAY

Anapamu 1996 Chardonnay, CA, $12

Baileyana 1996 Chardonnay, CA, $15

Benziger 1996 Chardonnay, CA, $13

Bogle 1996 Chardonnay, CA, $8

Bogle 1997 Chardonnay, CA, $8

Buehler 1996 Chardonnay, CA, $15

Canepa 1997 Private Reserve Chardonnay, Chile, $12.99

Canyon Road 1997 Chardonnay, CA, $7.99

Carta Vieja 1997 Reserve Chardonnay, Chile, $9

Casa LaPostolle 1995 Cuvée Alexandre Chardonnay, Chile, $15

Chamonix 1995 Reserve Chardonnay, South Africa, $15

Chandelle of Sonoma 1996 Pan American Dixie Chardonnay, CA, $11.95

Chateau La Joya 1997 Gran Reserva Chardonnay, Chile, $12.99

Chateau St. Jean 1996 Chardonnay, CA, $13

Chateau Souverain 1996 Chardonnay, CA, $14

Cloninger Cellars 1996 Estate Bottled Chardonnay, CA, $11

Clos du Bois 1996 Special Selection Chardonnay, CA, $15

Columbia Crest 1996 Chardonnay, WA, $9

Columbia Crest 1996 Estate Series Chardonnay, WA, $15

Concannon 1996 Chardonnay, CA, $9.95

Corbans 1996 Private Bin Oaked Chardonnay, New Zealand, $13.99

Corbett Canyon 1997 Chardonnay, CA, $9

D'Arenberg 1997 The Olive Grove Chardonnay, Australia, $15

DeLoach 1996 Sonoma Cuvée Chardonnay, CA, $13

Dunnewood 1996 Chardonnay, CA, $7.99

Eberle 1997 Chardonnay, CA, $14

Echelon 1997 Chardonnay, CA, $11

Eos Estate Winery 1996 Estate Bottled Chardonnay, CA, $14.99

Errazuriz 1997 Chardonnay, Chile, $9

Estancia 1996 Pinnacles Chardonnay, CA, $11

Etchart 1997 Cafayate Chardonnay, Argentina, $11.99

Etchart 1997 Rio de Plata Chardonnay, Argentina, $6.99

Fetzer 1997 Sundial Chardonnay, CA, $8.99

Flichman 1997 Chardonnay, Argentina, $9.95

Folie à Deux 1996 Chardonnay, CA, $14

Geyser Peak 1997 Chardonnay, CA, $14

Glen Ellen 1996 Expressions Chardonnay, CA, $10

Hardys 1996 Padthaway Chardonnay, Australia, $12.99

Husch 1996 Chardonnay, CA, $12.50

Jacob's Creek 1997 Chardonnay, Australia, $8.99

Lake Sonoma 1996 Heck Family Cellar Selection Chardonnay, CA, $15

Leasingham 1996 Chardonnay, Australia, $14

Lindemans 1997 Padthaway Chardonnay, Australia, $12

Madrona 1996 Estate Chardonnay, CA, $12

Mark West 1996 Chardonnay, CA, $15

Morton Estate 1996 Hawkes Bay Chardonnay, New Zealand, $10.99

Napa Ridge 1996 Chardonnay, CA, $9

Orfila 1995 Ambassador's Reserve Chardonnay, CA, $14.95

Pedroncelli 1996 Chardonnay, CA, $10

Pedroncelli 1996 F. Johnson Vineyards Chardonnay, CA, $12.50

Penfolds 1996 The Valleys Chardonnay, Australia, $12

Pintler Cellar 1996 Chardonnay, ID, $10.99

R.H. Phillips 1996 Estate Bottled "Toasted Head" Chardonnay, CA, $12

Raymond Vineyard 1996 Raymond Estate Chardonnay, CA, $13

Ste. Chapelle 1996 Barrel Fermented Chardonnay, ID, $9.89

Saint Clair 1996 Chardonnay, New Zealand, $15

Santa Barbara Winery 1996 Chardonnay, CA, $15

Santa Julia 1996 Oak Reserve Chardonnay, Argentina, $8.50

Santa Julia 1997 Chardonnay, Argentina, $6.99

Seven Peaks 1996 Chardonnay, CA, $12.99

Silver Ridge 1996 Barrel Fermented Chardonnay, CA, $10

Stag's Leap 1994 Barrel Fermented Chardonnay, CA, $10

Stone Creek 1997 Chardonnay, CA, $6.89

Sylvester Winery 1996 Kiara Reserve Chardonnay, CA, $12

Tasman Bay 1996 Chardonnay, New Zealand, $14

Temecula Crest 1997 Chardonnay, CA, $15

Trellis 1997 Chardonnay, CA, $8.50

Villa Mt. Eden 1996 Chardonnay, CA, $11

Viña Santa Carolina 1996 Reserva Chardonnay, Chile, $7.99

Viña Tarapaca 1997 Reserva Chardonnay, Chile, $10

Viu Manent 1997 Chardonnay, Chile, $8

Weinstock Cellars 1996 Chardonnay, CA, $10.99

Wild Horse 1996 Chardonnay, CA, $14

Windsor 1996 Chardonnay, CA, $10

Windsor 1997 Private Reserve Chardonnay, CA, $14

Wolf Blass 1997 President's Selection Chardonnay, Australia, $15

Yarra Ridge 1997 Chardonnay, Australia, $11.99

CHENIN BLANC

Alexander Valley Vineyards 1996 Dry Chenin Blanc, CA, $9

Chappellet 1995 Old Vine Cuvée Dry Chenin Blanc, CA, $12

Columbia Winery 1995 Chenin Blanc, WA, $5.99

Dry Creek Vineyard 1996 Clarksburg Dry Chenin Blanc, CA, $8

Fantaisie 1996 Chenin Blanc, CA, $8

Hogue 1997 Chenin Blanc, WA, $7

Husch 1997 La Ribera Vineyards Chenin Blanc, CA, $8.50

Navarro 1997 Chenin Blanc, CA, $9.50

Ventana 1997 Barrel Fermented Estate Bottled Chenin Blanc, CA, $10

Windsor 1996 Chenin Blanc, CA, $7.50

GEWURZTRAMINER

Adler Fels 1996 Gewurztraminer, CA, $11

Adler Fels 1997 Gewurztraminer, CA, $11

Alderbrook 1997 McIlroy Vineyard Gewurztraminer, CA, $12

Alderbrook 1997 Saralee's Vineyard Gewurztraminer, CA, $11

Alexander Valley Vineyards 1997 Wetzel Family Selection Gewurztraminer, CA, $9

Bargetto 1995 Gewurztraminer, CA, $10

Bayview Cellars 1997 Gewurztraminer, CA, $8.50

Beringer 1996 Gewurztraminer, CA, $7

Chateau St. Jean 1997 Gewurztraminer, CA, $9.50

Cosentino 1996 Gewurztraminer, CA, $14

DeLoach 1997 Early Harvest Gewurztraminer, CA, $12

Fetzer 1997 Gewurztraminer, CA, $6.99

Gan Eden 1996 Gewurztraminer, CA, $12

Geyser Peak 1997 Gewurztraminer, CA, $7.50

Gundlach-Bundschu 1997 Rhinefarm Vineyards Estate Bottled Gewurztraminer, CA, $12

Hoodsport 1997 Select Premium Gewurztraminer, WA, $8.99

Husch 1997 Estate Bottled Gewurztraminer, CA, $11

Kendall-Jackson 1996 Vintner's Reserve Gewurztraminer, CA, $10

Louis M. Martini 1996 Gewurztraminer, CA, $12

M.G. Vallejo 1996 Gewurztraminer, CA, $6

Mark West 1997 Reserve Gewurztraminer, CA, $15

Meridian 1997 Gewurztraminer, CA, $8

Mill Creek 1996 Estate Bottled Gewurztraminer, CA, $10

Navarro 1995 Gewurztraminer, CA, $14

Prejean Winery 1996 Dry Gewurztraminer, NY, $12

Standing Stone 1996 Gewurztraminer, NY, $10.99

Storrs 1996 Viento Vineyard Gewurztraminer, CA, $12

Thomas Fogarty 1997 Gewurztraminer, CA, $12.50

Ventana 1997 Estate Bottled Gewurztraminer, CA, $10

ITALIAN-VARIETAL REDS

Boeger 1995 Charbono, CA, $15

Boeger 1996 Barbera, CA, $13.50

Parducci 1994 Old Vines Charbono, CA, $10.75

Callaway 1994 Nebbiolo, CA, $12

Ehlers Grove 1996 Dolcetto, CA, $14

Martin Brothers 1996 Nebbiolo, CA, $11

Obester 1995 Twentieth Anniversary Sangiovese, CA, $13.95

Vino Noceto 1995 Sangiovese, CA, $12

Windwalker Vineyards 1996 Cooper Vineyard Barbera, CA, $12.50

MERLOT

Carta Vieja 1996 Reservado Merlot, Chile, $9

Casa LaPostolle 1996 Merlot, Chile, $10

Charles Shaw 1995 Barrel Select Merlot, CA, $8.99

Chateau La Joya 1995 Gran Reserva Merlot, Chile, $12.99

Chateau La Joya 1996 Gran Reserva Merlot, Chile, $12.99

Chateau La Joya 1996 Premium Merlot, Chile, $8.99

Cilurzo 1997 Reserve Merlot, CA, $12.95

Cuisine Cellars 1996 Merlot, CA, $8.99

Estancia 1995 Merlot, CA, $14

Fairview 1994 Merlot, South Africa, $14.99

Fetzer 1995 Barrel Select Merlot, CA, $14

Fetzer 1996 Eagle Peak Merlot, CA, $8.99

Gallo Sonoma 1995 Merlot, CA, $11

Geyser Peak 1995 Merlot, CA, $14.99

Glen Ellen 1995 Expressions Merlot, CA, $12.99

Hogue 1995 Barrel Select Merlot, WA, $15

J. Lohr 1996 Cypress Merlot, CA, $12

Jekel 1996 Sanctuary Estate Reserve Merlot, CA, $15

KWV 1995 Cathedral Cellar Merlot, South Africa, $12

Meerlust 1994 Merlot, South Africa, $11

Quatro 1994 Merlot, CA, $12.99

River Run Vintners 1996 Merlot, CA, $15

Rutherford Vintners 1996 Barrel Select Merlot, CA, $8.99

Silver Ridge 1996 Barrel Select Merlot, CA, $10

Talus 1995 Merlot, CA, $8

Tefft Cellars NV Merlot, WA, $15

Turning Leaf 1995 Reserve Merlot, CA, $9.99

MISCELLANEOUS REDS

Arciero 1995 Estate Bottled Cabernet Franc, CA, $10.50

Bogle 1996 Petite Sirah, CA, $9

Carmen 1995 Petite Sirah, Chile, $13.99

Concannon 1995 Petite Sirah, CA, $9.95

David Bruce 1996 Petite Syrah, CA, $15

Douglas Hill 1995 Cabernet Franc, CA, $14.99

Girardet Wine Cellars 1996 Baco Noir, OR, $14

Humberto Canale 1997 Malbec, Argentina, $7.99

Indian Springs Vineyards 1996 Cabernet Franc, OC, $15

Mirassou 1996 Family Selection Petite Sirah, CA, $11.95

Pagor 1996 "Vino Tinto" Tempranillo, CA, $10

Pepperwood Grove 1996 Cabernet Franc, CA, $6.99

Santa Julia 1996 Mendoza Malbec, Argentina, $5.99

Trentadue 1995 Carignane, CA, $12

Tupungato 1996 Mariposa Malbec, Argentina, $9.95

Van Roekel 1996 Grenache, CA, $12.95

Viu Manent 1996 Malbec, Chile, $8

W.B. Bridgman 1997 Lemberger, WA, $8.95

Wildhurst 1996 Cabernet Franc, CA, $13

Windsor 1996 Carignane, CA, $9.50

Yalumba 1996 Grenache, Australia, $15

MISCELLANEOUS WHITES

Concannon 1996 Marsanne, CA, $14.95

Etchart 1997 Torrontes, Argentina, $7.99

J. Lohr 1995 October Night Pinot Blanc, CA, $14

Mirassou 1996 Family Selection White Burgundy, CA, $10.95

Palmer 1996 Estate Pinot Blanc, NY, $11.99

Perry Creek 1997 El Dorado Estate Viognier, CA, $15

Phillips Farms Vineyards 1997 Highway 12 Vineyards Symphony, CA, $4.99

R.H. Phillips 1997 Estate Bottled Viognier, CA, $12

Robert Pepi 1996 Malvasia Bianca, CA, $14

Rosenblum 1996 Fleur de Hoof Palomino, CA, $18

Stony Ridge NV Malvasia Bianca, CA, $12

Thomas Coyne 1997 Viognier, CA, $15

Wild Horse 1997 Pinot Blanc, CA, $13

Willakenzie 1997 Pinot Blanc, OR, $14

Windsor 1997 French Columbard, CA, $6.75

PINOT GRIS

Cooper Mountain 1997 Estate Bottled Pinot Gris, OR, $12.75

Henry Estate 1997 Pinot Gris, OR, $13

Ivan Tamas 1996 Pinot Grigio, CA, $8.95

King Estate 1996 Pinot Gris, OR, $13

Lavelle Vineyards 1996 Winter's Hill Vineyard Pinot Gris, OR, $13

Willamette Valley 1996 Pinot Gris, OR, $12.50

PINOT NOIR

Anapamu 1995 Pinot Noir, CA, $11.99

Beaulieu Vineyard 1995 Pinot Noir, CA, $15

Beaulieu Vineyard 1996 Pinot Noir, CA, $15

Beringer 1996 Pinot Noir, CA, $15

Clos du Bois 1996 Pinot Noir, CA, $15

Concannon 1995 Reserve Pinot Noir, CA, $14.95

Gallo Sonoma 1996 Pinot Noir, CA, $10

Hacienda Wine Cellars 1996 Clair de Lune Pinot Noir, CA, $6.99

Hagafen 1996 Pinot Noir, CA, $13

Indigo Hills 1996 Pinot Noir, CA, $9

Lorane Valley 1995 Pinot Noir, OR, $10

Meridian 1995 Pinot Noir, CA, $15.50

Mirassou 1996 Family Selection Pinot Noir, CA, $10.95

Napa Ridge 1995 Reserve Pinot Noir, CA, $15

Napa Ridge 1996 Pinot Noir, CA, $11

Quatro 1995 Pinot Noir, CA, $12.99

Robert Mondavi 1995 Coastal Pinot Noir, CA, $10.95

Villa Mt. Eden 1996 Pinot Noir, CA, $12

Yarra Ridge 1997 Pinot Noir, Australia, $11.99

APPENDIX 1

RED BLENDS

Charles B. Mitchell NV Côtes du Cosumnes, CA, $9

Cuisine Cellars NV "Rich Red," CA, $6

Curtis 1996 Old Vines Heritage, CA, $10

Eberle 1996 Côtes Du Robles, CA, $13

Fenestra NV True Red, CA, $8

KWV Cathedral Cellar 1995 Triptych, South Africa, $12

Norman Vineyards 1996 No Nonsense Red, CA, $15

Rosemount 1997 Diamond Label Grenache Shiraz, Australia, $8.50

Sierra Vista 1997 Fleur de Montagne, CA, $14

Silverlake 1996 Cabernet-Merlot, WA, $13.99

Thomas Coyne 1996 Quest, CA, $10

Vigil 1996 Terra Vin, CA, $10

RIESLING

Amity 1995 Dry Riesling, OR, $9

Amity 1996 Riesling, OR, $9

Argyle 1995 Dry Reserve Riesling, OR, $12

Baily 1997 Mother's Vineyard Riesling, CA, $8.95

Beringer 1996 Johannisberg Riesling, CA, $7

Chateau St. Jean 1997 Riesling, CA, $9.50

Chateau Ste. Michelle 1997 Johannisberg Riesling, WA, $8

Concannon 1997 Limited Bottling Johannisberg Riesling, CA, $7.95

Dr. Konstantin Frank 1996 Semi-Dry Johannisberg Riesling, NY, $9.95

Fetzer 1997 Riesling, CA, $7.99

Gainey Vineyard 1997 Riesling, CA, $10

Greenwood Ridge 1997 Estate Bottled Riesling, CA, $10.50

Grove Mill 1996 Riesling, New Zealand, $14

Hagafen 1997 Johannisberg Riesling, CA, $10

Heron Hill 1995 Estate Bottled Johannisberg Riesling, NY, $8.49

Heron Hill 1996 Ingle Vineyard Riesling, NY, $8.99

Hogue 1997 Johannisberg Riesling, WA, $7

Kendall-Jackson 1996 Vintner's Reserve Johannisberg Riesling, CA, $11

Lamoreaux Landing 1996 Semi-Dry Riesling, NY, $10

Mirassou 1996 Fifth Generation Family Selection Johannisberg Riesling, CA, $7.50

Paraiso Springs 1995 Johannisberg Riesling, CA, $9

Paul Thomas 1997 Johannisberg Riesling, WA, $5.99

Penfolds 1997 Rawsons Retreat Bin 202 Riesling, Australia, $7

Renaissance 1996 Estate Bottled Riesling, CA, $9.99

Rusack Vineyards 1996 Lucas Select Riesling, CA, $12.50

Selaks 1997 Riesling, New Zealand, $12.99

Smith-Madrone 1997 Riesling, CA, $11

Stony Ridge 1997 Johannisberg Riesling, CA, $9

Swedish Hill 1997 Riesling, NY, $8.99

Temecula Crest 1997 Riesling, CA, $9.95

Unionville Vineyard 1997 Windfall Riesling, NJ, $7.99

Washington Hills 1997 Dry Riesling, WA, $5.99

Worden 1997 Cascade Collection Riesling, WA, $6.99

ROSÉ AND WHITE ZINFANDEL

Adam Puchta NV Riefenstahler, MO, $7.25

Augusta NV River Valley Blush, MO, $7

Barefoot Cellars NV Barefoot White Zinfandel, CA, $4.99

Baron Herzog 1997 White Zinfandel, CA, $7.49

Beaulieu Vineyard 1996 Signet Collection Pinot Noir Vin Gris, CA, $7.95

Beringer 1997 White Zinfandel, CA, $6

Blossom Hill 1996 White Zinfandel, CA, $4.49

Concannon 1996 Righteously Rosé, CA, $8.95

Corbett Canyon 1997 Coastal Classic White Zinfandel, CA, $4.99

DeLoach 1997 White Zinfandel, CA, $8

Fetzer 1996 White Zinfandel, CA, $6.99

Fetzer 1997 White Zinfandel, CA, $5.99

Glen Ellen 1996 Proprietor's Reserve White Zinfandel, CA, $5

Goose Watch Winery 1996 Rosé of Isabella, NY, $7.50

Hart Winery 1997 Collins Ranch Grenache Rosé, CA, $9

Heron Hill NV Bluff Point Blush, NY, $4.99

Les Vieux Cepages 1995 Ronfleur, CA, $6.99

Maurice Car'rie 1997 White Zinfandel, CA, $5.95

Paraiso Springs 1995 Baby Blush, CA, $12.50

Paraiso Springs 1997 Baby Blush Rides Again, CA, $15

Swanson Vineyards 1997 Rosé of Sangiovese, CA, $14

Sylvester Winery 1996 Kiara Reserve White Zinfandel, CA, $6

V. Sattui 1997 White Zinfandel, CA, $7.75

Weinstock Cellars 1997 White Zinfandel, CA, $6.49

Windsor 1997 Rosé du Soleil, CA, $11

Van Roekel Vineyards 1997 Estate Bottled Rosé of Syrah, CA, $9.95

SAUVIGNON BLANC

Adler Fels 1996 Organically Grown Grapes Fumé Blanc, CA, $10.50

Audubon Cellars 1997 Juliana Vineyards Sauvignon Blanc, CA, $11

Bellefleur Vineyards 1996 Sauvignon Blanc, CA, $11

Benziger 1996 Fumé Blanc, CA, $10

Beringer 1996 Sauvignon Blanc, CA, $9

Beringer 1997 Founder's Estate Sauvignon Blanc, CA, $8.99

Boeger 1997 Estate Bottled Sauvignon Blanc, CA, $9.50

Brutocao 1996 Estate Bottled Sauvignon Blanc, CA, $10.50

Cakebread 1996 Sauvignon Blanc, CA, $14

Callaway 1997 Sauvignon Blanc, CA, $8

Canyon Road 1997 Sauvignon Blanc, CA, $6.99

Chateau Los Boldos 1997 Sauvignon Blanc, Chile, $8.99

Chateau Souverain 1997 Sauvignon Blanc, CA, $8.50

Cloudy Bay 1996 Sauvignon Blanc, New Zealand, $14

Eos Estate Winery 1997 Sauvignon Blanc, CA, $12

De Lorimier 1997 Estate Bottled Sauvignon Blanc, CA, $10

Estancia 1996 Pinnacles Fumé Blanc, CA, $10

Fallbrook 1996 Sauvignon Blanc, CA, $7

Fetzer 1996 Echo Ridge Sauvignon Blanc, CA, $7.99

Filsinger 1997 Fumé Blanc, CA, $6

Foley Estates 1996 Sauvignon Blanc, CA, $14

Fountain Grove 1996 Sauvignon Blanc, CA, $9

Gan Eden 1995 Sauvignon Blanc, CA, $10

Gary Farrell 1997 Sauvignon Blanc, CA, $15

Geyser Peak 1997 Sauvignon Blanc, CA, $8.50

Greenwood Ridge 1997 Sauvignon Blanc, CA, $11

Handley Cellars 1996 Sauvignon Blanc, CA, $13

Hanna Winery 1996 Sauvignon Blanc, CA, $11

Hogue 1997 Fumé Blanc, WA, $7.95

Indigo Hills 1996 Sauvignon Blanc, CA, $8

Jory Winery 1996 Sauvignon Blanc, NM, $15

Kenwood 1997 Sauvignon Blanc, CA, $10

Lakespring 1996 Sauvignon Blanc, CA, $8

Lincoln 1997 Sauvignon Blanc, New Zealand, $14.99

Lolonis 1997 Organically Grown Grapes Fumé Blanc, CA, $11

Maurice Car'rie 1996 Sauvignon Blanc, CA, $6.95

Miguel Torres 1997 Santa Digna Sauvignon Blanc, Chile, $7.99

Murphy-Goode 1997 Fumé Blanc, CA, $11.50

Nautilus 1997 Sauvignon Blanc, New Zealand, $13.99

Navarro 1996 Sauvignon Blanc, CA, $12.50

Neil Ellis 1997 Sauvignon Blanc, South Africa, $12

Rodney Strong 1997 Charlotte's Home Sauvignon Blanc, CA, $10

Selaks 1997 Sauvignon Blanc, New Zealand, $12.99

Sierra Vista 1997 Estate Bottled Sauvignon Blanc, CA, $8.50

St. Supéry 1997 Dollarhide Ranch Sauvignon Blanc, CA, $10.55

Taltarni 1997 Victoria Estate Grown Sauvignon Blanc, Australia, $14.50

Temecula Crest 1997 Sauvignon Blanc, CA, $9.95

Trellis 1997 Special Selection Sauvignon Blanc, CA, $8.99

V. Sattui 1996 Suzanne's Vineyard Sauvignon Blanc, CA, $12.75

Viu Manent 1997 Sauvignon Blanc, Chile, $10

Voss 1997 Sauvignon Blanc, CA, $12.50

Windsor 1996 Middle Ridge Vineyards Fumé Blanc, CA, $11

SEMILLON

Barnard Griffin 1997 Semillon, WA, $9.95

Basedow 1996 Semillon, Australia, $9.99

Hogue 1996 Semillon, WA, $8

Indian Springs Vineyards 1997 Semillon, CA, $10.50

Kendall-Jackson 1996 Vintner's Reserve Semillon, CA, $12

Morris 1996 Semillon, Australia, $14

Rosenblum 1996 Semillon, CA, $14

Washington Hills Cellars 1996 Semillon, WA, $7.99

SPARKLING WINES

Cook's NV Spumante, NY, $4.49

Domaine St. George 1996 Premier Cuvée STG Pinot Noir, CA, $10

Gloria Ferrer Champagne Caves NV Blanc de Noirs, CA, $15

Hester Creek Estate Winery 1996 Blanc de Noir, Canada, $9.95

Korbel NV Méthode Champenoise Chardonnay Champagne, CA, $12.99

Korbel NV Méthode Champenoise Rouge Champagne, CA, $11.99

Laetitia NV Select Brut, CA, $13.99

Oasis NV Brut, VA, $12.50/375 ml

Seaview 1993 Pinot Noir–Chardonnay Brut, Australia, $13.50

Sutter Home NV Fre-Spumante, CA, $5.99

Swedish Hill NV Blanc de Blanc, NY, $10.99

Windsor 1994 Brut Méthode Champenoise, CA, $13

Windsor 1994 Private Reserve Blanc de Noirs, CA, $14

SYRAH/SHIRAZ

Columbia Winery 1996 Syrah, WA, $14

Correas 1996 Syrah, Argentina, $8.99

Curtis 1995 Ambassador's Vineyard Syrah, CA, $14

Deakin Estate 1997 Shiraz, Australia, $9.99

Fairview Estate 1993 Shiraz, South Africa, $14.99

Forest Glen 1996 Shiraz, CA, $10

Geyser Peak 1995 Shiraz, CA, $12.99

Geyser Peak 1996 Shiraz, CA, $12.99

Hermitage Road 1997 Shiraz, Australia, $12.99

Hogue 1995 Syrah, WA, $15

McDowell 1996 Syrah, CA, $10

Marietta 1995 Syrah, CA, $14.99

Meridian 1996 Syrah, CA, $15

Monthaven 1996 Syrah, CA, $9.99

Nevada City Winery 1996 Syrah, CA, $14

Silver Ridge 1996 Barrel Select Syrah, CA, $10

WHITE BLENDS

Alderbrook 1997 Tredici, CA, $10

Carmenet 1995 Paragon Vineyard White Meritage, CA, $15

Fantaisie 1996 Menage à Trois White Wine, CA, $8

Kingston Estate 1997 Semillon Sauvignon Blanc, Australia, $7.99

Rosemount 1997 Diamond Label Semillon-Chardonnay, Australia, $8

Washington Hills 1996 Semillion/Chardonnay, WA, $7.99

Handley 1997 Brightlighter White, CA, $8.75

ZINFANDEL

Amador 1995 Ferrero Vineyard Zinfandel, CA, $12.50

Barefoot Cellars NV Barefoot Zinfandel, CA, $5.99

Beringer 1995 Appellation Collection Zinfandel, CA, $12

Black Rock Wineworks 1996 Zinfandel, CA, $14.50

Castoro Cellars 1996 Tribute Estate Vineyard Zinfandel, CA, $15

Castoro Cellars 1996 Zinfandel, CA, $12

David Bruce 1995 Ranchita Canyon Vineyard Zinfandel, CA, $15

Deaver Vineyards 1995 Zinfandel, CA, $15

Deux Amis 1995 Zinfandel, CA, $15

Gallo Sonoma 1994 Frei Ranch Zinfandel, CA, $14

Gallo Sonoma 1995 Frei Ranch Zinfandel, CA, $14

Geyser Peak 1995 Zinfandel, CA, $12.99

Granite Springs 1995 Estate Bottled Zinfandel, CA, $11.50

Latcham Vineyards 1995 Special Reserve Estate Grown Zinfandel, CA, $14

Madrona 1996 Zinfandel, CA, $10

Obester Winery 1995 Zinfandel, CA, $14.95

Parducci 1996 Old Vines Zinfandel, CA, $10

Pedroncelli 1996 Mother Clone Special Vineyard Selection Zinfandel, CA, $12

Red Rock Winery 1994 Zinfandel, CA, $8

Rosenblum NV Vintner's Cuvée XVI Zinfandel, CA, $9.50

Sierra Vista 1996 Herbert Vineyard Zinfandel, CA, $15

Sierra Vista 1996 Reeves Vineyard Zinfandel, CA, $15

Windsor 1995 Zinfandel, CA, $14.50

Windsor 1996 Private Reserve Old Vines Zinfandel, CA, $13.50

Windsor 1996 Zinfandel, CA, $9.75

York Mountain 1996 Zinfandel, CA, $12

Best of the Best Wines:
Three or More Gold Medals

Once you realize that shopping for gold medal wines takes *all* of the anxiety and uncertainty out of wine buying, it's a great relief. I keep a dog-eared copy of *Best Wines!* in the glove compartment of my car so I'll always have it when I stop into the wine shop.

A potential problem with shopping this way, however, is that you might find yourself becoming obsessed with gold medal wines, as I have. When my companion chooses a bottle at the wine shop, I check the book to see if it's a gold medal winner. If not, I shrug my shoulders and tell him he'll have to take the blame if it's no good. Truth is, he's become a convert too. (Does he really have a choice, girls?)

A wine that's won one gold medal will rarely disappoint. But when I want *a stupendous wine,* a wine I know will be fantastic even if it's a type I don't normally drink or a label with which I'm unfamiliar, I seek out a BBW—Best of the Best Wines. These are bottles that walked away with *at least three gold medals from three different top competitions.* This means that no less than fifteen renowned wine authorities gave each of these wines their highest mark. Each was chosen best out of a combined field of anywhere from, say, 60 to 300 competing wines of the same type. Wow!

You'll be happy to discover, as I always am, that some of these BBWs are also great bargains as well.

The wines below are the crème de la crème, the killer wines, the ivy leaguers, *the bottles to stock.*

CABERNET SAUVIGNON

Beaulieu Vineyard 1994 Georges de Latour Private Reserve Cabernet Sauvignon, CA, $50

Belvedere 1995 Cabernet Sauvignon, CA, $17

Chateau Souverain 1994 Winemaker's Reserve Cabernet Sauvignon, CA, $35

Clos du Val 1993 Reserve Cabernet Sauvignon, CA, $48

Fetzer 1994 Usibelli Vineyard Reserve Cabernet Sauvignon, CA, $24

Fetzer 1995 Valley Oaks Cabernet Sauvignon, CA, $8.99

Gallo Sonoma 1993 Estate Cabernet Sauvignon, CA, $45

Gallo Sonoma 1994 Frei Ranch Vineyard Cabernet Sauvignon, CA, $18

Guenoc 1994 Bella Vista Vineyard Reserve Cabernet Sauvignon, CA, $30

Guenoc 1995 Cabernet Sauvignon, CA, $15.50

Meridian 1994 Coastal Reserve Cabernet Sauvignon, CA, $20

V. Sattui Winery 1996 Suzanne's Vineyard Cabernet Sauvignon, CA, $22.50

Venezia 1996 Meola Vineyards Cabernet Sauvignon, CA, $19.99

CHARDONNAY

Canyon Road 1997 Chardonnay, CA, $7.99

DeLoach 1996 O.F.S. Chardonnay, CA, $27.50

Dry Creek Vineyard 1996 Reserve Chardonnay, CA, $20

Gallo Sonoma 1995 Estate Bottled Chardonnay, CA, $35

Gary Farrell 1996 Allen Vineyard Chardonnay, CA, $28

Kendall-Jackson 1996 Camelot Vineyard Chardonnay, CA, $20

Monthaven 1996 Chardonnay, CA, $15.99

Seven Peaks 1996 Chardonnay, CA, $12.99

MERLOT

Bartholomew Park 1996 Alta Vista Vineyards Merlot, CA, $18

Benziger 1995 Reserve Merlot, CA, $32

Greenwood Ridge Vineyards 1995 Estate Bottled Merlot, CA, $22

MISCELLANEOUS REDS

Geyser Peak 1995 Trione Vineyards Winemaker's Selection Petite Verdot, CA, $20

Geyser Peak 1995 Winemaker's Selection Malbec, CA, $20

Robert Pepi 1995 Colline Di Sassi Sangiovese, CA, $25

Stag's Leap 1994 Petite Sirah, CA, $22

MISCELLANEOUS SWEET WINES

Chateau St. Jean 1994 Belle Terre Special Select Late Harvest Johannisberg Riesling, CA, $25/375 ml

Geyser Peak 1997 Preston Ranch Late Harvest Riesling, CA, $16/375 ml

Navarro 1996 Cluster Select Late Harvest White Riesling, CA, $19.50

Sumac Ridge 1996 V.Q.A. Pinot Blanc Ice Wine, Canada, (Can $) 49.95/ 375 ml

MISCELLANEOUS WHITES

Castelletto 1996 Cortese, CA, $16

Fetzer 1997 Riesling, CA, $7.99

St. James Winery 1997 Vintner's Reserve Vignoles, MO, $12.99

St. Supéry 1996 White Meritage, CA, $20

Ventana Vineyards 1997 Barrel Fermented Estate Bottled Chenin Blanc, CA, $10

MUSCAT

Gan Eden 1997 Black Muscat, CA, $12

Quady 1996 Essensia, CA, $13.50

Quady 1997 Elysium, CA, $13.50

Windsor 1996 Murphy Ranch LH Private Reserve Muscat Canelli, CA, $12.50

PINOT NOIR

Gary Farrell 1996 Bien Nacido Vineyard Pinot Noir, CA, $28

Gary Farrell 1996 Russian River Valley Pinot Noir, CA, $22.50

Greenwood Ridge 1996 Pinot Noir, CA, $22

Handley Cellars 1995 Pinot Noir, CA, $21

Hartford Court 1996 Arrendell Vineyard Pinot Noir, CA, $42

Hartford Court 1996 Sonoma Coast Pinot Noir, CA, $32

Meridian 1995 Pinot Noir, CA, $15.50

Stonestreet 1995 Pinot Noir, CA, $30

PORT AND SHERRY

Beringer 1994 Port of Cabernet Sauvignon, CA, $20

Ficklin Aged 10 Year Tawny Port, CA, $24

Sheffield Cellars NV Livingston Cream Sherry, CA, $3.99

RED BLENDS

Charles Krug 1994 Peter Mondavi Family Generations, CA, $30

Geyser Peak 1995 Reserve Alexandre, CA, $24.99

Kathryn Kennedy Winery 1996 Lateral, CA, $30

Sierra Vista 1997 Fleur de Montagne, CA, $14

St. Supéry 1994 Meritage, CA, $40

ROSÉ AND WHITE ZINFANDEL

Hart 1997 Collins Ranch Grenache Rosé, CA, $9

Laetitia 1993 Elegance Rosé, CA, $23

Swanson 1997 Rosé of Sangiovese, CA, $14

SAUVIGNON BLANC

Bellefleur 1996 Sauvignon Blanc, CA, $11

Canyon Road 1997 Sauvignon Blanc, CA, $6.99

Geyser Peak 1997 Sauvignon Blanc, CA, $8.50

Handley Cellars 1996 Sauvignon Blanc, CA, $13

St. Supéry 1997 Dollarhide Ranch Sauvignon Blanc, CA, $10.55

Voss 1997 Sauvignon Blanc, CA, $12.50

SPARKLING WINES

Jordan 1994 J, CA, $28

Windsor 1994 Private Reserve Blanc de Noirs, CA, $14

SYRAH/SHIRAZ

Benziger 1995 Syrah, CA, $16

Geyser Peak 1995 Reserve Shiraz, CA, $29.99

Geyser Peak 1996 Shiraz, CA, $12.99

Kathryn Kennedy 1996 Maridon Vineyard Syrah, CA, $30

Meridian 1996 Syrah, CA, $15

ZINFANDEL

Edmeades 1996 Zinfandel, CA, $19

Fanucchi 1996 Fanucchi-Wood Road Vineyard Old Vines Zinfandel, CA, $33.75

Gary Farrell 1996 Old Vine Selection Zinfandel, CA, $21.50

Hartford Court 1996 Hartford Vineyard Zinfandel, CA, $35

Rosenblum 1996 Richard Sauret Vineyard Zinfandel, CA, $17

Rosenblum 1996 Samsel Vineyard Maggie's Reserve Zinfandel, CA, $28

APPENDIX 3

A Glossary of Winespeak

I f you're not an avid reader and fan of wine magazines and wine guides, you may feel that wine writers belong to a secret society, one that excludes you with its enigmatic language. I used to shrug my shoulders, roll my eyes, and ask, "Who writes this stuff?"

The problem stems from the very thing that makes wine so special. As people have known since the dawning of Greek civilization and before, wine isn't merely a beverage. It's been imbued in people's hearts and minds with nearly divine qualities. It's been used and is still used in religious ceremonies; it's associated with love, happiness, passages, status, sin, decadence—you name it. So to describe its flavors and aromas, the effect it has in your mouth, the sensations it imparts beyond taste, and the other subtle, almost imperceptible feelings it evokes requires a special language.

Believe it or not, once you have the rosetta stone that unlocks the mysteries of winespeak, you'll find much of this once-boggling (and often goofy) set of terms quite useful. As with any other jargon, the better you can navigate in and around the terminology, the more you'll come to understand the subject itself.

Really grasping the most common terms will enhance your wine-tasting experience. For example, once I realized that vanilla refers to a subtle aroma imparted by oak barrel aging, I was able to train my nose to detect it, and then to pick up, for example, toasty scents too, also associated with oak.

The good news is that wine descriptions generally follow a simple—and, yes, logical!—six-part formulaic structure that exactly corresponds to how one experiences and tastes one's first sip of wine (see the Palate Secrets chapter). Each wine term in tasting notes will fall into one of six categories, as illustrated by the following chart:

TASTING TERM	TASTING STEP
Color	Look at the wine
Nose/aroma/bouquet	Swirl and sniff
Flavors	Sip and "whistle" in air
Body/texture	"Chew" the wine
Structure and balance (oak/tannins/acidity/ sugar/alcohol)	Consciously gather impressions while wine is in your mouth
Finish	Swallow the wine (or spit)

The following glossary will help to untangle some of the more common terms of winespeak.

acid/acidity   Acid is to wine what a good zing of lime juice is to food: it adds zest and liveliness. Terms such as *crisp, tart, lively,* and *refreshing* refer to wines that have a good balance of acidity. Acidity is what keeps sweet and semisweet wines from being too cloying, and it's what helps deliver the flavor in sparkling wines, since the mousse (foamy bubbles) can sometimes disperse the fruity elements. Acidity makes white wines a good dinner guest, since acid stimulates the appetite, cleanses the palate, and cuts through rich foods. Acidity is especially important in white wines, which lack the tannin levels of reds, because it contributes to white wine's ability to age well in your cellar.

aroma   How a wine smells after you pour it into a glass will tell much of the story, at least in terms of the kinds of flavors you can expect. A wine's aroma is often referred to as its *nose, bouquet,* or *scent.* Aromas in winespeak may include everything from saddle leather to flint, tropical fruits to common garden vegetables.

backbone Here's a term that can be taken rather literally. It generally refers to either tannin or acid levels that "hold up" or "support" the wine. A wine without adequate backbone might be too soft, too light bodied, too fruity, or too sweet. Wines with firm tannic or acidic backbones are *full bodied*.

balance This is a term of praise that describes that magic moment in a wine's development when its components— chiefly acid, sugar, alcohol and fruit—work together to achieve harmony. Acid is what balances sweetness; the concentration of fruit is what balances tannin and oakiness; and the overall flavor and acidity of the wine balance out the alcohol. It's reasonable to assume that all balanced wines won't have the same intensity. For example, a balanced light wine should be delicate, while a balanced full-bodied wine might inspire such adjectives as *blockbuster* and *powerhouse*.

barrel aging Most wines spend only a brief period of time in large vats or tanks to rid them of impurities and to prepare them for bottling. But the fuller-flavored reds and some whites, such as drier-style Chardonnays, Sauvignon Blancs, Chenin Blancs, and Pinot Blancs, are aged in large or small oak barrels or larger casks, which matures them, adds structure, and improves their taste, if done correctly.

Barrel aging requires time, money, knowledge, and considerable effort, so winemakers like to brag about what nationality of oak they used, how old their barrels were, how long their wine spent in the precious barrels, and so on. But there's another reason they mention it, especially in the case of white wines, which has to do with identifying a certain style of wine. Barrel-aged wines have specific flavor characteristics that nonbarrel-aged wines lack. Some terms that derive from oak barrel aging include *oak*, *vanilla, clove, nutmeg, cinnamon, toast, smoke,* and sometimes *chocolate.*

Oak barrel aging imparts all-important tannin necessary for longer shelf life to whites, but, oddly, mellows the sharp tannin levels in robust red wines.

big See **body**.

blend Blending is not too different in winemaking than it is in cooking up the perfect curry—a dash of this, a pinch of that, all to accomplish the perfect balance of flavors, bite, and piquancy. A wine might be a blend of the same varietal grown in different vineyards, a blend of the same wine aged in different casks, a blend of wines from different vintages, or a blend of two or more varieties.

The winemaker's goal in blending might be to produce a wine that consumers can depend on for flavor and quality consistency year after year. Often, though, blending is the art of maximizing the assets of each lot for the good of the whole. Certain varieties, such as Cabernet Sauvignon, simply become "friendlier" after marrying with, say, Merlot or Cabernet Franc in a Bordeaux-style blend. Most wines are blends of one type or another, and it is a perfectly legitimate practice for which every wine-producing country and region has laws that dictate how a blended wine can be labeled.

body This is a term for a sensation that's simple to identify if you pay attention. "Body" describes how a wine feels in your mouth—its texture, weight, and fullness—and refers to a combination of the wine's alcohol, sugar, and glycerin content (glycerin, a by-product of fermentation, is a colorless, sweet, slippery liquid that adds *smoothness* to wine). Body is substance; think of body as being the opposite of thin and watery. A light- and medium-bodied wine might be described as *soft, attractive, simple,* or *delicate.* A full-bodied wine might be called *brawny, mouth* *filling, chewy, big,* or *weighty*. Most wines are not full bodied, and there's no rule that says a medium-bodied wine is inferior to a full-bodied one. They are different, and will complement different foods. Remember that the key to a wine's greatness is its *balance,* not the measure of its body.

botrytis Its formal name is *Botrytis cinerea,* and it's also known as "noble rot." When wine grapes grow in just the right conditions—dry, sunny days alternating with damp, foggy mornings——they may become *botrytized,* or infected with the beneficial mold that transforms normal grape juice into a honeyed, aromatic, magical liquid. Since this condition is apt to happen after harvest season, as late as December in some places, the resultant wines are called *late harvest* wines, and they're prized the world over.

Here's how it works. The beneficial mold covers the grapes, sending little filaments into the skin that perforate the grapes and causes them to shrivel up. The mold doesn't rot the grapes, but 90 percent of the water evaporates, and the sugar and acids remain in the grape pulp. When this is pressed and fermented, you get very sweet wine (since all the sugar isn't fermented into alcohol) that has extremely concentrated flavors and aromas. Think, for example, of how intense a dried tomato or dried pear tastes compared to the fresh item, and you get the idea.

The most common grapes used to make late harvest wines are Semillon, Sauvignon Blanc, Riesling, Gewurztraminer, and Chenin Blanc, although there are others that are susceptible to the noble rot. These wines age extremely well in the bottle.

bouquet Most would argue that aroma and bouquet are basically the same thing. Others insist that bouquet refers to the range of scents associated with the vinification and aging processes, while aroma has more to do with the scent that emerges from the grapes. See also **aroma.**

brawny See **powerful**.

breathing/airing To breathe or not to breathe seems to be the question, and the answer, as far as I'm concerned, doesn't seem all that unclear. Breathing refers to the act of pouring wine into another container, such as a decanter, in order to allow the wine to aerate and mix with oxygen. This permits the aroma components of the wine to oxidize, thus intensifying them. (Breathing does *not* refer to uncorking a wine. The narrow neck of the bottle prohibits an adequate supply of oxygen from making any discernible difference in the wine's bouquet.)

But much of the material I've read seems to lean on the side of the pour-wine-into-your-glass-and-just-drink-it side of the argument. Only the surface is getting oxidized anyway, and some of the fruitiness and flavor is at risk if a wine is exposed to oxygen too long. (This makes sense; otherwise, why would we bother to recork a half-consumed bottle?) If you're serving a young, tannic red wine, breathing may lessen some of the tannins. If you're serving a very old wine, careful decanting should be done to separate the wine from the sediments in the bottom of the bottle.

In general, though, serve your wine in a large, wide wine glass (for maximum surface contact with the air), swirl it around a bit before sipping it, and your wine will get enough air to achieve the desired results. (For more on tasting and smelling wine, see the Palate Secrets chapter.)

brut This is a term that refers to the driest champagnes and other sparkling wine. In Europe, Common Market laws dictate that a sparkling wine labeled "brut" must have no more than 1.5 percent sugar. In America and elsewhere, the term is merely a descriptive one that means "very dry." There is no good way to tell if a non-European brut sparkling wine will be dry, very dry, or very, very dry without tasting it.

buttery See **creamy**.

chewy You'll know a chewy wine when you drink one. The term is used to describe red wines that have high levels of tannin and are rich, heavy, textured, and full of fruit extract. See also **body** and **mouth feel.**

cigarbox A term used to describe the aroma of cedar and/ or tobacco in a wine. It's not an uncomplimentary adjective.

citrus Although citrus fruits include oranges, lemons, and limes, among others, in winespeak the term *citrus* most often refers to grapefruit. Chardonnays grown in cool climates will often display a grapefruitlike character.

closed It may sound insulting to a layperson, but to say that a wine is closed implies that it has great potential. In other words, the wine has a loads of fruit concentration and good character, but needs more time in the bottle to mature to full intensity.

complex In a complex wine, layers and layers of flavors and aromas reveal themselves, the wine has just the right *mouth feel,* a lovely *finish,* and all of the components are in *balance.* Complexity is elusive, but the best wines have it.

concentrated Concentrated wines are not watery and thin, but possess intense fruit flavor components that jump out at you and make a distinct impression on your palate. The aftereffects of a concentrated wine tend to linger. See also **finish.**

creamy Some wines are described as having a creamy or *buttery* texture or flavors. In sparkling wines, this is a result of contact with the lees, or yeast cells. In certain whites, this creaminess may be a result of malolactic fermentation, a process by which malic acid, the acid in apples and other fruit, is converted into lactic acid, the acid found in milk, to create wines that are softer and more *supple* in texture, less harsh and less *tart*. In wine terms, creamy is the opposite of *crisp,* which refers to a wine's *lively acidity*.

crisp *Crisp* is a code word that indicates a wine's acid content, in this case a pleasing level of acidity. It is synonymous with *refreshing, fresh,* and *tart.* See **acid/acidity.**

cuvée This word comes from the French *cuve,* meaning vat or tank, particularly a large one used for blending or fermenting wines. In places other than Europe, the term has come to mean a specific lot or batch of a particular wine or blend.

delicate See **body**.

demi-sec Is the glass half full or half empty? *Demi* is from the French meaning "half," and *sec* means "dry." But demi-sec wines are closer to being half sweet than they are to being half dry. This term is usually applied to sparkling wines that are sweet to medium sweet.

depth Some of these wine terms get tricky, and you have to use your imagination a bit. Where *weight* refers to a wine's body, or how a wine "feels" in your mouth, depth has more to do with how *much* of your mouth experiences the wine. It's a subtle distinction, but a wine that has good depth is one full of layers of flavors that seem to fill your mouth from front to back.

dry The opposite of dry, in wine terms, is sweet. A still or sparkling wine in which an ordinary taster perceives no sweetness is dry, and that would fall somewhere between 0.5 and 0.7 percent *residual sugar,* which is the amount of sugar left after a wine has finished fermenting. Dry does not necessarily mean better; there are many wines that are supposed to be sweet. See **sweet**.

estate bottled In the United States, "estate bottled" on a label means that the wine comes from the winery's own vineyards, or from vineyards leased on a long-term basis, only if the vineyards and winery are both located within the appellation shown on the label. In other words, the grape juice wasn't purchased from a winery a thousand miles away, and then made into wine. Or conversely, the wine wasn't grown in the vineyards, and then made into wine a thousand miles away. Estate bottling is supposed to connote superior quality.

extract Elements that add flavor, aroma, and character to a wine are known as extract. A "highly extracted" wine, or one with "loads of extract," implies that the grapes used to make this wine had very concentrated juice, and this could be for any number of reasons, among them a great vintage; careful avoidance of overcropping; *old vines; late harvest;* or possibly because they were just great grapes.

fat Fat is good when it describes dessert wines. It refers to the naturally occurring glycerin in sweet dessert wines, the oily richness that coats your mouth. The term is less complimentary when it refers to nondessert wines that are medium to full bodied, slightly low in acid, and leave a fat or full impression on your palate.

filtered There's a lot of stuff floating around in wine after it's been fermented. After all, fermentation is caused by little living critters, and they don't just disappear, nor do their by-products. Therefore, most winemakers fine and filter their wine at least a little because most people expect their wine to be clear. Explaining the types of filters and extent to which wines should be filtered could fill the rest of this book. Know, however, that even as you read this, someone, somewhere is getting hot under the collar debating how extensively wines should be filtered. Why? Because wine lovers complain that *fining* and overfiltering wine removes from it the very thing we love: its character.

Therefore, many winemakers are moving back to the traditional (European, Old World) practice of not overdoing it, figuring that New World wine lovers would rather put up with a little sediment than drink something with no personality. Some wineries put "Unfined, Unfiltered" on their labels to alert consumers to a purist approach, a more hand-crafted winemaking method that, theoretically at least, leads to a higher-quality, more sensuous wine-drinking experience. See **fined**.

fined   Fining is similar to filtering, resultwise at least. As opposed to filtering, where the wine is poured through something that screens out the sediments and other junk, in fining something is *added* to the wine that captures the unwanted solid particles. It's the same process cooks use to clarify broth or to make jelly clear (by adding egg whites). In fact, winemakers also use egg whites sometimes, but more commonly gelatin or bentonite (a type of clay). Like filtering, it's a controversial practice if done to excess, because it's a bit like giving the wine a lobotomy: a lot of personality can get lost in the process. See **filtered**.

fine-grained tannins   When a winemaker refers to *tannins* as being fine-grained, he or she is saying that tannins are present, but they're smooth and refined, well behaved, and not overpowering.

finish   If only winespeakers would come up with some new ways to describe a great finish other than "long and lingering." After you swallow the wine, its finish is characterized both by how long the flavors linger in your mouth and by what kind of qualities are still perceptible. A finish in a quality wine might be medium or long, but it could also be soft, creamy, slightly tannic, or just "good." A wine's *length* or persistence is a component of its finish.

firm Used to describe a wine that hits your palate with an acidic or tannic bang, this is a complimentary term that implies your wine may be rather young, but will make a great accompaniment to strong-flavored foods.

fleshy/meaty These terms refer to *body* and texture, and often suggest a wine of great smoothness and richness, where suppleness and flavor are in harmony. See **chewy.**

fortified wine Sherry and port are the best-known examples of fortified wines in the New World. These are wines in which the alcoholic content has been increased to the tune of 17 to 21 percent in the finished product by the addition of brandy or neutral spirits. Because of their high alcohol, fortified wines are less likely to spoil after opening than table wines, and they also have long, long cellaring potential. In the United States, sweet fortified wines have to be labeled "Dessert Wine" because the federal authorities want to prevent street alcoholics from misunderstanding and then mistakenly buying up and glugging down all the expensive twenty-year-old rare port they can find.

fruity This is a term that often applies to young wines. A fruity wine is full of intense fruit flavors such as berries or apples, and possesses a quality of freshness.

glycerin A by-product of fermentation, glycerin is found in all wines, but is most obvious in higher-alcohol and late harvest wines. At high levels it feels slippery and smooth on the tongue, and adds fullness to the wine's body.

grassy You will often see this term when Sauvignon Blanc is being described because it is part of that wine's *varietal character*. Grassiness is a nice quality if you think of the light, fresh, green smell of a summer lawn being mowed. Sometimes "gooseberry" is used to describe a similar flavor/aroma. Too much grassiness is a negative.

grip When a wine, like a handshake, is forceful, it has grip. Grip is used to describe a red wine distinguished by rich texture and an assertive personality.

herbs/herbaceous Certain wines (for instance, Cabernet Sauvignon, Sauvignon Blanc, and Merlot) are sometimes described as having herbal aromas and/or flavors. Which herbs depends on the wine's *varietal character*.

hybrid When two or more grape varieties are genetically crossed by human intervention, you get a hybrid. The idea is to create a grape that's superior to the parents, or one that's better able to cope with such conditions as climatic extremes or proneness to disease. In the northern United States, French–native American hybrids have resulted in wines that are much better than those of native varieties in many cases. It may take thousands of crosses to come up with a commercially successful wine, and it takes about fifteen years to determine if that hybrid will produce consistently sound wine.

late harvest If harvest time is autumn, then grapes picked later than that would be late harvest, right? Well, yes, but late harvest on a label really refers to how *ripe* the grapes were at harvest time. If grapes are picked at a stage where they're riper than normal (i.e., they have a higher-than-normal sugar content), they'll be made into a late harvest wine. Often, but not always, these later-picked grapes have been infected with noble rot, or *botrytis*. Either way, *late harvest* on a label means that the wine will be sweeter than normal—possibly very, very sweet—or will have higher-than-normal alcohol levels. Most late harvest wines are after-dinner wines, sipped in place of dessert.

lees You'll often read that a wine "sat on the lees" or that it was "left in contact with the lees" for several months. Lees means sediment, or more precisely, dead yeast cells that are a by-product of fermentation. When wine ferments, this sediment sinks to the bottom of the barrel or tank and is promptly removed so as not to contribute unwanted odors or flavors. But some wines, particularly some Chardonnays and Sauvignon Blancs, are left in contact with the lees (called *sur lie*) after fermentation. This adds complexity and a lovely toasty, roasted grain character. Sparkling wines get much of their character from aging on the lees, done during a second fermentation inside the bottle—sediment and all—before the lees are removed. This is why the best sparkling wines taste akin to freshly toasted homemade bread. The lees contact also contributes richness and creaminess to these sparkling wines.

length The amount of time the aftertaste lingers in your mouth after swallowing your wine is a wine's length. Ten seconds is good, fifteen is great, and twenty seconds is spectacular. See **finish**.

méthode champenoise All champagnes from France are produced by the *méthode champenoise*. For producers of sparkling wine in the New World (some of whom insist on calling their sparklers "champagne," which is punishable by law in France if not produced in that eponymous region!), this wine term has definite snooty connotations. In fact, wines made by this method take a lot more expertise, time, and money, so the resultant sparklers are generally of higher quality.

After the wine has fermented it is bottled, and a measured amount of sugar and yeast is added. When the bottle is corked, fermentation occurs, but the carbon dioxide that is produced gets trapped inside, thus creating those great bubbles. The sediment that is a by-product then must be expelled. These champagnes are marketed in the very bottle in which the second fermentation took place.

mouth feel/mouth filling Wine writers love this term, which refers to wines with intense, round flavors, often in combination with glycerin or slightly low acidity. The idea here is that the wine's various characteristics seem to expand in the mouth, thus "filling" it up (as opposed, say, to an acidic wine that would have a distinct cutting or biting edge). Mouth feel is often used in conjunction with the modifiers *chewy* or *fleshy*. See **body.**

must The juice of grapes produced by pressing or crushing, before it is fermented.

natural In *méthode champenoise* sparkling wines, after the lees have been removed, a small amount of wine is lost. So winemakers commonly add a mixture of wine and sugar (known as the dosage) to fill up the bottle and to add some degree of sweetness, depending on how dry they want the final sparkler to be. Natural (sometimes spelled naturel) sparkling wines have no sweetener added. Thus, a natural champagne or sparkling wine is driest of all. Winemakers sometimes refer to these as "no dosage" wines.

New World wines The world of fine wine is no longer dominated by Italy and France. Open up any wine magazine and you'll see article after article about New World wines. New World, as it refers to wines, means Australia and New Zealand, South Africa, and the winemaking regions of North and South America—

primarily Canada, the U.S., Chile, and Argentina. The term refers to the colonies that were established as a result of European exploration starting around the 15th century.

Wine writers love to compare New World with Old World wines. To do so here would take up an entire chapter. Suffice it to say that like every other industry, the wine industry exchanges technology, tradition, know-how, and capital and human resources left and right across the oceans and back. Excellence, when it comes to wine nowadays, is global.

noble rot See **botrytis**.

no dosage See **natural**.

nose See **aroma**.

NV These initials, commonly seen on labels, stand for nonvintage. The word means that the wine you're drinking is a blend of several different vintages, usually based mainly on the most recent one, with the products of some past vintages, sometimes called "reserve wines," blended in. Just because a wine has no vintage does not mean it is of lower quality. Indeed, some winemakers attempt to produce wines year after year that will be consistent and always excellent. NV is often seen on sparkling wines or champagnes.

oak/oaky Aging in oak barrels imparts certain flavors and aromas to wines, including, obviously, oakiness. Vanillin, which comes from the oak itself, and toasty or roasted qualities, derived from the charring that comes from the open flames used to heat the barrel staves during barrel making, are common ways to describe oaky wines. *Woody* is another word for oaky.

oenology   Also spelled enology, this is the study and knowledge of wine, and includes both viticulture (wine growing) and winemaking.

old vines   Like classic, well-cared-for cars, old grapevines are considered valuable. The reason, oddly enough, is that the older a vineyard becomes, the lower its yield. But since each vine has to devote all of its energy into producing fewer grapes, those fewer grapes will have a higher level of *extract*. Since conventional wisdom would state unabashedly that old vines make better wines, you'll often see "Old Vines" or "80 Year Old" or some such right on the label to announce to potential buyers that this wine should be jam-packed with flavor.

phylloxera   If you're seeking revenge on a mean and nasty winemaker who has dis'd you, whisper "phylloxera" in his ear and walk away. He'll turn several shades of white, for this vine disease, brought about by tiny aphids or lice that attack the roots of most grapevines, was responsible for wiping out virtually all vineyards in France and America in the last century. Grape growers are deadly afraid of it, and for good reason. The little pests live on in the soil, and will attack *Vitis vinifera* vines (which includes all of the European varieties from which the finest wines in the world are made) like there's no tomorrow.

In the late nineteenth century, it was discovered that most native American varieties were immune to phylloxera, so grafting the European varieties onto American rootstock was done, both in America and throughout Europe. Unfortunately, that didn't solve the problem completely, since the little devils have found a way to show up again on the American rootstock that was widely used in the 1980s. (By the year 2000, for instance, 30 to 50 percent of all U.S. coastal vineyards will have to be systematically replanted because of phylloxera.) Some varieties are more resistant than others, and some regions—Chile, for example—have never had the problem at all.

powerful Powerful red wines are ones that are high in alcohol and tannin, also sometimes called *brawny* reds. A powerful white wine would be a dry wine with lots of body.

private reserve See **reserve**.

proprietary wine This is a name or brand dreamed up by a producer that's exclusive to that producer, and is used instead of the varietal name. So, for example, if a producer wants his 1993 Cabernet Sauvignon to stand out from the pack, he might name it Midnight Red, and the next year's wine would be the 1994 Midnight Red. It's a bit like trademarking your wine. The problem for consumers, of course, is that it's impossible to determine from the proprietary name what kind of wine they're buying. On the other hand, this growing trend has added some sparkle, fun, and mystique to the formerly stuffy wine world.

proprietor's reserve See **reserve**.

reserve Although there's no official regulation governing how this term is used, a reserve wine usually represents a wine of higher quality than the regular bottling of that same variety. You'll see the term alone, or sometimes as Grand Reserve, Private Reserve, Proprietor's Reserve, Special Reserve, Vintner's Reserve, Winemaker's Reserve, and the like. A high-quality producer with a conscience won't abuse the term; it should be merited.

Reserve wines get their name because the wine has been separated out, or reserved, from the rest of the batch. It might be aged longer or differently. It might be from selected vineyards, or from selected lots of wine. Or sometimes reserve wines are merely chosen and bottled from the top 5 to 10 percent of the existing batches.

Regardless, expect to pay more for reserve wines. If both the reserve and the regular bottling have won gold medals, try both and see if the difference in quality warrants the difference in price.

residual sugar After a wine is done fermenting, there's usually at least a small amount of unfermented grape sugar, known as residual sugar. Winemakers put this statistic in their notes, and occasionally on their labels, especially for dessert wines, to let consumers know how sweet they can expect the wine to be and how and with what foods to enjoy it. It's expressed as a percentage by volume or weight. See **sweet.**

roasted See **oaky.**

round A wine described as being round has enough residual sugar to balance out any rough edges such as tannin and acid, and may be rich and ripe, leaving a full sensation in your mouth. The key word here is *balance,* since round wines have a quality of fullness or completeness, without any one taste or tactile sensation dominating.

sec Applied to sparkling wines, *sec,* which in French means "dry," actually means sweet or very sweet. You'll have to figure it out.

soft See **body**.

spicy Certain varietals are often, and appropriately, described as being spicy. Gewurztraminer's *varietal character* evokes such a description, as do Zinfandel, Shiraz, and red Rhône blends. Spicy generally refers to pungent, attractive aromas and flavors including black pepper, clove, cinnamon, anise, cardamom, and caraway, depending on the wine.

structure How body, acid, alcohol, glycerin, and tannin interact in a wine make up its structure. A good wine will have "firm" or "good" structure.

supple This is a complimentary term that's generally used to describe full-bodied reds that have achieved a kind of softness, in spite of high levels of *tannin* and *acidity,* and a fairly firm *structure.*

sur lie See **lees**.

sweet As I've mentioned, sweetness is not a fault. Sweet wines are *supposed* to be sweet. The key is to have enough *acid* present to maintain *balance.* Many wines will have the residual sugar levels right on their label. If you happen to love Riesling, but not supersweet Riesling, you'll need to know about residual sugar (RS):

Less than 0.5% RS	=	dry
0.6% to 1.4% RS	=	slightly sweet
1.5% to 2.9% RS	=	medium sweet
3.0% to 5.9% RS	=	sweet
More than 5.9% RS	=	very sweet

tannin Tannin, or tannic acid, comes from the stems, seeds, and skins of grapes, as well as the wooden barrels in which the wines are stored and aged. Red wines have about five times more tannin than whites.

Tannins are detected not by taste but by *feel*. That puckery feeling in your mouth, also known as astringency, is from tannin. Brawny young reds will often have overpowering tannin, which means you should cellar them until the tannins soften and make room for the fruit. If the tasting notes say the wine is fairly tannic, that's winespeak for "don't touch this bottle for a year or two at least." Since tannin is a natural preservative, it's a necessary component of wines that are meant to have a very long life.

However, in order to age gracefully, a tannic wine must have adequate acid, sugar, and alcohol to stay in *balance*.

tart See **acid/acidity**.

texture See **body**.

toasted Caramel and toffee are toasty aromas. See also **oaky** and **yeasty.**

vanilla/vanillin When you see vanilla or vanillin in tasting notes, think oak. The reason is because aromas of vanilla come from the vanillin that is contributed by oak barrel staves. Just as in food, a whiff of vanilla, however subtle, gives an impression of sweetness. See **oaky**.

varietal A varietal wine takes its name from the grape variety of which it's primarily composed.

varietal character Each variety of grape has a distinct set of flavor and aroma characteristics when picked at the optimum moment of ripeness. Occasionally a winemaker will say that a wine "displays typical varietal *characteristics*," (or *bouquet* or *flavors*), which means, in effect, that he or she feels the wine is a typical but brilliant example of its variety. Once you know, for example, that California Zinfandels are spicy and berrylike, the phrase is convenient shorthand for all the spicy/berry flavors you're already likely to encounter and expect.

vinifera Short for *Vitis vinifera*, this is the species of grape used for the world's finest and most acclaimed wines. Except for the native American species, all the wines in this book are made from vinifera grapes.

vinification The act of turning grape juice into wine. This is the winemaker's domaine. See **viticulture.**

vintage Vintage basically means year, so a vintage 1993 bottle would contain wine that was grown and harvested in 1993. The rule is that at least 95 percent of that wine has to have come from 1993-grown grapes.

vintner's reserve See **reserve**.

viticulture The science of growing grapevines, as opposed to making wine. Viticultural practices such as cloning, cropping, pest control, etc. are the responsibilities of the grapegrower.

weight See **body**.

winemaker See **vinification**.

yeast/yeasty Commonly used to describe sparkling wines, yeastiness comes from—you guessed it—the yeast that is part of the fermentation process. "Toastiness" and "fresh baked bread" express the same aromas.

young To say that a wine is "still young" means that it could benefit from more time in the bottle to reach its full potential. A young wine might be good, but will be better still if given time to mature.

APPENDIX 4

Mail-Order/Internet Wine Buying

In sleepy little Woodstock, New York, there are three really excellent wine shops. Not only do they have remarkable selections, but they're always willing to go out of their way to order special wines I want and to make any number of calls to locate the exact vintage I seek. I like to patronize them because they offer something a mail-order outlet can't: hands-on service and personal attention.

But what if you live in Podunk, Nebraska, where you'd be as likely to find a ski resort nearby as a bottle of fine wine? Or what if you just feel like wine shopping in your pajamas in front of the cool computer screen one late and snowy night? Go for it, I say. But be aware that the state you live in may severely limit your wine-buying options (see Reciprocal States, below).

There are alarmists who try to make you feel guilty for shopping by Internet. "You'll put our mom and pop stores out of business!" they cry. These people envision ghost towns where all the stores are crumbling shells, the lonely and alienated residents at home huddled around computer stations.

It's just not going to happen. It didn't happen with the advent of mail-order catalogs, and it's not going to happen because of Internet retailers either.

One of the fun things about wine shopping on the Internet is browsing these sites, many of which have information about wine, wine clubs, listings of wine-related events, newsletters I can subscribe to, gift ideas, recipes, and more. If you've become a fan of a particular gold medal winery, you can also call them directly. Most wineries have free newsletters you can get and clubs you can join for discounts on their wines. Make sure you ask them if they can legally ship to you.

RECIPROCAL STATES

What is a reciprocal state anyway? Basically, a reciprocal wine state is one that allows residents to legally receive direct shipments of wine from other states that offer "reciprocal" shipping privileges to their residents.

There's a big hubbub going on around direct wine shipping. At issue is the survival of the three-tier system: producer (winery), wholesaler, and retailer. The latter two miss out when the winery sells directly to the customer without a middleman. Powerful lobby groups have tried to enact legislation that would make it a crime to ship or to receive wine, and they've succeeded in making it a felony in Florida, Georgia, Kentucky, North Carolina, and Tennessee. In some states the practice is "forbidden" but laws are not enforced.

To keep up with all the pending legislation and subtle shades of interpretation in the wine-shipping laws state-by-state would require a law degree. If you're thinking of buying wine by phone or online, here are steps you should take before doing so:

1. Get the most current wine-shipping regulations from Wine Institute's website. That address is http://www.wineinstitute.org. This excellent organization provides up-to-date, state-by-state, consumer-friendly information on the subject. Click on your own state to find out its legal status vis-à-vis direct wine shipping.

2. Ask the retailer, wine club, or winery whether or not they can ship to your state. These sources don't want to get into legal hot water, so they can either do it or they can't. Some of the firms listed below have found ways to be in legal compliance in getting the wine to you even if you live in a non-reciprocal state.

A CAVEAT

My research has shown that these are reputable places with good customer service people and policies. However, I can't make any guarantees. Be a smart shopper before you spend your hard-earned money. Find out if the retailer has a minimum order. Find out what the shipping costs are. Chat with the customer service person about how their company packs the wines, how the wines are stored, shipped, and when you can expect to receive them. A reputable firm will guarantee safe delivery and should allow you to return bottles that get broken or otherwise damaged in transit.

Brown Derby

International Wine Center
2023 South Glenstone
Springfield, MO 65804
(417) 883-4066
fax: (417) 883-3073
http://www.brownderby.com

Brown Derby has been around since 1937 and takes pride in its in-depth selection of wines from all over, including some of the uncommon wines from its region. All wines are shipped in preapproved boxes and go second-day air. Also, if you're in the market for Riedel crystal from Austria, this is one of the top retailers. Check out the website for more about these top-of-the-line wine glasses. Call to get on Brown Derby's mailing list. You'll receive the annual catalog and monthly flyers.

Calwine.com

1215 Silverado Trail
Napa, CA 94559
(888) CALWINE
fax: (707) 226-2086
http://www.calwine.com

I love sites like this one, which features a WineFinder, an easy way to look up the bottles you want, and an efficient way to just browse the selection. Calwine.com's wine list is good, and the site features gift baskets and a food shop too. The Wine Shop has a nifty Wine Club you can join. If the wine's available, they say, they'll find it for you.

City Wine
347 South Colorado Boulevard
Denver, CO 80246
(303) 393-7576
fax: (303) 393-1725
http://www.citywine.com

If City Wine is as good as its website, go no further. It's easy to look up wines in the wine portfolio, and if there's a wine you want that's not listed, contact the City Wine folks and they'll get it for you. On the website you'll find lots of good deals, discounted items, and specials. The people at City Wine personally taste and select every wine they carry, and the selection changes constantly.

Duke of Bourbon
20908 Roscoe Boulevard
Canoga Park, CA 91304
(800) 4FINE-WINE
fax: (818) 341-9232
http://www.dukeofbourbon.com

The Duke of Bourbon is an award-winning family-run retail wine and spirits enterprise established in 1967. It specializes in personalized service and offers a hand-picked selection of unique and rare California wines as well as a fine selection of French, Italian, and other world-class wines. Among the offerings: a newsletter, events, wine club, California wines matched with gourmet recipes, and custom gift baskets. To get on their mailing list, just give them a call. Definitely check out the website.

Geerlings and Wade, Inc.
960 Turnpike Street
Canton, MA 02021
(800) 782-WINE
fax: (781) 821-4153
http://www.geerwade.com

This is a big, reputable company with connections galore and a comprehensive and informative website. If G&W

can't get a wine, it probably can't be got! Mix a 3-, 6-, or 12-bottle case. Ask for the full list of imported and domestic wines. Subscribe to their monthly newsletter and also get a free wine accessories catalog. Become a G&W member and save. Satisfaction is guaranteed, and they'll accept most major credit cards.

The Great House of Wine
88101 Overseas Highway
Islamorada, FL 33036
(888) 853-5155 or (305) 853-5155
fax: 305-852-3280
http://www.tghwine.com
e-mail: info@tghwine.com

What if you live in New York State, where direct wine shipments are prohibited, and you're dying for a case of gold medal California wine that your local wine shop doesn't carry? Or say you live in Florida, where it's a felony to get wine by mail? Attorney Jim Mattson, co-founder of The Great House of Wine, had a great idea. He started a company in 1997 that currently makes it legal and convenient for residents of Florida, New York, and Connecticut to receive shipments of wine and be in total compliance with those state's laws. Over the next year, TGHWine plans to expand into another nine states; check out the website for updates. TGHWine *does not* sell wine directly to consumers. Rather, you place your order with the winery, who then ships your order through TGHWine. TGHWine loads the wine onto a constant-temperature truck, ships to a constant-temperature warehouse, and gets it to you one day after it reaches the warehouse. The cost? It ends up about the same as if you bought the wine locally. The advantage, of course, is that you'll be able to get the wines you want delivered directly to your doorstep—quickly, legally, and in excellent condition. At this writing, The Great House of Wine is working with dozens and dozens of top wineries, most of whom are in this book. To find out how to use TGHWine, call them or visit their informative website. Better yet, call the winery you want to order from and ask them if they use TGHWine's services. If they don't, they should.

K&L Wine Merchants
3005 El Camino Real
Redwood City, CA 94061
(800) 247-5987
fax: (650) 364-4687
http://www.klwines.com

I loved K&L's website, which was designed for readers who want an easy way to search the store's inventory, but have other interests besides just drinking wine. For example, you can browse the site for wine books, wine accessories, wine software, and more. K&L also offers single malt scotch and other spirits, and has a wine club you can join and a monthly newsletter.

Mr. Liquor
250 Taraval Street
San Francisco, CA 94116
(800) 681-WINE
fax: (415) 731-0155
http://www.mrliquor.com

Mr. Liquor's philosophy is simple: "big enough to serve you, small enough to know you." Mr. Liquor gives personalized service to all customers and ships just about anywhere. "Introduce yourself" over the phone and they'll definitely take care of all your wine needs. Call the store to get on the mailing list, or sign up on the website, which is really excellent, easy to use and understand, and very comprehensive.

Red Carpet Wines
400 East Glenoaks Boulevard
Glendale, CA 91207
(800) 339-0609
fax: (818) 247-6151
http://redcarpetwine.com

If you're looking for a California wine that's from a small producer, a so-called boutique winery, look no further than Red Carpet. This retailer specializes in California wineries whose case productions are from 100 to 1,000. Red Carpet also carries hard-to-find New World and Old World wines as well. Log on to the exciting website for a listing of wines it stocks. You can get on the mailing list by e-mail or phone. The site also features wonderful writers, wine events listings, travel features, wine reviews, and more. All in all, an enjoyable Internet experience. Red Carpet ships just about anywhere in the world.

Sam's
1720 N. Marcey Street
Chicago, IL 60614
(800) 777-9137
fax: (312) 664-7037
http://www.sams-wine.com

Sam's website is user-friendly, with easy-to-access lists of wines you can browse. They have it all: wines, spirits, cigars, accessories, gift baskets, books, gourmet cheese, coffee, olive oil, links to other wine sites, and more. You can also sign up to receive their electronic newsletter. Their motto is: "No order too big, no destination too far." Inquire for shipping specifications.

301 Wine Shop
301 L Street
Eureka, CA 95501
(800) 404-1390, ext. 108 or (707) 445-0311
fax: (707) 444-8067
http://www.301wines.com

These people offer a really enjoyable Internet shopping experience. In fact, they were just awarded the Wine Spectator Grand Award for their restaurant site (only five awards are given). Their wine list is excellent, and they have a wine club you can join for special values. The monthly newsletter (you can subscribe to it right on their website) lists their top picks each month along with recipes, travel-related articles, winemaker profiles, chef profiles, and more. Here's a real thinking man's (and woman's) wine shop. Give them a call, or pay them a visit.

APPENDIX 4

Virtual Vineyards
3803 East Bayshore Road, Suite 175
Palo Alto, CA 94303
(800) 289-1275 or (650) 938-9463
fax: (650) 919-1977
http://www.virtualvin.com

Here's a fun site. Virtual Vineyards tries to make wine shopping entertaining as well as easy. The site features an excellent wine list that's easy to use, and various food items as well as other gifts. While you're at it, go into their Q&A section, or learn about food pairings, recipes, travel information, and more.

Wally's
2107 Westwood Boulevard
Los Angeles, CA 90025
(888) 9-WALLYS or (310) 475-0606
fax: (310) 474-1450
http://www.wallywine.com

The people at Wally's are great. This is a huge wine store rated number one wine store in LA by Zagat's guide. In addition to carrying a huge selection of wine, they sell books, Riedel glassware, gourmet food, cigars in Wally's Cigarbox, gift baskets, and more. Call them up to receive their free newletter. The new website is definitely worth checking out.

Wine Cask
813 Anacapa Street
Santa Barbara, CA 93101
(800) 436-9463
fax: (805) 568-0664
http://www.winecask.com

This wine store has an extensive wine list, which you can browse in their website that also features information on travel and wine-related events. If you're in the Santa Barbara area, check out the store, which sells some gourmet food items and has a cafe/bar/tabac joint next page called Intermezzo, open until midnight every night. By the way, the wine site is great, and the store is recommended by wine guru Robert Parker.

Wine Country
2301 Redondo Avenue
Signal Hill, CA 90806
(800) 505-5564
fax: (562) 597-9493

This sounds like a great place to visit if you're in the area. They just added a 90-foot mural of the California wine region to their collection of other murals, Spanish tiles, and their 3-D replica of the Mondavi arch. The Wine Country folks aren't driven by reviews; in fact, they ignore them. Instead, they try to find wines from all regions that offer a "lot of goodness" for the value, according to the owner. You'll find discounted prices on many of their selections, which spans the 6,000-square-foot store. Call for a free monthly newsletter. They also sell microbeers, imported beers, and some gourmet food items.

Wine Exchange
2368 N. Orangemall
Orange, CA, 92865
(800) 76-WINEX
fax: (714) 974-1792
http://www.winex.com

Wine Exchange carries "the best, the most interesting, the most famous, and the rarest in wines and spirits." Their buying power enables them to get substantial discounts, which they pass on to you. One can browse their website for new arrivals, premium imported cigars, glassware, caviar and other specialty foods, and lots more. They also have a great monthly newsletter.

Gold Medal Wineries by Region

ARGENTINA

Caballero de la Cepa

Correas

Etchart

Flichman

Grove Street Winery

Humberto Canale

Santa Ana

Santa Julia

Tittarelli

Tupungato

AUSTRALIA

Basedow

Chapel Hill

Chateau Reynella

Clarendon Hills

Cullen

D'Arenberg

De Bortoli

Deakin Estate

Ebenezer

Eileen Hardy (Hardy's)

Elderton

Evans & Tate

Goundrey

Hamilton

Hardys

Henschke

Hermitage Road

Hillstowe

Howard Park

Jacob's Creek

Jamieson's Run

Jim Barry

Kaesler Winery

Katnook Estate

Kingston Estate

Lawson's

Leasingham

Lindemans

Maglieri

Morris

Mount Prior

Norman's

Orlando

Parker

Penfolds

Penley Estate

Pepper Tree Wines

Peter Lehmann

Robertson's Well

Rosemount

Rymill Winery

St. Hallett

Seaview

Seppelt

Stanley Brothers

Taltarni

Tim Adams

Vasse Felix

Wolf Blass

Wyndham Estates

Wynns

Yalumba

Yarra Ridge

CANADA

Calona

Cedar Creek

Colio Estate Wines

Gehringer Brothers

Hawthorne
Mountain Vineyards

Henry of Pelham

Hester Creek Estate
Winery

Hillebrand Estates

Inniskillin Wines

Jackson-Triggs

Konzelmann

Magnotta

Mission Hill

Peller

Pillitteri Estates

Quails' Gate

Reif Estate

Stoney Ridge

Strewn

Sumac Ridge

Summerhill Estate
Winery

Thirty Bench

Tinhorn Creek
Vineyards

Vineland Estates

CHILE

Canepa

Carmen

Carta Vieja

Casa Lapostolle

Chateau La Joya

Chateau Los Boldos

Foxridge

Manso De Velasco

Miguel Torres

Santa Rita

Stonelake

Viña Calina

Viña Errazuriz

Viña Santa Carolina

Viña Tarapaca

Viu Manent

NEW ZEALAND

Ata Rangi

Brancott

C.J. Pask

Cloudy Bay

Cooper's Creek

Corbans

De Redcliffe

Giesen

Grove Mill

Lincoln

Morton Estate

Nautilus

Palliser Estate

Saint Clair

Seifried Estate

Selaks

Tasman Bay

Vavasour

Villa Maria

SOUTH AFRICA

Chamonix

Clos Malverne

Eikendal

Fairview

Kanonkop

KWV Cathedral Cellar

Laborie Estate

Meerlust

Neethlingshof

Neil Ellis

Rust en Vrede

Stellenzicht

Swartland

UNITED STATES

CALIFORNIA

Adelaida

Adler Fels

Alban

Alderbrook

Alexander Valley
Vineyards

Altamura

Amador

Anapamu

Anderson's Conn
Valley Vineyards

Antares

Arciero

Arrowood

Atlas Peak

Au Bon Climat

Audubon Cellars

B.R. Cohn

Baileyana

Baily

Barefoot Cellars

Bargetto

Baron Herzog

Bartholomew Park

Bayview Cellars

Baywood

Beaucanon

Beaulieu Vineyard

Bella Vista

Bellefleur

Belvedere

Benziger

Beringer

Black Rock Wineworks

Blossom Hill

Boeger

Bogle

Bonterra

Bouchaine

Brutocao

Buehler

Buttonwood Farm
Winery

Byington

Cain

Cakebread

Callaway

Cambria

Canyon Road

Cardinale

Carmenet

Carmody McKnight

Castelletto

Castle

Castoro Cellars

Caymus

Cedar Mountain

CALIFORNIA con't

Chalk Hill	Concannon	Dominus
Chalone	Conn Creek	Douglas Hill Winery
Chameleon Cellars	Cooper-Garrod	Dry Creek Vineyard
Chandelle of Sonoma	Corbett Canyon	Duckhorn
Chappellet	Cornerstone	Dunn
Charles B. Mitchell	Cosentino	Dunnewood
Charles Krug	Cottonwood Canyon	Eberle
Charles Shaw	Coturri	Echelon
Chateau Montelena	Cronin	Edgewood
Chateau Potelle	Cuisine Cellars	Edmeades
Chateau St. Jean	Curtis	Edna Valley Vineyard
Chateau Souverain	Cuvaison	Ehlers Grove
Chimney Rock	Dalla Valle	El Molino
Chouinard	David Bruce	Elkhorn Peak Cellars
Christian Brothers	Davis Bynum	Eos Estate Winery
Christopher Creek	De Lorimier	Eric Ross Winery
Cilurzo	De Rose	Estancia
Cinnabar	Deaver	Fallbrook
Cline	Deer Valley	Fantaisie
Cloninger Cellars	Dehlinger	Fanucchi
Clos du Bois	DeLoach	Far Niente
Clos du Val	Deux Amis	Fenestra
Clos LaChance	Diamond Creek	Ferrari Carano
Clos Pegase	Dolce	Fess Parker
Cloudy Cellars	Domaine Carneros	Fetzer
Cobblestone	Domaine St. George	Ficklin

CALIFORNIA con't

Fieldbrook

Fife

Filsinger

Firestone

Fisher

Flora Springs

Foley

Folie à Deux

Forchini

Forest Glen

Fountain Grove

Franciscan

Freemark Abbey

Frick

Gainey

Galleano

Gallo Sonoma

Gan Eden

Gary Farrell

Geyser Peak

Girard

Glen Ellen

Gloria Ferrer
Champagne Caves

Godwin

Granite Springs Winery

Greenwood Ridge

Grgich Hills

Guenoc

Gundlach-Bundschu

Hacienda

Hagafen

Handley

Hanna

Hart

Hartford Court

Hawley Wines

Heitz

Helena View

Hendry

Herzog

Hess Collection

Hidden Cellars

Hop Kiln

Husch

Indian Springs
Vineyards

Indigo Hills

Iron Horse

Ivan Tamas

J. Lohr

J. Runquist Wines

Jarvis

Jekel

Jordan

Jory

Joseph Filippi

Joseph Phelps

Joseph Zakon

Justin

Kathryn Kennedy
Winery

Kendall-Jackson

Kenwood

Kistler

Korbel

Kunde

La Crema

Laetitia

Lake Sonoma

Lakespring

Lambert Bridge

Lamborn Family

Landmark

Langtry

Latcham

Laurel Glen

Lava Cap Winery

Le Ducq

Les Vieux Cepages

Lin Court Vineyards

CALIFORNIA con't

Lockwood

Lolonis

Louis M. Martini

M.G. Vallejo

MacRostie

Madrona

Marcelina

Marietta

Mark West

Markham

Martin Brothers

Martin Ray

Martinelli

Martini & Prati

Matanzas Creek

Maurice Car'rie

Mazzocco Vineyards

McDowell

McIlroy Wines

Mer et Soleil

Meridian

Merryvale

Michel-Schlumberger

Mill Creek

Mirassou

Montevina Winery

Monthaven

Monticello

Morgan

Mount Eden

Mount Palomar

Mumm Napa

Murphy-Goode

Murrieta's Well

Napa Creek Winery

Napa Ridge

Navarro

Nelson Estate

Nevada City Winery

Newlan

Nichelini

Nichols

Niebaum-Coppola

Norman Vineyards

Oakstone

Obester

Opus One

Orfila

Page Mill

Pagor

Paraiso Springs

Parducci

Pedroncelli

Peju Province

Pepperwood Grove

Pepperwood Springs

Perry Creek

Peter Michael

Pezzi King

Phillips Farms Vineyards

Phoenix Vineyards

Pine Ridge

Plam

Prager Winery & Port Works

Preston

Quady

Quail Ridge

Quatro

Quivira Vineyards

R.H. Phillips

Rabbit Ridge

Rancho de Philo

Ravenswood

Raymond

Red Rock Winery

Renaissance

Renwood

CALIFORNIA con't

Richardson

Ridge

River Run Vintners

Robert & Hunter Winery

Robert Craig

Robert Keenan

Robert Mondavi

Robert Pepi

Rocking Horse

Rodney Strong

Roederer Estate

Rombauer

Rosenblum

Rusack Vineyards

Rutherford Hill

Rutherford Ranch

Rutherford Vintners

S. Anderson

Saddleback Cellars

St. Clement

St. Francis

St. Supéry

Saintsbury

San Antonio

Sanford

Santa Barbara Winery

Savannah

Scharffenberger

Schramsberg

Sea Ridge Coastal Winery

Seavey

Sebastiani

Sequoia Grove

Seven Peaks

Shafer

Sheffield Cellars

Shenandoah Vineyards

Sierra Vista

Signorello

Silver Oak

Silver Ridge

Silverado

Silverado Hill Cellars

Simi

Smith & Hook

Smith-Madrone

Solis Winery

Sonoma Creek Winery

Sonoma-Loeb

Sonora Winery & Port Works

Soquel

Sparrow Lane

Spottswoode

Staglin

Stag's Leap

Steele

Sterling

Stevenot

Stone Creek

Stonestreet

Stony Ridge

Storrs

Storybook Mountain

Sunstone

Sutter Home

Swanson

Sylvester

Talbott

Talus

Temecula Crest

Thackrey

Thomas Coyne

Thomas Fogarty

Thornton

Titus

Topolos

Trellis

CALIFORNIA con't

Trentadue	Vichon	Wildhurst
Truchard	Vigil	William Hill
Turley	Villa Mt. Eden	Windemere Winery
Turning Leaf	Vino Noceto	Windsor
Twin Hills Winery	Von Strasser	Windwalker Vineyards
V. Sattui	Voss	Woodside
Valley of the Moon	Weinstock Cellars	York Mountain Winery
Van Roekel	Wellington	Yorkville Cellars
Venezia	Wente Vineyards	Zaca Mesa
Ventana	Whitehall Lane	ZD
Viano	Wild Horse	

IDAHO

Pintler Cellar	Ste. Chapelle

MICHIGAN

St. Julian

MISSOURI

Adam Puchta Winery	St. James Winery
Augusta Winery	Stone Hill

NEBRASKA

Cuthills Vineyard

NEW JERSEY

Unionville Vineyard

NEW YORK

Cook's	Lakewood Vineyards	Standing Stone
Dr. Konstantin Frank	Lamoreaux Landing	Swedish Hill
Glenora	Palmer	Taylor Wine Cellars
Goose Watch Winery	Peconic Bay	Widmer's Wine Cellars
Heron Hill	Prejean	

OHIO

Breitenbach Wine Cellars	Lonz Winery
Ferrante Wine Farm	Meier's Wine Cellars

OREGON

Adelsheim	Elk Cove	Panther Creek
Amity	Girardet Wine Cellars	Ponzi
Archery Summit	Henry Estate	Seven Hills
Argyle	Ken Wright	Silvan Ridge
Beaux Frères	King Estate	St. Innocent
Benton Lane	La Garza	Willakenzie
Cooper Mountain	Lavelle Vineyards	Willamette Valley Vineyards
Domaine Drouhin	Lorane Valley	
Domaine Serene	Oak Knoll	

TEXAS

Messina Hof

VIRGINIA

Horton	Oasis
Jefferson Vineyards	Prince Michel Vineyards

WASHINGTON

Andrew Will	Hyatt Vineyards	Tefft Cellars
Apex	Kiona	W.B. Bridgman
Barnard Griffin	L'Ecole No. 41	Washington Hills
Chateau Ste. Michelle	Leonetti	Waterbrook
Columbia Crest	Paul Thomas	Woodward Canyon
Columbia Winery	Portteus	Worden
Gordon Brothers	Preston	Yakima River
Hogue	Silverlake Winery	
Hoodsport	Staton Hills Winery	

WISCONSIN

Botham	Wollersheim Winery

WINE
▬▬ INDEX/SHOPPING ▬▬
GUIDE

$	bargain wines—$15 and under
✳	Best of the Best Wines - 3 or more gold medals
℘	non-American wines
(Can $)	price in Canadian dollars; sold only in Canada

- A -

$ Adam Puchta NV Riefenstahler, MO, $7.25, **235**

Adelaida 1993 Cabernet Sauvignon, CA, $19, **58**

Adelaida 1995 Sangiovese, CA, $24, **90**

Adelsheim 1995 Pinot Noir, OR, $18.99, **121**

$ Adler Fels 1996 Gewurztraminer, CA, $11, **195**

$ Adler Fels 1996 Organically Grown Grapes Fumé Blanc, CA, $10.50, **216**

Adler Fels 1996 Sangiovese, CA, $20, **90**

$ Adler Fels 1997 Gewurztraminer, CA, $11, **195**

Alban 1995 Grenache, CA, $28, **112**

Alban 1995 Reva Estate Syrah, CA, $21, **143**

Alban 1996 Viognier, CA, $20, **227**

Alderbrook 1996 George's Vineyard Zinfandel, CA, $24, **152**

Alderbrook 1996 Kunde Vineyard Merlot, CA, $22, **97**

Alderbrook 1996 Pinot Noir, CA, $18.95, **121**

$ Alderbrook 1997 McIlroy Vineyard Gewurztraminer, CA, $12, **195**

$ Alderbrook 1997 Saralee's Vineyard Gewurztraminer, CA, $11, **195**

$ Alderbrook 1997 Tredici, CA, $10, **253**

$ Alexander Valley Vineyards 1996 Dry Chenin Blanc, CA, $9, **192**

$ Alexander Valley Vineyards 1997 Wetzel Family Selection Gewurztraminer, CA, $9, **195**

Altamura 1994 Sangiovese, CA, $28, **90**

$ Amador 1995 Ferrero Vineyard Zinfandel, CA, $12.50, **152**

Amity 1993 Winemaker's Reserve Pinot Noir, OR, $35, **121**

$ Amity 1995 Dry Riesling, OR, $9, **211**

$ Amity 1996 Riesling, OR, $9, **211**

$ Amity 1997 Gamay Noir, OR, $9, **53**

$ Anapamu 1995 Pinot Noir, CA, $11.99, **121**

$ Anapamu 1996 Chardonnay, CA, $12, **167**

Anderson's Conn Valley Vineyards 1994 Estate Reserve Cabernet Sauvignon, CA, $40, **58**

Andrew Will 1994 Cabernet Sauvignon, WA, $30, **58**

Andrew Will 1994 Reserve Cabernet Sauvignon, WA, $40, **58**

- D -

David Bruce 1995 Reserve Pinot Noir, CA, $26, **123**

$ David Bruce 1996 Petite Syrah, CA, $15, **118**

David Bruce 1996 Shell Creek Vineyard Petite Syrah, CA, $18, **118**

Davis Bynum 1994 Hedin Vineyard Cabernet Sauvignon, CA, $24, **64**

Davis Bynum 1995 Laureles Vineyard Merlot, CA, $22, **100**

Davis Bynum 1995 Limited Edition Pinot Noir, CA, $28, **123**

℘   De Bortoli 1994 "Noble One" Australian Botrytis Semillon, Australia, $19.99, **254**

℘   De Bortoli 1995 Cabernet Sauvignon, Australia, $21, **64**

℘   De Bortoli 1995 "Noble One" Australian Botrytis Semillon, Australia, $19.99, **254**

℘   De Bortoli 1996 Chardonnay, Australia, $21, **173**

De Lorimier 1995 Mosaic, CA, $24, **134**

De Lorimier 1996 Estate Bottled Chardonnay, CA, $16, **173**

$ De Lorimier 1997 Estate Bottled Sauvignon Blanc, CA, $10, **217**

℘   De Redcliffe 1996 Reserve Sauvignon Blanc, New Zealand, $16, **218**

De Rose 1995 Cedolini Family Vineyard Old Vines Zinfandel, CA, $17.95, **153**

$℘ Deakin Estate 1997 Shiraz, Australia, $9.99, **144**

$ Deaver Vineyards 1995 Zinfandel, CA, $15, **153**

$ Deer Valley 1995 Cabernet Sauvignon, CA, $4.99, **64**

Dehlinger 1995 Chardonnay, CA, $18, **173**

DeLoach 1993 O.F.S. Cabernet Sauvignon, CA, $25, **64**

DeLoach 1994 O.F.S. Estate Bottled Cabernet Sauvignon, CA, $27.50, **64**

DeLoach 1996 Barbieri Ranch Zinfandel, CA, $20, **153**

DeLoach 1996 Estate Bottled Merlot, CA, $18, **100**

✳   DeLoach 1996 O.F.S. Chardonnay, CA, $27.50, **173**

DeLoach 1996 O.F.S. Zinfandel, CA, $27.50, **153**

DeLoach 1996 Saltone Ranch Zinfandel, CA, $20, **153**

$ DeLoach 1996 Sonoma Cuvée Chardonnay, CA, $13, **173**

$ DeLoach 1997 Early Harvest Gewurztraminer, CA, $12, **196**

$ DeLoach 1997 White Zinfandel, CA, $8, **236**

$ Deux Amis 1995 Zinfandel, CA, $15, **154**

Diamond Creek 1994 Volcanic Hill Cabernet Sauvignon, CA, $50, **65**

Dr. Konstantin Frank 1995 Cabernet Sauvignon, NY, $22, **65**

$ Dr. Konstantin Frank 1996 Semi-Dry Johannisberg Riesling, NY, $9.95, **212**

Dolce 1995 Late Harvest Semillon, CA, $60/375 ml, **254**

Domaine Carneros 1993 Sparkling Brut, CA, $17.95, **242**

Domaine Carneros 1994 Pinot Noir, CA, $20, **123**

Domaine Drouhin 1995 Laurene Pinot Noir, OR, $45, **123**

$ Domaine St. George 1996 Premier Cuvée STG Pinot Noir, CA, $10, **123**

- G -

Gainey 1995 Cabernet Franc, CA, $20, **55**

Gainey 1995 Limited Selection Chardonnay, CA, $25, **176**

$ Gainey 1997 Riesling, CA, $10, **212**

Galleano NV Barrel Aged "Crema" Sherry, CA, $16.95, **264**

Gallo Sonoma 1992 Estate Cabernet Sauvignon, CA, $40, **68**

✱ Gallo Sonoma 1993 Estate Cabernet Sauvignon, CA, $45, **68**

Gallo Sonoma 1993 Frei Ranch Vineyard Cabernet Sauvignon, CA, $18, **68**

Gallo Sonoma 1994 Barelli Creek Vineyard Cabernet Sauvignon, CA, $20, **68**

✱ Gallo Sonoma 1994 Frei Ranch Vineyard Cabernet Sauvignon, CA, $18, **68**

$ Gallo Sonoma 1994 Frei Ranch Zinfandel, CA, $14, **154**

Gallo Sonoma 1994 Laguna Ranch Chardonnay, CA, $16, **176**

$ Gallo Sonoma 1995 Barelli Creek Vineyard Valdiguié, CA, $12, **53**

✱ Gallo Sonoma 1995 Estate Bottled Chardonnay, CA, $35, **176**

$ Gallo Sonoma 1995 Frei Ranch Zinfandel, CA, $14, **155**

Gallo Sonoma 1995 Laguna Ranch Vineyard Chardonnay, CA, $18, **176**

$ Gallo Sonoma 1995 Merlot, CA, $11, **102**

Gallo Sonoma 1996 Estate Chardonnay, CA, $39.99, **176**

Gallo Sonoma 1996 Laguna Ranch Chardonnay, CA, $16, **176**

$ Gallo Sonoma 1996 Pinot Noir, CA, $10, **124**

Gallo Sonoma 1996 Stefani Vineyard Chardonnay, CA, $16, **176**

$ Gan Eden 1995 Sauvignon Blanc, CA, $10, **218**

$ Gan Eden 1996 Gewurztraminer, CA, $12, **196**

$✱ Gan Eden 1997 Black Muscat, CA, $12, **258**

Gary Farrell 1995 Allen Vineyard Pinot Noir, CA, $40, **125**

Gary Farrell 1995 Anderson Pinot Noir, CA, $30, **125**

Gary Farrell 1995 Hillside Selection Cabernet Sauvignon, CA, $24, **68**

Gary Farrell 1995 Rochioli Vineyard Pinot Noir, CA, $50, **125**

✱ Gary Farrell 1996 Allen Vineyard Chardonnay, CA, $28, **176**

✱ Gary Farrell 1996 Bien Nacido Vineyard Pinot Noir, CA, $28, **125**

✱ Gary Farrell 1996 Old Vine Selection Zinfandel, CA, $21.50, **155**

✱ Gary Farrell 1996 Russian River Valley Pinot Noir, CA, $22.50, **125**

$ Gary Farrell 1997 Sauvignon Blanc, CA, $15, **219**

♎ Gehringer Brothers 1996 V.Q.A. Pinot Noir, Canada, (Can $) 12.95, **125**

♎ Gehringer Brothers 1997 Riesling Ice Wine, Canada, (Can $) 43, **250**

$ Geyser Peak 1995 Cabernet Sauvignon, CA, $15, **68**

$ Geyser Peak 1995 Henry's Reserve Shiraz Port, CA, $15, **260**

$♎ Geyser Peak 1995 Merlot, CA, $14.99, **102**

✱ Geyser Peak 1995 Reserve Alexandre, CA, $24.99, **135**

$ Granite Springs 1995 Estate Bottled Zinfandel, CA, $11.50, **155**

Greenwood Ridge 1995 Estate Bottled Cabernet Sauvignon, CA, $32, **69**

✳ Greenwood Ridge 1995 Estate Bottled Merlot, CA, $22, **103**

Greenwood Ridge 1996 Estate Bottled Late Harvest Riesling, CA, $18, **254**

✳ Greenwood Ridge 1996 Pinot Noir, CA, $22, **125**

Greenwood Ridge 1996 Scherrer Vineyards Zinfandel, CA, $18, **155**

$ Greenwood Ridge 1997 Estate Bottled Riesling, CA, $10.50, **212**

$ Greenwood Ridge 1997 Sauvignon Blanc, CA, $11, **219**

Grgich Hills 1994 Cabernet Sauvignon, CA, $35, **69**

Grgich Hills 1994 Late Harvest Violetta, CA, $35/375 ml, **254**

Grgich Hills 1995 Zinfandel, CA, $20, **155**

Grgich Hills 1996 Fumé Blanc, CA, $16, **219**

🍷 Grove Mill 1996 Chardonnay, New Zealand, $20, **177**

$🍷 Grove Mill 1996 Riesling, New Zealand, $14, **212**

🍷 Grove Mill 1996 Sauvignon Blanc, New Zealand, $17, **219**

🍷 Grove Mill 1997 Sauvignon Blanc, New Zealand, $18, **219**

🍷 Grove Street Winery 1996 Cabernet Sauvignon, Argentina, $17, **69**

✳ Guenoc 1994 Bella Vista Vineyard Reserve Cabernet Sauvignon, CA, $30, **69**

Guenoc 1994 Vintage Port, CA, $25, **260**

✳ Guenoc 1995 Cabernet Sauvignon, CA, $15.50, **69**

Guenoc 1995 Petite Sirah, CA, $15.50, **118**

Guenoc 1996 Chardonnay, CA, $15.50, **177**

Guenoc 1997 Chardonnay, CA, $15.50, **178**

Gundlach-Bundschu 1996 Barrel Fermented Sangiacomo Ranch Chardonnay, CA, $16, **178**

$ Gundlach-Bundschu 1997 Rhinefarm Vineyards Estate Bottled Gewurztraminer, CA, $12, **197**

$ Gundlach-Bundschu 1997 Rhinefarm Vineyards Gamay Beaujolais, CA, $9, **53**

- H -

$ Hacienda 1996 Clair de Lune Pinot Noir, CA, $6.99, **125**

Hagafen 1995 Cabernet Sauvignon, CA, $20, **70**

$ Hagafen 1996 Pinot Noir, CA, $13, **126**

$ Hagafen 1997 Johannisberg Riesling, CA, $10, **212**

🍷 Hamilton 1996 Leconfield Cabernets, Australia, $19.50, **135**

Handley Cellars 1993 Brut, CA, $22, **243**

Handley Cellars 1995 Estate Reserve Pinot Noir, CA, $29, **126**

✳ Handley Cellars 1995 Pinot Noir, CA, $21, **126**

Handley Cellars 1996 Estate Grown Chardonnay, CA, $16, **178**

Handley Cellars 1996 Handley Vineyard Chardonnay, CA, $16, **178**

✳🍷 Handley Cellars 1996 Sauvignon Blanc, CA, $13, **219**

- L -

La Crema 1996 Reserve Chardonnay, CA, $27, **179**

La Crema 1996 Reserve Pinot Noir, CA, $27, **127**

La Crema 1996 Reserve Zinfandel, CA, $22, **156**

$ La Garza 1996 Cabernet Sauvignon, OR, $15, **73**

$℘ Laborie Estate 1996 Cabernet Sauvignon, South Africa, $14, **73**

✱   Laetitia 1993 Elegance Rosé, CA, $23, **244**

Laetitia 1996 La Colline Vineyard Pinot Noir, CA, $29, **127**

Laetitia 1996 Reserve Pinot Blanc, CA, $28, **206**

Laetitia 1996 Reserve Pinot Noir, CA, $19, **127**

$ Laetitia NV Select Brut, CA, $13.99, **244**

$ Lake Sonoma 1996 Heck Family Cellar Selection Chardonnay, CA, $15, **179**

Lake Sonoma 1995 Zinfandel, CA, $17, **156**

$ Lakespring 1994 Cabernet Sauvignon, CA, $10, **73**

$ Lakespring 1996 Sauvignon Blanc, CA, $8, **220**

$ Lakewood Vineyards 1996 Delaware, NY, $5.49, **237**

Lambert Bridge 1995 Merlot, CA, $20, **104**

Lambert Bridge 1996 Zinfandel, CA, $20, **157**

Lamborn Family 1995 French Connection Zin., CA, $22.50, **157**

$ Lamoreaux Landing 1996 Semi-Dry Riesling, NY, $10, **213**

Landmark 1996 Overlook Chardonnay, CA, $20, **179**

Langtry 1995 Meritage, CA, $48, **136**

Langtry 1996 Meritage, CA, $21, **136**

$ Latcham 1995 Select Port, CA, $15, **261**

$ Latcham 1995 Special Reserve Zinfandel, CA, $14, **157**

Laurel Glen 1994 Cabernet Sauvignon, CA, $38, **73**

Lava Cap Winery 1996 Reserve Zinfandel, CA, $25, **157**

$ Lavelle 1996 Winter's Hill Vineyard Pinot Gris, OR, $13, **209**

℘   Lawson's 1992 Shiraz, Australia, $35, **146**

Le Ducq 1992 Le Ducq 92, CA, $68.99, **137**

Le Ducq 1993 Le Ducq 93, CA, $69, **137**

Le Ducq 1994 Le Ducq 94, CA, $65, **137**

Le Ducq 1994 Sylviane Merlot, CA, $30, **104**

Le Ducq 1995 Sylviane Cabernet Sauvignon, CA, $30, **73**

$℘ Leasingham 1996 Chardonnay, Australia, $14, **179**

L'Ecole No. 41 1994 Cabernet Sauvignon, WA, $24, **73**

L'Ecole No. 41 1995 Merlot, WA, $24, **104**

Leonetti 1994 Cabernet Sauvignon, WA, $45, **73**

$ Les Vieux Cepages 1995 Ronfleur, CA, $6.99, **237**

Lin Court Vineyards 1996 Chardonnay, CA, $16, **180**

$℘ Lincoln 1997 Sauvignon Blanc, New Zealand, $14.99, **220**

℘   Lindemans 1993 Limestone Ridge Shiraz-Cabernet, Australia, $27.99, **137**

℘ Manso de Velasco 1995 Cabernet Sauvignon, Chile, $18.99, **74**

Marcelina 1993 Cabernet Sauvignon, CA, $20, **74**

Marcelina 1995 Chardonnay, CA, $18, **180**

$ Marietta 1995 Syrah, CA, $14.99, **146**

Mark West 1995 Reserve Chardonnay, CA, $20, **180**

$ Mark West 1996 Chardonnay, CA, $15, **180**

$ Mark West 1997 Reserve Gewurztraminer, CA, $15, **197**

Markham 1995 Zinfandel, CA, $16, **157**

Martin Brothers 1994 Vecchio Nebbiolo, CA, $20, **92**

$ Martin Brothers 1996 Nebbiolo, CA, $11, **92**

Martin Ray 1995 Pinot Noir, CA, $36, **127**

Martinelli 1996 Jackass Vineyard Zinfandel, CA, $25, **157**

Martini & Prati 1996 Reserve Zinfandel, CA, $18, **157**

Matanzas Creek 1996 Sauvignon Blanc, CA, $18, **220**

$ Maurice Car'rie 1996 Sauvignon Blanc, CA, $6.95, **220**

$ Maurice Car'rie 1997 White Zinfandel, CA, $5.95, **237**

Mazzocco Vineyards 1994 Matrix-Estate, CA, $30, **137**

McDowell 1995 Estate Syrah, CA, $16, **147**

$ McDowell 1996 Syrah, CA, $10, **147**

McDowell 1996 Viognier, CA, $16, **228**

McIlroy Wines 1996 Aquarius Ranch Chardonnay, CA, $18, **181**

McIlroy Wines 1996 Aquarius Ranch Pinot Noir, CA, $18, **127**

McIlroy Wines 1996 Porter-Bass Vineyards Zinfandel, CA, $18, **157**

℘ Meerlust 1991 Cabernet Sauvignon, South Africa, $22, **74**

℘ Meerlust 1992 Rubicon, South Africa, $22, **137**

$℘ Meerlust 1994 Merlot, South Africa, $11, **104**

$ Meier's Wine Cellars NV Concord, OH, $3.99, **116**

$ Meier's Wine Cellars NV Pink Catawba, OH, $3.99, **237**

Mer et Soleil 1995 Chardonnay, CA, $35, **181**

✳ Meridian 1994 Coastal Reserve Cabernet Sauvignon, CA, $20, **74**

$ Meridian 1995 Cabernet Sauvignon, CA, $12, **74**

$✳ Meridian 1995 Pinot Noir, CA, $15.50, **127**

Meridian 1995 Reserve Pinot Noir, CA, $20, **127**

Meridian 1996 Coastal Reserve Chardonnay, CA, $16, **181**

Meridian 1996 Pinot Noir, CA, $15.50, **128**

$✳ Meridian 1996 Syrah, CA, $15, **147**

$ Meridian 1997 Gewurztraminer, CA, $8, **197**

Merryvale 1995 Reserve Chardonnay, CA, $30, **181**

Merryvale 1995 Reserve Merlot, CA, $32, **104**

Merryvale 1996 Vignette, CA, $22, **230**

Merryvale 1995 Reserve Cabernet Sauvignon, CA, $32, **74**

Merryvale 1996 Startmont Chardonnay, CA, $18, **181**

Messina Hof 1996 Late Harvest "Glory" Muscat Canelli, TX, $16.99, **258**

℘   Mount Prior 1994 Durif, Australia, $28.50, **113**

     Mumm Napa NV Blanc de Noirs, CA, $15.95, **244**

     Mumm Napa NV Cuvée Blanc de Blancs, CA, $19, **244**

     Mumm Napa NV Cuvée Prestige Brut, CA, $15.95, **244**

     Murphy-Goode 1994 Brenda Block Cabernet Sauvignon, CA, $30, **75**

     Murphy-Goode 1995 Zinfandel, CA, $18, **158**

     Murphy-Goode 1996 The Deuce Fumé II, CA, $24, **221**

     Murphy-Goode 1996 The Reserve Fumé, CA, $16.50, **221**

     Murphy-Goode 1996 Zinfandel, CA, $16, **158**

$ Murphy-Goode 1997 Fumé Blanc, CA, $11.50, **221**

     Murrieta's Well 1995 Estate Vineyard Vendimia, CA, $28, **137**

- N -

$ Napa Creek Winery 1997 Chardonnay, CA, $8.99, **182**

$ Napa Ridge 1994 Reserve Cabernet Sauvignon, CA, $15, **75**

$ Napa Ridge 1995 Reserve Pinot Noir, CA, $15, **128**

$ Napa Ridge 1996 Chardonnay, CA, $9, **182**

$ Napa Ridge 1996 Oak Barrel Cabernet Sauvignon, CA, $10, **75**

$ Napa Ridge 1996 Pinot Noir, CA, $11, **128**

$℘   Nautilus 1997 Sauvignon Blanc, New Zealand, $13.99, **221**

     Navarro 1993 Cabernet Sauvignon, CA, $20, **75**

$ Navarro 1995 Gewurztraminer, CA, $14, **198**

✳   Navarro 1996 Cluster Select Late Harvest White Riesling, CA, $19.50, **256**

     Navarro 1996 Cluster Select Riesling, CA, $35, **213**

$ Navarro 1996 Late Harvest White Riesling, CA, $9.75, **256**

$ Navarro 1996 Napa Gamay, CA, $12, **53**

$ Navarro 1996 Sauvignon Blanc, CA, $12.50, **221**

     Navarro 1996 Zinfandel, CA, $18, **158**

$ Navarro 1997 Chenin Blanc, CA, $9.50, **193**

     Navarro 1997 Cluster Select Late Harvest Gewurztraminer, CA, $25, **256**

$ Navarro 1997 Late Harvest Sweet Gewurztraminer, CA, $9.75, **256**

℘   Neethlingshof 1996 Noble Late Harvest White Riesling, South Africa, $19.50/375 ml, **256**

℘   Neethlingshof 1997 Weisser Late Harvest Noble Riesling, South Africa, $29.99/375 ml, **256**

℘   Neil Ellis 1993 Cabernet Sauvignon, South Africa, $16.99, **75**

$℘   Neil Ellis 1997 Sauvignon Blanc, South Africa, $12, **221**

     Nelson Estate 1995 Merlot, CA, $19, **105**

     Nevada City Winery 1994 Director's Reserve Claret, CA, $16, **138**

$ Nevada City Winery 1996 Syrah, CA, $14, **147**

     Newlan 1995 Pinot Noir, CA, $19, **128**

     Nichelini 1995 Nichelini Vineyard Petite Sirah, CA, $17.50, **119**

Nichols 1996 Cottonwood Canyon Vineyard Pinot Noir, CA, $33, **128**

Nichols 1996 Pisoni Vineyard Pinot Noir, CA, $42, **128**

Nichols 1996 Reserve Pinot Noir, CA, $45, **128**

Niebaum-Coppola 1995 Francis Coppola Family Wines Merlot, CA, $32, **105**

Niebaum-Coppola 1996 Black Label Claret, CA, $17, **138**

Norman Vineyards 1995 Estate Bottled Cabernet Sauvignon, CA, $17, **76**

$ Norman Vineyards 1996 No Nonsense Red, CA, $15, **138**

Ῥ Norman's 1995 Chais Clarendon Shiraz, Australia, $17.99, **147**

Ῥ Norman's 1996 Chais Clarendon Cabernet Sauvignon, Australia, $17.99, **76**

Ῥ Norman's 1996 Chais Clarendon Shiraz, Australia, $17.99, **147**

Ῥ Norman's 1996 White Label Cabernet Sauvignon, Australia, $9.99, **76**

- O -

Oak Knoll 1994 Vintage Reserve Pinot Noir, OR, $34, **129**

Oak Knoll 1996 Vintage Reserve Pinot Gris, OR, $17, **209**

Oakstone NV Merlot Port, CA, $16, **261**

$ Oasis NV Brut, VA, $12.50/375 ml, **244**

$ Obester 1995 Twentieth Anniversary Sangiovese, CA, $13.95, **92**

$ Obester 1995 Zinfandel, CA, $14.95, **158**

Opus One 1994, CA, $90, **138**

$ Orfila 1995 Ambassador's Reserve Chardonnay, CA, $14.95, **182**

Orfila 1996 Merlot, CA, $15.98, **105**

Orfila 1996 Pinot Noir, CA, $16, **129**

Ῥ Orlando 1993 St. Hugo Cabernet Sauvignon, Australia, $28.99, **76**

Ῥ Orlando 1994 St. Hugo Cabernet Sauvignon, Australia, $28.99, **76**

Ῥ Orlando 1997 St. Hilary Chardonnay, Australia, $22, **182**

- P -

Page Mill 1996 Bien Nacido Vineyard Chardonnay, CA, $18, **182**

$ Pagor 1996 "Vino Tinto" Tempranillo, CA, $10, **113**

Ῥ Palliser Estate 1996 Pinot Noir, New Zealand, $29.99, **129**

Ῥ Palliser Estate 1997 Estate Sauvignon Blanc, New Zealand, $19, **221**

Palmer 1995 Reserve Merlot, NY, $29.99, **105**

$ Palmer 1996 Estate Pinot Blanc, NY, $11.99, **207**

Panther Creek 1995 Freedom Hill Vineyard Pinot Noir, OR, $27.99, **129**

$ Paraiso Springs 1995 Baby Blush, CA, $12.50, **237**

$ Paraiso Springs 1995 Johannisberg Riesling, CA, $9, **213**

$ Paraiso Springs 1997 Baby Blush Rides Again, CA, $15, **237**

Paraiso Springs 1997 Reserve Pinot Blanc, CA, $22.50, **207**

✳ Robert Pepi 1995 Colline Di Sassi Sangiovese, CA, $25, **92**
Robert Pepi 1995 Due Baci, CA, $25, **139**
Robert Pepi 1995 Two-Heart Canopy Sangiovese, CA, $18, **93**

$ Robert Pepi 1996 Malvasia Bianca, CA, $14, **200**

𝒫 Robertson's Well 1996 Cabernet Sauvignon, Australia, $16, **78**
Rocking Horse 1996 Lamborn Vineyard Zinfandel, CA, $18, **160**
Rodney Strong 1993 Reserve Cabernet Sauvignon, CA, $40, **78**
Rodney Strong 1994 Reserve Cabernet Sauvignon, CA, $35, **79**

$ Rodney Strong 1995 Cabernet Sauvignon, CA, $13, **79**

$ Rodney Strong 1997 Charlotte's Home Sauvignon Blanc, CA, $10, **222**

Roederer Estate 1991 L'Ermitage Brut, CA, $33, **245**

Rombauer 1995 Chardonnay, CA, $23.75, **184**

𝒫 Rosemount 1994 Roxburgh Chardonnay, Australia, $35, **184**

𝒫 Rosemount 1995 "GSM" Grenache Shiraz Mourvèdre, Australia, $18.95, **139**

𝒫 Rosemount 1995 Balmoral Shiraz, Australia, $40, **148**

𝒫 Rosemount 1995 Mountain Blue Shiraz Cabernet Sauvignon, Australia, $30, **139**

𝒫 Rosemount 1995 Reserve Shiraz, Australia, $22.95, **148**

𝒫 Rosemount 1995 Traditional Cabernet Sauvignon Merlot Petite Verdot, Australia, $18.95, **139**

$𝒫 Rosemount 1997 Diamond Label Grenache Shiraz, Australia, $8.50, **139**

$𝒫 Rosemount 1997 Diamond Label Semillon Chardonnay, Australia, $8, **231**

Rosenblum 1995 Hendry Vineyard Reserve Cabernet Sauvignon, CA, $40, **79**

Rosenblum 1995 Holbrook Mitchell Trio, CA, $35, **139**

Rosenblum 1995 Lone Oak Vineyard Merlot, CA, $20, **107**

Rosenblum 1996 Annette's Reserve Vineyard Zinfandel, CA, $20, **160**

$ Rosenblum 1996 Fleur de Hoof Palomino, CA, $8, **200**

Rosenblum 1996 Harris Kratka Vineyard Zinfandel, CA, $22, **160**

Rosenblum 1996 Kenefick Ranch Petite Sirah, CA, $18, **119**

Rosenblum 1996 Pato Vineyard Zinfandel, CA, $19, **160**

✳ Rosenblum 1996 Richard Sauret Vineyard Zinfandel, CA, $17, **160**

Rosenblum 1996 Rockpile Vineyard Zinfandel, CA, $22, **160**

✳ Rosenblum 1996 Samsel Vineyard Maggie's Reserve Zinfandel, CA, $28, **160**

$ Rosenblum 1996 Semillon, CA, $14, **225**

Rosenblum 1996 White Cottage Vineyard Zinfandel, CA, $21, **160**

$ Rosenblum 1997 Viognier, CA, $15, **228**

$ Rosenblum NV Vintner's Cuvée XVI Zinfandel, CA, $9.50, **160**

$ Rusack Vineyards 1996 Lucas Select Riesling, CA, $12.50, **214**

𝒫 Rust en Vrede 1992 Estate Red, South Africa, $25, **140**

𝒫 Rust en Vrede 1993 Estate Selection, South Africa, $25, **140**

Rutherford Hill 1995 21ˢᵗ Anniversary Sangiovese, CA, $30, **93**
Rutherford Hill 1995 Reserve Merlot, CA, $44, **107**
$ Rutherford Ranch 1994 Cabernet Sauvignon, CA, $10, **79**
$ Rutherford Vintners 1996 Barrel Select Merlot, CA, $8.99, **107**
℗ Rymill Winery 1995 Cabernet Sauvignon, Australia, $16.50, **79**
℗ Rymill Winery 1995 Coonawarra Shiraz, Australia, $16.50, **148**

- S -

S. Anderson 1994 Richard Chambers Vineyard Cabernet Sauvignon, CA, $54, **79**
S. Anderson 1993 Brut, CA, $25, **245**
S. Anderson 1996 Estate Bottled Chardonnay, CA, $22, **184**
Saddleback Cellars 1995 Cabernet Sauvignon, CA, $27, **79**
$℗ Saint Clair 1996 Chardonnay, New Zealand, $15, **185**
St. Clement 1994 Howell Mntn. Cabernet Sauvignon, CA, $45, **79**
St. Clement 1994 Napa Cabernet Sauvignon, CA, $25, **79**
St. Clement 1995 Merlot, CA, $24, **107**
St. Clement 1996 Abbotts Vineyard Chardonnay, CA, $20, **185**
St. Francis 1994 Reserve Cabernet Sauvignon, CA, $30, **80**
St. Francis 1994 Reserve Merlot, CA, $29, **107**
$ St. Francis 1995 Cabernet Sauvignon, CA, $12, **80**
St. Francis 1995 Merlot, CA, $18, **107**
St. Francis 1996 Old Vines Zinfandel, CA, $20, **161**
St. Francis 1996 Reserve Pagani Vineyard Zinfandel, CA, $28, **161**
℗ St. Hallett 1993 Old Block Shiraz, Australia, $30.99, **148**
St. Innocent 1995 Freedom Hill Vineyard Pinot Noir, OR, $24.99, **129**
St. Innocent 1995 O'Connor Vineyard Pinot Noir, OR, $19.99, **130**
St. James 1993 Norton, MO, $30, **116**
$ St. James 1994 Norton, MO, $14.99, **116**
St. James 1994 Private Reserve Norton, MO, $19.99, **116**
$ St. James 1997 Vintner's Reserve Seyval Blanc, MO, $9.99, **203**
$✷ St. James 1997 Vintner's Reserve Vignoles, MO, $12.99, **203**
$ St. James NV Country White, MO, $5.99, **203**
$ St. James NV Pink Catawba, MO, $6.99, **237**
$ St. James NV Sparkling Blush, MO, $6.99, **245**
$ St. James NV Velvet Red Concord, MO, $5.99, **116**
$ St. Julian 1997 Sweet Reserve Seyval Blanc, MI, $6.50, **203**
$ St. Julian NV Solera Cream Sherry, MI, $12, **264**
St. Supéry 1994 Cabernet Sauvignon, CA, $90, **80**
✷ St. Supéry 1994 Red Meritage, CA, $40, **140**
St. Supéry 1996 Red Meritage, CA, $20, **140**
✷ St. Supéry 1996 White Meritage, CA, $20, **231**
$✷ St. Supéry 1997 Dollarhide Ranch Sauv. Blanc, CA, $10.55, **222**

About the Author

Gail Bradney has edited numerous books, among them many well-known cookbooks and five books by leading wine authority Robert Parker. This is her third edition of *Best Wines!* She lives in Woodstock, New York.

The Print Project, an independent publisher, has an outstanding reputation for assembling and presenting consumer information in a way that's useful and appealing. They're best known for *Buy Wholesale by Mail* (formerly *The Wholesale-by-Mail Catalog*), the leading consumer guide to discount shopping by mail, phone, or online, now in its twenty-first consecutive edition.

Feedback

We welcome your feedback. To contact Gail Bradney or The Print Project with comments or questions, or for information on bulk purchases of *Best Wines!,* please write or e-mail:

> The Print Project
> P.O. Box 703
> Bearsville, NY 12409
> bestwines@ulster.net